A MIRROR FOR SOCIALISM

• GILBERT ROZMAN •

A Mirror for Socialism

Soviet Criticisms of China

Princeton University Press
Princeton, New Jersey

Published by Princeton University Press, 41 William Street,
Princeton, New Jersey 08540

Library of Congress Cataloging in Publication Data will be
found on the last printed page of this book

ISBN 0-691-09411-X

This book has been composed in Linotron Baskerville

Clothbound editions of Princeton University Press books
are printed on acid-free paper, and binding materials are
chosen for strength and durability

Printed in the United States of America by Princeton University Press
Princeton, New Jersey

CONTENTS

PREFACE

The first half of the 1980s has been marked by frequent international tensions and heightened doubts about the prospects for a secure world order in the final period of the century. In this atmosphere, the almost simultaneous news in the fall of 1982 of the beginning of Sino-Soviet negotiations and the death of Leonid I. Brezhnev centered attention on two uncertainties of importance to world affairs: 1) what direction would be taken by the post-Brezhnev leadership in the Soviet Union? and 2) what relationship would result from Sino-Soviet negotiations no longer encumbered by Maoist rule in China? The answers to these questions could still not be clearly discerned in early 1984 after Iuri V. Andropov's brief tenure and the selection of Konstantin U. Chernenko as his successor, and from the indecisive progress reports on the negotiations—now in Moscow, now in Beijing—conducted by deputy foreign ministers. Given the penchant for secrecy in communist capitals and the difficulty of redirecting policies entrenched over two decades, it is doubtful that these uncertainties will be soon dispelled.

What made the situation in 1983 and 1984 different from earlier speculation about a redirection of Soviet policy and a reconciliation between the two powers in the communist world was the realization that strikingly new opportunities existed. Even the slightest indication of change in either of these matters had aroused outside observers since Nikita Khrushchev's 1956 de-Stalinization speech and the 1960 open split of the two giant, communist-led states. However, because of Leonid Brezhnev's status-quo leadership and Mao Zedong's deep-seated hostility to the Soviet Union, for a long time little happened to suggest the need for intensive investigation. Even so, Kremlinologists wrote a great deal about possible Soviet interest groups and leadership rifts, while foreign policy analysts produced a large literature that traced the Sino-Soviet dispute year by year. Since few published sources gave much direct indication of differences within Soviet opinion, specialists failed to penetrate very far through the veil of secrecy that hides the inner debates in Moscow and Beijing. Nevertheless, despite the dearth of data and the lack of movement toward major policy changes the subjects remained intriguing.

Suddenly in the final months of 1982 the way was opened for far-reaching changes. In October, after a year of gradually improving relations between China and the Soviet Union and periodic speeches including remarks on China by Leonid Brezhnev, negotiations between the two powers began. A month later, Brezhnev died and was succeeded by Yuri Andropov. Much speculation centered on the post-Brezhnev leadership. Would reformers have a major role? Would a new vision of socialism appear as it had after each previous leadership change in the Soviet Union? Would the new leadership take a more conciliatory position toward China? Could the rift between these two countries, the single most important shift in world alliances since the postwar alignments were set in the second half of the 1940s, be healed? Even if, in 1984, with Chernenko in power these questions are scarcely closer to being answered, their importance has in no way diminished. It remains imperative to find information that could help to answer them, and, in the process, to enhance our ability to predict world affairs.

In sharp contrast to the Western democracies, where the programs of aspiring leaders and rival parties highlight the differences among them, Russian publications are carefully censored to omit references to variations of opinion about issues as sensitive as the agenda for improving socialism and the correct policy toward China. Soviet spokesmen insist that the resulting façade of unanimity is an accurate reflection of reality. From reports by émigrés and private conversations with current Soviet citizens, we know, however, that the reality is different. But how can we go about systematically proving it and demonstrating the range of opinions that are expressed in official circles? How can we understand the forces in the USSR that might provide guidance for redirecting Soviet society and support for a new relationship with the PRC (People's Republic of China)?

While engaged in research on eighteenth- and nineteenth-century Chinese and Russian societies, I made a discovery that promised to provide insight into these elusive themes. I learned that Soviet writings on China are more than a source of information on China; they serve also as a forum for discussing how socialism can fail and, in turn, how it can be improved. I first found sources that search for the roots deep in Chinese history of the Maoist deviation from socialism; then I turned to writings on contemporary China for a fuller explanation of how a country can go astray on the path to socialism. I became aware that Soviet indictments of Chinese society bear a strong resemblance to Western criticisms of Soviet society (and of communist-led systems in general), and I began to wonder if Soviet perceptions of contemporary China might not offer an unexpected bonus—a forum for debating the shortcomings of the Soviet Union.

The more I read on this topic, the more I realized that these Soviet materials convey sharp, if indirectly expressed, differences of opinion on two themes: the meaning of socialism, and the prospects for Sino-Soviet relations. This literature contains what may be the clearest statement in any area of Soviet publishing of differences concerning the past, present, and future of socialism. By analyzing these differences, we can establish how orthodox and reform viewpoints disagree on the fundamental problems of a socialist society. Moreover, the Soviet literature on China reveals two conflicting assessments of what is happening in that country, each with implications for the future of Sino-Soviet relations. In other words, without actually debating the sensitive topics of socialism in the USSR and Soviet foreign policy, these publications manage to present many of the main arguments pertinent to these debates.

As a sociologist, I will not directly address questions of leadership and foreign policy differences. Instead, I will adopt a form of social class analysis to study policies directed at social change. This approach is particularly well suited for the study of communist-led countries, which give high priority to concealing divisions over leadership agendas and foreign policy. I will examine what Soviets write about socialism in China and will focus particularly on the development of social classes and the relations among them. These are the fundamental issues of communist ideology; yet they are sufficiently far removed from the proscriptions on sensitive matters set down by Soviet leaders that diverse interpretations are permitted. After all, it was long in the interest of Soviet leaders to build a persuasive case to rally public opinion against their Chinese rivals.

Through views expressed about China, we learn what Soviet reformers identify as the dangers inherent in a communist-led system and how these dangers should be combatted. We find an agenda for reform that is of immediate application to post-Mao China but also of considerable relevance to the Soviet Union. It is an agenda for de-Maoization and also, I believe, for a revival of de-Stalinization. The reform perspective on China, in contrast to the orthodox viewpoint, also suggests a basis for improved relations in the 1980s. It offers hope for cooperative coexistence within a pluralistic communist bloc in a world in which tensions are relaxed. But it is a minority view. The orthodox group in the Soviet Union retains its dominant position and maintains its harsher line against recent reforms in China.

My purpose in this book is not to analyze the accuracy of Soviet criticisms of China. To compare Soviet writings to Western and Japanese (or Chinese) writings and to try to assess their accuracy on hundreds of separate issues would be a large undertaking, and a diversionary one for the aims of this study. Even in comparing Soviet criticisms of China and what Soviets call anticommunist criticisms of the Soviet Union, I have relied only on Soviet restatements of the views they attack. This method highlights the Soviet views and allows us to understand them better. Whatever the value (and I think it is considerable) of Soviet writings for comprehending the reality of China, this study focuses elsewhere—on the Soviet perceptions themselves. The exceptions to this approach are my attempts to show parallels between the views Soviets label anticommunism and the Soviet conclusions about China and to assess the differences between orthodox and reform viewpoints. Study of these two themes enables us to ascertain what is most significant about Soviet studies of China.

Soviet writings on so-called anticommunism are methodologically flawed because they give little space to the arguments they criticize while resorting to one-sided and distorted arguments in refutation. I try to avoid these suspicious methods by presenting the Soviet views at length. Given the repeated Soviet charges of distortions and falsifications in the coverage of their society and their views (and given, more generally, the mutual suspicions of inaccurate assessments of each other among Soviets, Chinese, and Westerners), I have accepted it as my first obligation to paraphrase and quote extensively from Soviet sources. My purpose is to understand what Soviets are really saying when they write about Chinese social classes. This information can, I believe, tell us a lot about differences of opinion within Soviet official circles and about the internal debates that form the background of the Sino-Soviet negotiations. In short, this book provides information about Soviet thinking, largely from the late 1970s and early 1980s, of importance for understanding the decisions likely to be faced in the mid and late 1980s for redirecting Soviet socialism and improving Sino-Soviet relations.

G. R.
April 1984

ACKNOWLEDGMENTS

This volume is the result of a two-year project, 1981-1983, assisted with funds provided by the National Council on Soviet and East European Research. I am grateful to the National Council for providing support for my research. I also want to express my appreciation to the International Research and Exchanges Board (IREX) for its encouragement of academic exchanges with the Soviet Union in Chinese studies. I gathered materials and learned about the organization of Soviet research on China through the auspices of the American Council of Learned Societies—Soviet Academy of Sciences Binational Commission in the Humanities and Social Sciences administered by IREX.

The Institute of Oriental Studies of the Soviet Academy of Sciences served as my host during two visits to the Soviet Union. The staff of the Department of China and the department head, Professor L. P. Deliusin, facilitated my efforts to become informed about a subject that few Americans have studied. I greatly appreciate their cooperation. Gracious assistance in obtaining materials was also provided by L. S. Kiuzadjan of the Institute of Scientific Information in the Social Sciences, Academy of Sciences, as part of the exchange of materials on China arranged through the Binational Commission. I am indebted to other Soviet scholars too who met with me and answered my questions about their field of study.

Of course, neither the American organizations that supported my research nor the Soviet organizations and scholars who helped me to obtain information are responsible for the conclusions I have reached. This volume represents my own attempt to bring together the available information, mostly publications readily acquired in the West, in order to understand how Soviets view China.

xiii

ACKNOWLEDGMENTS

I want to thank Blanche Anderson, Theresa Kuzianik, Gladys Starkey, and Gail Wenrich for helping with the preparation of my manuscript. I especially want to thank Gail Filion Ullman for her editorial assistance in revising the manuscript for publication.

A MIRROR FOR SOCIALISM

· 1 ·

INTRODUCTION

The official Soviet worldview—like the consumer products turned out by Soviet industry—is not manufactured to withstand open, international competition. It is an artificial creation imposed and supported by national planning, tight internal censorship, and persistent controls on the flow of information from outside. It is, of course, not a properly scientific understanding, subject to unlimited revision on the basis of independent scholarship. Nor can one show convincingly that it is accepted unqualifiedly by large numbers of educated Soviet citizens. Nevertheless, this worldview establishes the terms of discourse and helps shape internal change within the USSR, and at the same time it affects relations with other countries.

The Soviet view of historical change and world forces is not static. It has been continually modified in response to challenges posed by new information to which Soviet specialists and, often, large numbers of citizens have access. One of the most serious and persistent challenges from outside the borders of the USSR has come from developments in China. One unexpected occurrence has followed another: China's Great Leap Forward in 1958, the open split with the Soviet Union in 1960, the Cultural Revolution in 1966, the dangerous border skirmishes of 1969, the Sino-American rapprochement of 1972, and the abrupt reversal of leadership and policies in the aftermath of Mao's death in 1976. As the Chinese experience with socialism and as Sino-Soviet relations have changed, Soviet spokesmen have had to account in diverse ways for the wayward path of a rival communist-led society. No less in the post-Mao era than before, new demands are placed on China watchers in defense of the communist leadership's beleaguered worldview. The Chinese heresy has had a profound effect

3

on Soviet orthodoxy, perhaps as profound as any other development since the de-Stalinization movement of the 1950s.

For about a quarter-century the Sino-Soviet dispute has been one of the driving forces in international relations. Soviet leaders have sought to channel this force. Using China as an example of social change, specialists have reinterpreted the regularities of historical development in order to show why China has deviated while the Soviet Union has followed the correct path. They have analyzed many facets of life in China in support of their conclusions. In this way, the Soviet leaders have tried to strengthen the legitimacy of their own system and to rally the international communist movement behind them. The struggle against China has, of course, included troop deployments and occasional border skirmishes, but the primary battleground for the Soviets has occurred in publications that interpret social change in that country.

This is a study of Soviet perceptions of China after the rupture of the Sino-Soviet alliance in 1960. The primary aim is to convey accurately the views presented in Soviet publications about what has gone wrong in the People's Republic of China. Because, according to the perspective of both Chinese authorities and Soviet analysts, social classes are the principal units of society, I have divided this treatment into separate discussions of five social classes or groups in the population. For each social group, I review what Soviet authors contend were the incorrect policies adopted in China and the explanations the Soviets offer for them.

In no way should these separate discussions of social classes and groups be construed as an attempt to represent Soviet views on the PRC in their entirety. Perhaps the most glaring omission is a discussion of what the Soviets consider to have gone right in the period 1949-1957 as a result of Soviet and communist bloc assistance. Nor does this book examine international relations. Nevertheless, we should bear in mind that Soviet writers regard close relations with the Soviet Union as a precondition for China's advance to socialism. During the early and mid-1950s Soviet advisers helped set a course for labor unions and worker relations in China, for the organization of intellectuals, and for the establishment of departments in which cadres worked. This assistance is described in Soviet writings as an unqualified blessing for China's march toward socialism. In general, however, much more can be learned from the creative process of identifying what went wrong in China than from the rote application of formulas assumed to assure success in any communist-led society. For that reason, the following chapters concentrate on the topics about which there is greatest diversity of opinion as authors suggest various reasons why China deviated from the path of socialism.

We will examine especially the writings of Soviet specialists on China—officials, journalists, and, above all, academics—and will review how these specialists have exposed the failings of Chinese society. But this theme itself fits into a broader context, which forms the core of the Soviet worldview. We will also explore, therefore: 1) the current Soviet understanding, based on the official interpretation of Marxism-Leninism, of the transition from feudalism and capitalism to socialism, and the character of a socialist society; 2) the recent Soviet attempts to refute the views labeled "anticommunist," which are critical of Soviet history and contemporary society; 3) the evolution of the Sino-Soviet dispute in which each has accused the other of deviating from the path of socialism; and 4) the sociological study of China, the world's largest society. To understand how these themes fit together, it is necessary to cut through the dense jargon used by communists—and demanded by censors—to rationalize their methods and discredit their opponents. When this is done, the surprising result is a striking resemblance between Soviet criticisms of Chinese society and Western criticisms of Soviet society.

THE SOVIET WORLDVIEW

By worldview I mean an outlook on historical development, on the contemporary world order, and on the nature of one's own society. This outlook explains social change and anticipates the future social system. The Soviet worldview differs from any others because it is grounded in a large body of writings that are claimed to provide a systematic and consistent understanding—a scientific understanding—of human existence.

The current Soviet perspective on historical development recognizes four primary forces: 1) *technology*; 2) *class struggle*; 3) *scientific understanding* of social change; and 4) *planned transformation* under communist leadership. According to this materialist conception of history, technological change basically determines the nature of production and greatly influences patterns of ownership and property relations. As technology advances, the relations between individuals engaged in production change. Increasingly individuals become conscious of serious barriers to the further development of production and to improvement in their well-being—barriers that result from existing forms of property and distribution. Technology advances but the organization of society fails to change substantially. The resulting contradictions aggravate relations between social classes. Oppressed working people resort to class struggle. Their actions eventually lead to revolution and a victory for a new socioeconomic formation that conforms to the level of technology. As a rule, three successive formations based on class antagonisms emerge: slavery gives way to feudal society, which in turn is replaced by capitalism.

In the mid-nineteenth century, as capitalist society was establishing the technological and class relations that are prerequisites for a transition to socialism, founders of Marxism added a vital new force for progress. In the words of Khachik N. Momjan, the president of the Soviet Sociological Association, "At last, mankind had at its command a science of society, which made it possible to rise to new stages of historical progress in the shortest possible period."[1] Those who achieved a scientific understanding banded

[1] Khachik N. Momjan, *Landmarks in History: The Marxist Doctrine of Socio-Economic Formations*, p. 22.

together to form the communist movement. They were able to lead the working classes to victory in revolutionary struggle.

According to this conception, following a communist-led revolution, changes in the economic base or the substructure are for the first time accelerated by a fourth force: the planned development of the superstructure (the other basic element of a socioeconomic formation; it includes the state, the dominant ideology, the legal system, the educational system, the mass media, and the arts). Just as major technological breakthroughs and revolutionary victories are the landmarks of earlier history, each congress of the Communist Party of the Soviet Union has represented a twentieth-century landmark in propelling Soviet society forward and in leading the way for other communist parties at their own congresses to follow the same successful path. For example, in the aftermath of the Twenty-sixth Congress of the CPSU in 1981 it was claimed that, on the basis of a careful examination of all areas of social life, a scientifically based strategy had been worked out and was embodied in decisions that would favorably influence world social progress.[2] The Soviet view holds that a communist future looms ahead, following the inevitable historical progression that is brought about by these four moving forces of history.

Although this Soviet perspective is basically deterministic, elements of uncertainty are present. It recognizes that the speed of transformation can be affected by factors such as a country's distinctive historical legacy, the role of individual leaders, and international forces. Each country's history must be examined in detail in order to determine variations in timing and even short-term or local deviations from the general path. The Marxist view labeled "historical materialism" is not all-inclusive and is "not meant to substitute for historical science, or for the whole system of social sciences. Historical materialism is a general methodology for the study of history, its motive forces and main

[2] *Problemy nauchnogo kommunizma*, vol. 15, p. 3.

stages, its general direction, global sociological uniformities, and forms of their manifestation."[3]

The need for specific analysis is evident from many qualifications noted in Soviet writings: Some countries may bypass a particular formation, such as capitalism; "there is no mechanical dependence of consciousness on the economic order"; "the socialist order in itself cannot guarantee men against mistakes in questions of economics, politics, culture and ideology";[4] and the role of a "great man" may determine if an historical event takes place earlier or later, even if the basic direction of historical development remains as predicted and, in the final determination, the decisive role is that of the working masses. The possibility exists that all four of the moving forces of history may vary from their expected pattern in certain historical circumstances, leading to different outcomes in different countries.

The inevitability of socialism and communism is premised on the following assumptions. First, communist parties, because of the composition of their membership and the structure of their organization, will not make serious mistakes in building a socialist superstructure and in transforming the inherited substructure. Second, if communist parties and their leaders should make serious mistakes, the existence of a scientific understanding of social relations in the Marxist-Leninist literature will impel other communists to redirect them on a proper course. Third, if for any reason, the ideology continues to be incorrectly interpreted, class struggle will ensue as the working classes battle to establish a system consistent with their interests. Finally, if all else fails in the short-run, the persistence of technological change will eventually transform the working classes into a decisive revolutionary force. The four moving forces continue to operate in all periods prior to full-fledged communism. As a rule, one takes over from the next as the guiding force. But should a breakdown somehow occur,

[3] Momjan, *Landmarks in History*, p. 246.
[4] *Social Science*, pp. 94, 116.

the others wait in reserve, prepared to set the progress of society back on course.

The application of this approach by specialists on particular countries requires what Soviets call "historical sociological research." According to this approach, the general sociological laws are understood but it remains to be determined how these laws operate in concrete conditions of place and time. This is not viewed as a deductive process, because in the short-term occur "temporary deviations under the influence of various kinds of chance events" (*sluchainosti*) and all kinds of zigzags, and only in the final analysis is the basic direction of development evident.[5] It is up to the specialists to investigate concrete historical events, including what are widely referred to as "regressions," "contradictory forces," "multi-formations," "deviations," "disproportions," and "deformations."[6] Of course, they may do so only so long as they raise no direct challenges to the general sociological laws, i.e. the essence of Marxism-Leninism as currently interpreted.

Implicitly or explicitly the application of this approach calls for comparisons. To the extent that individual Soviet writers reject mere illustrations of general sociological laws, they base their generalizations on a comparative approach. The comparisons mostly rely on Vladimir I. Lenin's findings from Russian history or Karl Marx's earlier interpretations of Western Europe's history, but increasingly a wider range of historical experience has been incorporated. The regularities that operate as the basis for comparative analysis fall into three primary categories, each focusing on a separate period of a society's evolution: the legacy of feudalism, the transition to socialism, and the building of communism.

---

[5] E. M. Zhukov, et al., *Teoreticheskie problemy vsemirno-istoricheskogo protsessa*, pp. 17, 22.

[6] All of these expressions can be found in the volume published by Zhukov, et al., and they are commonly encountered in the literature on China.

The Legacy of Feudalism

In the past three centuries, the forces of capitalism and imperialism have confronted feudal societies one after another throughout the world. By "feudal," Marxists mean largely agrarian settings in which the primary class antagonism is between landlords and peasants. Increasingly Soviet area specialists accept as the starting point of analysis a need to specify the nature of that confrontation and of the preceding period of feudalism. Different approaches can be found in the literature. Some specialists prefer alternatives to the pure notion of feudalism as a socioeconomic formation. Various points of view center on the concept of the Asiatic mode of production, which was introduced by Marx.[7] One view is that there was an independent Asian formation, which was an alternative to slaveholding society as the first class formation. A second view is that the Asiatic mode was a transitional step either to slaveholding or to feudalism. V. P. Iliushechkin, one of two China specialists who have published analyses of the materials on the Asiatic mode of production, rejects the separate categories of slave, feudal, and Asiatic and proposes a third view that there was a single prebourgeois class formation in which renters, serfs, or slaves were exploited by a class of large-scale landowners.[8] In contrast, V. N. Nikiforov, the other China specialist who has written extensively on this concept, offers a fourth view that there is no distinctive Asiatic formation.[9] No concept has drawn more attention to the consequences of historical conditions that deviate from the "normal" course than the notion of the Asiatic mode of production, and no country is more important than China to the debate over this concept.

[7] V. Ia. Izraitel', *Problemy formatsionnogo analiza obshchestvennogo razvitiia*, pp. 147-49.

[8] V. P. Iliushechkin, "Obshchee i osobennoe v razvitii doburzhuaznykh klassovykh obshchestv," in *Sotsial'naia i sotsial'no-ekonomicheskaia istoriia Kitaia*, pp. 5-24.

[9] V. N. Nikiforov, *Vostok i vsemirnaia istoriia*.

Associated with the concept of the Asiatic mode of production are at least five social conditions: 1) community
property with much actual ownership in the hands of central authorities (the use of irrigation supports community
ownership); 2) exploitation of labor by a despot who rules
through a bureaucracy and maintains a superstructure of
Eastern despotism; 3) inertia and conservatism in technology or the means of production; 4) unity of farming and
crafts on a small scale, which signifies a weakly developed
division of labor and domestic market; and 5) overlapping
of socioeconomic contradictions in which the transition from
kin to class relations is more complex than usual, which
signifies a distortion of class relations and class struggle.[10]
This legacy is associated with backwardness in modern societies, especially in the delayed and distorted emergence
of capitalism. Even among the majority of specialists who
eschew the Asiatic mode as a separate formation, these
same conditions are widely accepted as part of the legacy
of Eastern feudalism.

Throughout the 1970s continued efforts were made to
integrate sociology and oriental studies and sociology and
history. In both cases, it was recognized that prior failures
to unite these approaches had produced a negative effect
on scholarship. In short, the legacy of feudalism had been
neglected. The most fruitful results in the integration of
sociology and oriental studies are considered to be "the
complex study of the genesis, the formation and the evolution of the socio-class structure of multi-formation countries of Asia and Africa."[11] Soviets claim that this combi-
nation of fields can clarify the mixture of elements of the
old and the new in societies with multi-formations, i.e. all
of the Third World. They also argue that the convergence
of sociology and history is a recent development that is
absolutely necessary for both disciplines.[12]

[10] Izraitel', *Problemy formatsionnogo analiza obshchestvennogo razvitiia*, pp.
152-53. I have combined two of the author's six conditions.

[11] *Issledovaniia sotsiologicheskikh problem razvivaiushchikhsia stran*, p. 5.

[12] *Sotsiologiia i problemy sotsial'nogo razvitiia*, p. 26.

Out of new combinations of these three fields arises a heightened interest in the character of traditional society, in factors operating as barriers to progressive development, and in the weakness of conditions deemed important for the transition to capitalism. Thus the Soviet view of history now draws attention to the "peculiarities" of a country's premodern social structure in explanations of its contemporary development. This legacy of the past is obviously not the only factor that matters in a society's current development. While the legacy primarily affects the level of technology and the class struggle, leaders with a scientific understanding of society and planned development can do much to overcome it, especially with the assistance of the Soviet Union.

The Transition to Socialism

After 1917 a new epoch began, which occupies a preeminent place in the Soviet view of the world. It is the transitional period of change guided by a Marxist-Leninist party that has already gained power. The rationale for this period is that revolution alone is not sufficient to bring about socialism. Because socialist property cannot grow under capitalism as opposed to capitalist property under feudalism, a transition is necessary until the time is reached when socialism exists in the main. Soviet spokesmen insist that the transition requires a dictatorship on behalf of the proletariat, liquidation of capitalist property, the establishment of collective ownership over the basic means of production, the collectivization of agriculture, central planning, a cultural revolution, and much more. The length of the transition varies with the circumstances in a given country, especially the level of technology and the related balance of social classes. In this stage, countries (the Soviet Union included) often face a major contradiction between their advanced political authority based on a scientific understanding of society and their backward technical, economic base.[13] For the first time in history the superstructure is well ahead of the substructure.

Recognition of diverse paths to socialism is now commonplace in Soviet writings. For example, V. E. Kozlovskii writes that he cannot agree with some Soviet authors who consider the transition from feudalism to capitalism to be more varied than the transition from capitalism to socialism.[14] In the latter, there may be a multiparty system, coexistence of diverse types of agriculture including private ownership, inclusion of former kulaks in cooperatives, and many other notable variations. The battle for a complete transition to socialism varies with the historical circumstances. "Socialism does not appear automatically and with dispatch. . . . It is possible quickly, in a matter of days, or sometimes even of hours, to seize power. But the old society, consisting, as any society, of a most intricate complex of diverse components, is impossible to break up, to destroy with one storming, with one—even the most decisive—attack."[15]

Acknowledgment of diversity, however, only goes so far. Communists warn against revisionists who exaggerate national peculiarities and reject the regularities of history, i.e. revisionists commit the error of losing sight of the scientific understanding of human existence that Marxism-Leninism has gained. This danger may result in an underestimation of the contradiction between the emerging socialist formation and the surviving capitalist and, perhaps, pettytrade (feudal) formation. At the same time, communists also warn against dogmatists, who blindly adhere to the general scheme while overlooking variations in historical conditions. The Soviet worldview in recent decades has shifted in the direction of revisionism, but there remain contending points of view ready to label further shifts in

[13] V. E. Kozlovskii, *Dialektika perekhoda ot kapitalizma k sotsializmu*, p. 7.
[14] Ibid., p. 11.
[15] *Ot kapitalizma k sotsializmu: osnovnye problemy istorii perekhodnogo perioda v SSSR 1917-1937 gg.*, I, pp. 6-7.

either direction as antithetical to scientific Marxism-Leninism.

The transition to socialism in the main in the Soviet Union required about two decades. With the experience of the first socialist country available to other communist parties and with generous Soviet assistance, this process can be accelerated in other societies. (Indeed, by 1957, only eight years after the Chinese Revolution was victorious, the communist world recognized the completion of this transition in China.) But there is a need to be vigilant against difficulties that may arise. Above all, the Soviets warn, any weakening of the leading role of the ruling Marxist-Leninist party causes enormous losses.[16] The overthrown, exploiting classes will continue to resist; class struggle does not disappear in this period. Under these circumstances, class enemies must be liquidated, and policies directed at workers, peasants, the old intelligentsia, and the new cadres must be worked out in accordance with a general strategy for strengthening the forces of socialism. The transition may be complicated by a country's backwardness and the proportion of its population who are peasants.[17] However, because some peoples have proceeded directly to socialism without experiencing capitalism, backwardness is not an insurmountable obstacle.[18] In this period, the development of the material-technical base of socialism is essential, e.g. in the collectivization of agriculture and the realization of a cultural revolution. A new order is constructed through conscious and planned actions directed by the leaders of the communist party.

The Building of Communism

Even after the transition to socialism ("socialism in the main") is largely complete, there is danger of a reversal. A period

[16] Ibid., p. 45.

[17] Ibid., pp. 27-28.

[18] F. Kh. Kasymov, *Minuia kapitalizm: sovetskaia istoriografiia perekhoda narodov Srednei Azii k sotsializmu.*

of building full socialism ensues, then comes a period of irreversible socialism, and finally a period of developed socialism. These distinctions are rather fuzzy. As each leader tries to show how new policies and priorities help to define the current stage of socialism the meaning of these slogans continues to change. From stage to stage, however they are divided, a society moves ever closer to communism. But in the first of these stages of socialism, the situation remains somewhat precarious. Prior to the full and final victory of socialism, which was proclaimed in the USSR in 1959, the danger remains serious. As in the transition to socialism, in this stage the primary needs are party leadership and policies directed at strengthening the working class and its support from other classes. The composition of the communist party, fraternal relations with other communist parties, especially that of the Soviet Union, and party strategy all matter. Moreover, the continued impact of the level of economic development is great; backwardness has many negative consequences. The methods adopted to overcome these problems, if not carefully formulated, may even threaten the existence of socialism.

Discussions of dangers that lurk in socialist societies appear in Soviet justifications of policies adopted in their country, and by their close allies, and also in criticisms of Chinese mistakes. This is the primary subject of Soviet writings on contemporary China, but it is often treated in relation to China's precapitalist legacy and its transition to socialism in the years after 1949. China has enormous importance for the Soviet worldview because it is a central example in the enduring debate over the Asiatic mode of production and the impact of traditional society, in the analysis of the impact of backwardness on the transition to socialism, and in the sensitive discussion of how socialism can reach a crisis. Indeed, it is possible that abstract discussions and studies devoted to Soviet history fail to express implicit points in this worldview that can be discerned more fully in Soviet writings on China.

Soviet interpretations of China are tightly interlocked

with Sino-Soviet relations and conflicting views of socialism. Indeed, Nikita Khrushchev's reinterpretation of the Stalinist era proved to be one of the factors that exacerbated relations between the two countries in this period. Only two years after the de-Stalinization speech at the Twentieth Party Congress in 1956, Mao Zedong proposed a new vision of the transition from socialism to communism that called for people's communes to serve as an advanced form of organization. Since this initial clash of views in which the Chinese were hesitant to reject Stalinism and the Soviets were irritated by China's grandiose claims to be moving ahead to communism, each side has greatly revised its approach to the process of building communism. But the conflict between different perspectives on socialism has persisted. The Soviets have sought to answer such questions as: Is China a socialist society? What accounts for its policies that do not follow the socialist course of development? What forces will return China to this course? The answers depend not only on the Soviet analysis of Chinese society but also on the official view of Soviet society since the 1950s.

In a socialist society there are no enemy classes—no landlords, no *kulaks*, no capitalists. But a great deal may still need to be accomplished before the victory of socialism is deemed irreversible and the building of communism is regarded as well along. Technological changes are necessary to achieve a predominance of factory production and mechanized agriculture. Educational advances result in a skilled and specialized labor force. The intelligentsia grows most rapidly, followed by the workers. Cities must also grow rapidly; they house the most advanced groups and pull the rural areas in their wake. Ethnic minorities, women, and other previously disadvantaged groups should take advantage of growing opportunities as inequalities diminish. During the course of this second transition after the victory of a communist revolution, individual personalities are transformed, collectives gain in importance, equality increases, and prosperity including social welfare benefits reaches the

16

population. Those are the claims that Soviets make. They argue that all of these goals continue to be approached in the stage of developed socialism that the Soviet Union has been in since the late 1960s.

Social problems persist even after socialism exists in the main. Upbringing work (*vospitanie*, including not just child-rearing but education of the entire population through all available channels) must be given ever greater attention to overcome "remnants of the past" in individual attitudes. There is a need for countermeasures against bourgeois ideology originating from outside the country. The communist party must also avoid mistakes that could create new tensions and inefficiencies, exacerbating existing social problems. These problems justify centralized control and ideological struggle by the party as it increases its demands on citizens. According to the current Soviet worldview, the party's role grows from: 1) the interpreter of scientific laws and the vanguard of the revolution; to 2) the exposer of class enemies and the voice of the proletariat in reorganizing and planning society; and 3) finally in a socialist society to the pervasive force in overseeing all areas of life.

The official Soviet worldview bombards each Soviet citizen from all directions. Through repetition and reinforcement, it shapes the learning of school children and the acquisition of news from the mass media by the entire population. More sophisticated versions of this worldview reach an educated audience. In the scholarly literature, the detailed treatments of feudal legacies, diverse transitions to socialism, and complexities of socialism are intended for a limited reading public. In comparison to the Stalinist generation, this educated minority is better informed about international events and has a broader perspective on the shortcomings of its own society. Without abandoning their goal of orchestrating the availability and interpretation of knowledge, Soviet leaders have decided to provide these readers with a wide range of specific information, including hundreds of specialized books on China.

Citizens eager to learn about China are likely to be well read in Soviet history and international affairs. Their outlook matters a great deal to the Soviet leadership because many of them are involved in academic research and education or have responsible positions as officials. They shape the thinking of others and find guidance in their reading for leading others as well as motivation for individual performance. Even when educated readers have doubts about some of what they read, the leadership can measure success in their general acceptance of the broad contours of the official worldview. Because the specialists themselves debate numerous specific points, the reader's doubts can often be attributed to a lower level of understandable, and still unresolved, uncertainty rather than to the highly generalized level of fundamental principles. In this way, detailed presentations (and recognition of uncertainties and limited disagreements) are intended to save the credibility of the official worldview among a well-educated readership. At the same time, the information provided has the potential to extend or modify the official viewpoint. While leaders are on guard against challenges to the official worldview, it is difficult to draw the line in this field.

In short, because of the claims made for the communist party's role, the Soviet Union requires an elaborate worldview. This viewpoint needs to account for the split with China—a society once considered to be following in the footsteps of the Soviet Union and, outside of the Soviet bloc, widely compared to the Soviet Union to determine which one more faithfully upholds the principles of Marxism-Leninism. To reach relatively informed and influential citizens, Soviet leaders must back up their criticisms of China with detailed studies. For these to be most effective, they should focus on problems of socialism that have direct meaning to Soviet citizens. As a result, writings on China provide an unusual challenge for treating issues of great sensitivity, and, in the process, an exceptional opportunity for revealing variations that qualify or even, in limited ways, contradict the official worldview.

REFUTATIONS OF ANTICOMMUNISM

Soviet leaders and spokesmen repeatedly insist that the ideological struggle between socialism and capitalism intensifies in the current period. They accuse Sovietologists, Western specialists on the USSR, of being in the forefront of the opposition, and they demand that all Soviet citizens become actively engaged in this struggle. Treated as bourgeois ideologists, Sovietologists and other perceived critics of socialism are labeled "anticommunists" who distort, slander, and falsify the facts about Soviet society in an effort to reduce the appeal of this progressive system. Their method is "mechanically to transfer to socialist society phenomena peculiar to capitalism."[19] They hide "behind ostentatious objectivity," operate "under the guise of impartiality," and offer "a tendentious selection of facts."[20] In the Soviet Union a great deal of effort is invested in the refutation of foreign assessments labeled "anticommunist."

Studies of the Soviet Union

Bourgeois sources on Soviet society are identified in Soviet books as making the following false accusations: 1) The Soviet Union is a *dictatorship of a minority*; the communist party and Soviet officials represent a new class or elite that through anti-democratic methods oppresses the working people, who do not take an active part in running the country. 2) The country is run by an *unchecked leader*, who rules through the cult of personality and the great power invested in him as the party leader. 3) It exhibits *bureaucratism*: economic life is on command from above and is inefficient. 4) The Soviet system is *exploitative*, the people's well-being is ignored, and material incentives are underestimated. 5) There is *racism* based on the suppression of

---

[19] A. A. Amvrosov, *Ot klassovoi differentsiatsii k sotsial'noi odnorodnosti obshchestva*, p. 270.

[20] N. P. Mikeshin, *History versus Anti-History: A Critique of the Bourgeois Falsification of the Postwar History of the CPSU*, p. 10.

national minorities. 6) The Soviets have *forced industriali-zation*, in which administrative, noneconomic means replace market mechanisms. 7) The system is guided by an *anti-scientific ideology*, with dogmatism and canonization of ideas supported by references to the writings of leaders. 8) Ignorant officials make a practice of *interference in science*, operating as a brake on scientific progress. 9) The Soviet Union has a *totalitarian culture*, marked by a loss of freedom and creativity as ideology stifles diversity. 10) There is *militarism*; the military priority means concentration of investment in heavy industry. 11) One observes a *suppression of individuality*, resulting from a sacrifice to collectivism and a loss of human rights. These are among the major Western criticisms leveled against Soviet society, and they form the essence, if not the entirety, of what Soviets call anticommunism.[21]

Of course, Western criticisms of the Soviet Union also find fault with the dominant place of the communist party, the unscientific nature of Marxism-Leninism as the official ideology, the negative impact on incentives from state and collective ownership of the means of production, and the inefficiency of centralized planning. Even without attacking these four shibboleths, however, it is still possible to oppose the existing structures and functions of a communist-led society, i.e. to engage in a wide range of criticisms that Soviets label anticommunism. For this reason, I refer to criticisms that concentrate on the eleven areas identified above, without challenging these four basic institutions, as echoes of anticommunism. As we see in the following chapters, Soviet writings are critical of China in each of these eleven areas. They repeat the criticisms lodged against their own system in charges they make against the Chinese system.

This similarity of criticisms is, as I conclude in Chapter 7, not coincidental. Soviets are writing for a domestic audience familiar with the mistakes of Soviet history. They

---

[21] *Sovremennyi antikommunizm: politika, ideologiia*, pp. 165-73.

are seeking to shape Soviet public opinion against Chinese policies. There are other objectives as well, which differ among Soviet authors. These objectives pertain, above all, to Soviet history and to contemporary attitudes toward reform in Soviet society. While finding fault with China, Soviets are fully aware that similar criticisms have been leveled against their own country. When they repeat these criticisms it does not mean that they identify themselves with the camp of "anticommunism." Yet, how they treat these themes is significant as a contribution to Soviet policy debates and especially to molding Soviet public opinion. On the basis of close familiarity with Soviet writings on China, it is possible to search for the significance of the echoing effect—to understand the purposeful nature of airing and transposing criticisms widely seen as applicable to Soviet history.

The manner of criticism also enters into Soviet discussions of anticommunism. Soviet publications suggest that primitive anticommunism has given way to "academic" anticommunism or that "primitive slander is replaced now by pseudo-scientific studies."[22] Appealing to science, this newer approach gives the pretense of strict impartiality. According to the Soviets, the central place in anticommunist historiography is held by studies on the USSR. After 1950 the number of foreign specialists and publications in this area expanded many times. Through increasingly detailed studies, these critics have launched a massive effort to deceive people throughout the world about the true nature of a socialist society. This is the perceived threat from anticommunism.

Among the falsifications of which Sovietologists are accused, many of the most prominent center on the relations among social classes. Soviet writers depict anticommunism as a distortion of the harmonious relations and the true

---

[22] B. I. Marushkin, *Istoriia v sovremennoi ideologicheskoi bor'be (stroitel'stvo sotsializma v SSSR skvos' prizmu antikommunisticheskoi istoriografii SShA)*; and *Real'nyi sotsializm v SSSR i ego burzhuaznye fal'sifikatory*, p. 23.

nature of social classes in the Soviet Union. First, it portrays rural oppression, with peasants looked down upon, living in wretched conditions under surveillance, and herded together against their will in collectives. A build-up of heavy industry and military might takes place on the backs of the peasantry. Second, bourgeois Sovietologists assert that the working class does not occupy the leading place in social life, has a poor attitude toward labor, and has been slow to gain materially from the expansion of the Soviet economy.[23] Workers remain passive or alienated in politics and production. Third, anticommunists concentrate on the intelligentsia as a group opposed to the officials and eager for a relaxation of restrictions. Fourth, there are attacks on the leading role of the party and accusations that its officials and other state bureaucrats represent a new ruling class. These accusations insist that the true nature of the system is repressive on behalf of a small number of privileged leaders who receive disproportionate benefits and wield virtually unchecked power. Soviets refer briefly to the "pseudo-scientific studies" of so-called bourgeois falsifiers on each of these themes and respond with justifications of their society. Refutations of those studies play an important role in the Soviet worldview.

Criticisms of "Anticommunism": Commentaries on Peasants

Soviet writings are of special interest because of their dual role as defenders and critics of policies that bear some resemblance. On the one hand, they justify the rural programs of the CPSU against critics whom they accuse of anticommunism. On the other hand, they condemn rural policies in the PRC, appropriating as their own many of the charges that have been leveled against the Soviet Union and redirecting them against China. Both pursuits are essential for the Soviet worldview. Soviet spokesmen are simultaneously mobilized in a counteroffensive against for-

---

[23] *Real'nyi sotsializm v SSSR i ego burzhuaznye fal'sifikatory*, pp. 187-204.

22

eign criticisms in a drive to rationalize their own rural past and in an offensive to discredit the deviations from the socialist path in China. The following quotations indicate what is considered anticommunist.

• Sovietologists cast monstrous aspersions on the CPSU and the Soviet state, accusing them of hostility to peasants, of putting these policies [collectivization] into effect not for the benefit, but to the detriment of rural laborers. The basic meaning of their assertions comes down to the following: "exploitation of the peasantry as it was the cornerstone of traditional Russian society," so it remains to this day the basic policy of the party in the village, and that the Soviet state treats the peasants antagonistically. . . . Collectivism is presented as not only "forced," but even as a "real war" between the government and the peasants.[24]

• Stressing the idea of collectivization "from above" Sovietologists are silent about support from below, picturing a "revolution from above" by force over the masses.[25]

• A. Nove considers the only economic aim of "forced collectivization" the provision of government requirements for agricultural production. This, in his opinion, leads to a low survival minimum for the peasant and conversion of his labor in the collective farms (for the state) to feudal duty.[26]

• In this way, M. Lewin propagates the myth that the *kolkhoz* system suppressed the work initiative of peasants, not arousing in them interest in the development of public production.[27]

[24] Ibid., p. 217.
[25] A. D. Smirnov, ed., *Kritika antimarksistskikh ekonomicheskikh teorii v prepodavanii politicheskoi ekonomiki*, p. 223.
[26] Ibid.
[27] I. I. Klimin, *Agrarnaia politika KPSS (1917-1937 gg.): deistvitel'nost' i burzhuaznye vymysly*, p. 127.

- The Soviet Union's ideological opponents attribute to agriculture the role of a "buffer sector" that absorbs all the blows of a "discriminatory" economic policy.[28]

- The anticommunists' sociological "studies" are capped by their treatment of the role and place of the collective farm peasantry in socialist society. They harp on the false thesis that the peasantry is the most exploited part of Soviet society.[29]

- "Sovietology" traditionally describes the CPSU's attitude to the Soviet peasantry as "hostile," "unjust," etc. while the peasantry is in turn depicted as a force opposing the party, a force aggravated by its situation.[30]

- Open hostility to the Soviet formation permeates anticommunist propaganda, depicting the position of collective farmers as "citizens of a second sort" deprived of any kind of democratic rights. Sovietologists assert that the chairman of the collective farm is not elected by the farmers, but is designated by higher organizers.[31]

- The party is depicted by Sovietologists as a force having its interest opposed to the collective farmers, exercising "surveillance" and "control" over the collective farmers.[32]

Criticisms of "Anticommunism": Commentaries on Workers

Foreign criticisms of Soviet and Chinese treatment of workers have much in common. Although not as severe as criticisms against rural policies, these criticisms highlight many of the same themes, e.g. state coercion and inadequate incentives. What Soviets write about the situation of workers in China often appears to echo the criticisms by other for-

[28] Mikeshin, *History versus Anti-History*, p. 58.
[29] Ibid., p. 99.
[30] Ibid., p. 118.
[31] *Real'nyi sotsializm v SSSR i ego burzhuaznye fal'sifikatory*, p. 223.
[32] Ibid., pp. 225-26.

eigners. At the same time, Soviet accusations in response to Western criticisms of Soviet conditions are punctuated with charges that they are both baseless and anticommunist. Their vigorous rejection of the "fabrications" of Sovietologists concerning Soviet workers provides an instructive starting point for examining what the Soviets write about China.

• Bourgeois Sovietologists, attempting to describe the Soviet formation as "antisocialist socialism," try to prove that no liberation of the working class in our country has occurred and that it never played or will play a leading role in society. Over the decades there have been propagated and continue to be propagated fabrications of the appearance in the USSR of a "new ruling class," of the "elite's oppression of workers," of the latter having received nothing from the socialist transformation of society, of "differences of opinion" among the working class, the collective farmers, the intelligentsia, etc.[33]

• A large place in the writings of Sovietologists is occupied by attempts to distort the interrelations of the Communist Party of the Soviet Union and the working class: they strive to suggest to the foreign reader poorly informed about the USSR the thought that the CPSU is not interested in the living requirements of the workers, it only tries to manipulate them with the aim of increasing the productivity of labor.[34]

• In works of Sovietology over the last years are repeated fabrications on the low political consciousness and "social passivity" of the working class.[35]

• Intentionally falsifying reality, "Sovietologists" have often undertaken to demonstrate that Soviet trade unions

[33] Ibid., pp. 187-88.
[34] Ibid., p. 198.
[35] Ibid., p. 201.

concern themselves only with production matters, not with the defense of working people's interests.[36]

- Accusing the Soviet state system of "totalitarianism," "Sovietologists" attempt to extend this pseudo-totalitarianism to socialist production relations. This is expressed especially in the anticommunists' allegation that labor in the USSR is of a forced character and is coercion by the CPSU with respect to Soviet working people.[37]

According to these summaries and refutations of Western writings about Soviet workers, "anticommunism" manifests itself in many ways. First, the workers are seen as oppressed and unrewarded by the existing system. They are also portrayed as divided in their outlook from other classes. Second, the leadership is viewed as exploitative, concerned not with the well-being of the workers but with the extent to which production can be increased. Third, the working class appears apathetic and passive rather than as an active participant in the political process. Fourth, Sovietologists portray trade unions as pawns in the hands of leaders interested only in production. The workers are not properly represented. Finally, critics assert that labor is forced rather than freely volunteered. Soviet spokesmen insist that these accusations are false. They are not based on facts, but on distortions of Soviet reality.

Criticisms of "Anticommunism": Commentaries on the Intelligentsia

Similarities in the position of educated persons in China and the Soviet Union are identified in Western publications. Although Westerners are generally much harsher on the treatment of intellectuals in Maoist China, they point to some basic similarities between the two countries in ed-

---

[36] Mikeshin, *History versus Anti-History*, p. 123.
[37] Ibid., p. 136.

ucation, the arts, the mass media, management, and academic research. They accentuate the controls placed on creative endeavors and scientific investigations. Critics also emphasize censorship and heavy-handed bureaucratic methods. Soviet publications vigorously reject the Western criticisms of the role of the intelligentsia in their country, while, at the same time, finding fault with China for many of the same shortcomings.

- The Sovietological falsification of relations of the intelligentsia to the communist party leads to the line of rejection of the unity of ideas and the political unity of the intelligentsia and the party and distortion of the character of the party-political leadership of the intelligentsia.[38]

- Sovietologists energetically spread a myth about the isolation of the intelligentsia from the remaining workers of Soviet society.[39]

- The thesis of "ideological coercion" allegedly carried out by the CPSU by means of propaganda is becoming increasingly widespread in the present-day literature of anticommunism. Professor Carl Friedrich of Harvard University substitutes coercion for persuasion, which is the only and permanent method of party propaganda. This advocate of the "theory of totalitarianism" singles out coercion as the dominant feature of the Soviet education system. In his opinion, it manifests itself primarily in the coercion of minds, in the compulsory submission of men to a single ideology. . . . "Ideological coercion" is manifested concretely, in the view of "Sovietologists," in the struggle of Soviet Communists against such allegedly inherent human qualities as individualism, egoism, money-grubbing, career seeking, and so on. . . . "Sovietologists" conclude that there is an inevitable "psychological coercion" of Soviet

[38] *Real'nyi sotsializm v SSSR i ego burzhuaznye fal'sifikatory*, pp. 242-43.
[39] Ibid., p. 246.

27

citizens in the name of the attainment of communist goals. A consequence of this is the alleged "apoliticism" of Soviet citizens.[40]

Criticisms of "Anticommunism": Commentaries on Officials

The consensus in Western political writings about both the Chinese and Soviet political systems is that a small group of communist party leaders, who actually wield power, has recruited and promoted officials largely on the basis of their unquestioning support. Aspiring officials join the party less out of idealism than out of cynicism and career aspirations. Once in the party, they must offer unswerving support to their superiors and to central decisions. Discipline is tight, with little or no opportunity to voice disagreement or, except at the higher levels, to represent divergent interests on important national matters. Officials, including some who are not party members, are under close scrutiny in the most fundamental pursuits, but at the same time may be given considerable leeway to achieve various day-to-day objectives. Because there are no checks and balances, party officials are able, without much likelihood of getting caught, to make arbitrary demands and to do favors for those close to them. In the Western view, the system breeds abuse of power, corruption, and a feeling by the majority that they are pawns.

In the recent outpouring of refutations of so-called anticommunist writings, Soviet authors sharply refute charges that their system is not democratic and just. They condemn any attempt to oppose the interests of officials to those of others in the society. Perhaps even more than in responses to other charges, the Soviet critics of "anticommunist" assertions about the role of the party, and other organs of power, quickly brush aside the arguments they are refuting. They have no intention of fully summarizing criticisms in such a sensitive area. Nor do they give credence to these

[40] Mikeshin, *History versus Anti-History*, pp. 148-49.

INTRODUCTION

analyses of Soviet society by separately discussing socialist officials as if they could form an independent class. However, as we see below, in some Soviet analyses of China the *ganbu* or cadres are singled out for separate discussion. Arguing that the workers, the peasants, and the intelligentsia of China have all been oppressed, the Soviets are hard-pressed to identify the oppressors. In addition to Chinese official circles—the central leadership, the CCP (Chinese Communist Party), the PLA (People's Liberation Army), the local cadres, etc.—Soviets sometimes work the bourgeoisie into their discussions of class struggle in China.

In defense of their own class system, Soviets place their officials within the intelligentsia. They reject the charge that a new ruling class emerges in the transition from capitalism to socialism. Rather they proclaim the emergence of a new type of selfless and dedicated public servant, recruited largely from the working class, trained according to new principles of "upbringing," and organized in ways that promote the interests of society. Without examining the conditions that might cause officials to go astray from the loftiest of principles, Soviet writers concentrate on what is necessary in the transition to socialism and the buildup of a developed socialist society to achieve a just and selfless group of employees of administrative institutions.[41]

Only when we turn to Russian writings on China can we obtain a clearer impression of what can go wrong. No mention is made of a new class in China; one does not find repeated the Western vocabulary about totalitarianism and class conflict in communist-led systems. Nevertheless, the substance of the criticisms leveled against Chinese leaders and officials repeats much that is familiar in Western studies of both China and the Soviet Union.

• Attempts "to split up" the Soviet people into an elite— the intelligentsia—and a counterelite—the workers and

---

[41] *Izmeneniia sotsial'noi struktury sovetskogo obshchestva: oktiabr' 1917-1920*, p. 295. *Ot kapitalizma k sotsializmu: osnovnye problemy istorii perekhodnogo perioda v SSSR 1917-1937 gg.*, I, pp. 299-355; II, pp. 190-233.

peasants—serve as the point of departure of contemporary bourgeois conceptions.[42]

• The Soviet administrative apparatus is depicted by anticommunists as a ruling and moreover a bureaucratic machine, harmful to the masses.[43]

• All these facts debunk the schemes of the "Sovietologists" who maintain that the communist party is a nonworker, nonpeasant party, that it is a "caste," an "elite" made up of a closed group of intelligentsia administrators.[44]

• The "exploitative minority"—by which is meant the Soviet intelligentsia, or a part of it—that the falsifiers have invented is presented in the guise of a "special social stratum" that is alleged to wield political, economic and ideological power over the people.[45]

• "Sovietologists," of course, in addition to reducing the Soviet working class to an "exploited" status, maintain that the working class lacks the opportunity to take part in managing production or to deal with affairs of state.[46]

• All the links between the communist party and the people are crudely falsified by anticommunists . . . in "Sovietology" there are no few specialists who attempt to demonstrate that the party represents no one but itself.[47]

• In the struggle against socialism, bourgeois "Sovietology" launches especially intensive attacks on the CPSU, falsifying above all its social essence, organizing principles, leading role in communist construction.[48]

[42] *Problemy nauchnogo kommunizma*, vol. 15, pp. 187-88.
[43] *Real'nyi sotsializm v SSSR i ego burzhuaznye fal'sifikatory*, p. 240.
[44] Mikeshin, *History versus Anti-History*, p. 119.
[45] Ibid., p. 92.
[46] Ibid., p. 97.
[47] Ibid., p. 113.
[48] *Real'nyi sotsializm v SSSR i ego burzhuaznye fal'sifikatory*, p. 70.

- Party leadership of civic organizations is falsified to an extreme by "Sovietologists." Seeking to cast a shadow over the CPSU, they spread the lie of the "dictatorship of the party," of the conversion of these organizations into "appendages of the party without rights," they seek to show the "illegitimacy" of the CPSU's leadership of them.[49]

- The Soviets, declares T. von Laue, do not at all "reflect the will of the people," they "are simple conveyer belts for transmitting the will . . . of the center."[50]

Criticisms of "Anticommunism": Commentaries on Ethnic Minorities

In refuting criticisms leveled against the history of Soviet ethnic policies, spokesmen reject the following negative themes: 1) the theme that the nationality question remains unresolved and that centrifugal forces operate in the socialist world as well as in other multi-ethnic states; 2) the idea that Soviet policies are a continuation of tsarist oppression, in which colonialist forces prevail with the support of military might; 3) the notion that the economic and political relations among nationalities are advantageous only to Moscow; 4) the theme of forced assimilation against the will of the minority peoples, in which coercion is used to eliminate national customs; 5) the argument that the minorities do not participate in any significant way in the major decisions that affect their way of life. The following quotations from sources that seek to refute "bourgeois anti-Soviet falsifications" set forth the major viewpoints with which there is disagreement.

- There are certain bourgeois ideologists who as before remain fixed on the thought that the "tsarist policies of oppression of nationality regions," their "economic

---

[49] Mikeshin, *History versus Anti-History*, p. 120.
[50] Marushkin, *Istoriia v sovremennoi ideologicheskoi bor'be*, p. 145.

exploitation," continues in the USSR, with the result that they cannot take off onto the path of industrial development and provide for their own political and cultural growth; that the unification of many nationalities in the structure of the USSR is "profitable only to Moscow," etc.[51]

- In statute 36 [of the 1977 Soviet Constitution] the policies of the convergence of all nations and peoples of the USSR are recalled. These theses testify, according to his [B. Meissner's] words, to "the further development in the Soviet multinational state of the process of assimilation" supposedly intended as justification for "having continued in the country the process of Russification of the population under the flag of internationalism." He sees a "turnabout" in the area of nationality policy in the USSR from the principle of self-determination of nations to "affirmation of the priority of the Russian nationality." Anti-Soviets spread slanderous distortions about "the departure of the CPSU from Marxism-Leninism on the nationality question" and even about "the presence of racism" in the USSR.[52]

- Accusations against Soviet authority for carrying out colonial policies toward the non-Russian nations and peoples are contained in many works of Western ideologists, where are pointed out the "monocultural" direction in the agriculture of Central Asian republics, the "absence" here of an industrial complex, and also that the economic level of certain republics of Central Asia is on the whole somewhat lower than the all-union.[53]

- All these facts [Soviet election results and minority representation in government positions] show the far-

[51] A. I. Luk'ianov, G. I. Denisov, E. L. Kuz'min, and N. N. Razumovich, *Sovetskaia konstitutsiia i mify sovetologov*, pp. 161-62.
[52] Ibid., p. 167.
[53] Z. S. Chertina, *Natsional'nye otnosheniia pri sotsializme v burzhuaznoi istoriografii SShA*, p. 77.

fetchedness of the distortion of Western authors that in the USSR non-Russian peoples "do not have" political strength in discussions of important questions and their representation is "absent" in the supreme organs of state authority.[54]

• Speaking of the successes of socialist nations in the area of cultural life, bourgeois specialists in the process propagate ideas of the "domination of Russian culture," "the forcing out of the traditional cultures of non-Russian peoples," their "forced assimilation."[55]

• American Sovietologists assert that an all-Soviet culture is not the result of the convergence of all cultures of the Soviet peoples, that it is the culture of the Russian people, forcibly implanted in other nations and peoples.[56]

• T. Rakowska-Harmstone affirms, following Pipes, that the establishment of the Soviet system in the nationality regions was achieved with the help of "military actions of Russians to a significant extent against the will of the local population," which "in the majority was hostile to the new authority."[57]

• Anticommunists present the advancement of the Russian language as the language of international contact and collaboration in the guise of an obvious example of "Russification," "force," "the imposition of the Russian language."[58]

A number of nationalities reside on both sides of the Sino-Soviet border. Unfortunately there have been no detailed comparisons of their experiences under the two

[54] Ibid., p. 89.
[55] Ibid., p. 98.
[56] Ibid., p. 100.
[57] Marushkin, *Istoriia v sovremennoi ideologicheskoi bor'be*; p. 130.
[58] K. Kh. Khanazarov, *Reshenie natsional'no-iazykovoi problemy v SSSR*, p. 216.

separate systems. However, Soviet studies of national minorities in China insist that the policies of the two systems have been diametrically opposed. Their accusations against the leaders of China bear remarkable resemblance to the charges against their own country's policies that Soviets so vociferously deny.

Studies of China

Publications written in the West and even in China about Chinese society are considered to be part of the ideological struggle associated with anticommunism. Chinese falsifiers are seen as anti-Soviet and allied with the imperialists in their distortions of Soviet history and also seriously in error in their writings on Chinese history. Bourgeois China specialists are accused of attempting "to prove that socialism was in principle unacceptable for China."[59] Their views of the history of socialism in China are perceived as second only to Sovietology in the forefront of anticommunism. Soviet writings on China are called upon to refute both Chinese and bourgeois anticommunist writings.

How can a reappraisal of Chinese history reinforce the Soviet outlook on the world? This is the question that Soviet specialists on China have worked hard to answer since the 1960s. They have analyzed the legacy of feudalism (or the Asiatic mode of production) and the peculiarities of capitalism's origins in China to explain both the victory of the Chinese Revolution and the difficulties of building socialism and communism after 1949. In the process, Soviet specialists have attacked Chinese writings on the history of the communist movement and Western studies of Chinese policies both before and after the split with the Soviet Union.

Soviet specialists keep close tabs on Chinese writings about the Soviet Union. According to O. B. Rakhmanin (writing under the pseudonym, O. B. Borisov), in 1980 *People's Daily*

[59] O. B. Borisov, "Polozhenie v KNR i nekotorye zadachi sovetskogo kitaevedeniia," *Problemy Dal'nego Vostoka* 1982:2, p. 9.

contained more than 3,400 attacks on the internal and external policies of the USSR and on the leaders of the CPSU and the Soviet government, while in 1981 about 2,500 anti-Soviet materials were published.[60] Moreover, he accuses the PRC of distributing fabrications by anticommunist centers.[61] In a continuation of charges against Maoism in the 1960s and 1970s, Soviets lump Chinese publications with those of the West in their anti-Soviet and even anticommunist approach.

Varied interpretations of China in the West, including positive assessments in the early 1970s of Maoism as a purer form of Marxism-Leninism than the Soviet version and the varied post-Mao reevaluations, are linked by Soviets to anticommunism. "Myths about China, are spread by those who consciously pursue the goal of discrediting the theory and practice of socialism."[62] The struggle against bourgeois interpretations of China is given high priority and is repeatedly mentioned in the plans for Chinese studies within the Soviet Union.

THE SINO-SOVIET DISPUTE

In the first decade after the Chinese communists won power in October 1949, they enjoyed the benefits of friendship with the Soviet Union. By "leaning to one side," as Mao put it, they gained the security of a 30-year Treaty of Friendship, Alliance, and Mutual Assistance. In return for China's involvement in the Korean War, the People's Liberation Army received modern armaments from the Soviet Union. Stalin granted modest economic assistance, and then Khrushchev in 1954 offered increased aid and reduced Soviet interference, including the elimination of Sino-Soviet joint companies. A large number of modern factories

---

[60] O. B. Borisov, "Nekotorye aspekty politiki Kitaia," *Kommunist* 1981:6, reprinted in *Opasnyi kurs* 11, p. 23; and "Polozhenie v KNR i nekotorye zadachi sovetskogo kitaevedeniia," p. 13.

[61] Borisov, "Nekotorye aspekty politiki Kitaia," p. 23.

[62] *Sovremennyi Kitai v zarubezhnykh issledovaniiakh*, p. 7.

were built with the help of Soviet advisers, who also contributed to the reorganization of Chinese government, education, and science. In 1957, more economic aid was promised along with assistance in building nuclear weapons. Close ties with the Soviet Union helped the Chinese communists to build up their urban organizational structure after two decades of rural isolation, to achieve extraordinary rates of industrial growth, and to enjoy military security despite U.S. containment policies.

During this period there were also developments that reduced China's gratitude to its ally. First, the Chinese objected to interference in their country, especially to Soviet involvement in regions along the border from Sinjiang to Manchuria in the early 1950s. Second, Mao and his supporters resented the limitations on their foreign policy and ideological claims imposed by Soviet leadership in the communist bloc. When China sought to regain islands in the Taiwan Straits and to extend its influence in Asia, it found that the Soviet Union was unsupportive despite Mao's claim that "the east wind prevailed over the west wind." Third, the Chinese leaders had increasing doubts from the mid-1950s about the applicability of the Soviet model of development with its primary reliance on heavy industry, central planning, and the urban sector. Nationalistic motives intensified China's reactions to the dependent relationship that had developed.

Three key issues drove the two countries apart between 1956 and 1960: de-Stalinization, détente, and development. Stalin's death and, more directly, Khrushchev's February 1956 speech to the Twentieth Party Congress of the CPSU set in motion a process of reordering relations in the communist world and rewriting Marxist-Leninist ideology. By the end of the year, Polish riots, the Hungarian uprising, and the divisive de-Maoization of China's official ideology at China's Eighth Party Congress all reveal the turmoil and reconsiderations that followed. By proceeding independently in revising the communist movement's ideology and view of history—both deeply embedded in Stalinism—Khrushchev posed a serious challenge to China's leaders, who had created an ideology over several decades and believed that they had won widespread popular support to their cause. Eventually the response to de-Stalinization was re-Maoization in China. In the late 1950s the Soviet leaders gave high priority to improving relations with the United States and also attached importance to better relations with India; these foreign policy objectives clashed with China's interests. Finally the Chinese leaders in 1958 launched the Great Leap Forward to solve their developmental needs, infuriating the Soviet leaders with their claims to more advanced forms of organization in the transition to communism.

The Course of Hostile Relations

The years from the open split of 1960 to 1983 can be divided into many periods, as relations between the Soviet Union and China changed, but three major divisions should be noted: the 1960s, when relations between the two countries were on a downward spiral; the 1970s, when relations remained poor at the same time China's relations with the United States and its allies were improving; and the early 1980s, when Sino-Soviet relations were normalizing.

From 1960 to 1963 the split was still indirect and not at full intensity. The Soviets stopped all economic assistance to China and withdrew their advisers in July 1960. The Twenty-second Congress of the CPSU in October 1961 reopened wounds about de-Stalinization. The war between China and India in October 1962 and the Chinese criticisms of Khrushchev's handling of the Cuban missile crisis exacerbated differences in foreign policy. In July 1963 delegations headed by Deng Xiaoping and Mikhail A. Suslov met to try to work out differences, but the talks were broken off by the Chinese, who opposed the almost simultaneous opening of negotiations between the Soviet Union and the United States over a partial nuclear test ban. From 1963 to 1966, relations were characterized by open hostility and direct clashes. The dispute widened to encompass what Suslov regarded as Mao's cult of personality and also Chinese territorial claims resulting from unequal treaties under the tsars and Chinese rejections of the new Brezhnev leadership as "Khrushchevism without Khrushchev." The low point in Sino-Soviet relations was from 1966 to 1969. Anti-Soviet incidents occurred during the Cultural Revolution, and the Soviets retaliated by expelling Chinese students. Each country sharply attacked the other as having deviated from socialism. Finally in early 1969 military clashes took place on the Ussuri river, and the possibility of war between the countries threatened. Only in September 1969 did the two sides agree to border talks and a return of ambassadors to their embassies.

In the decade of the 1970s Chinese relations with the United States, Japan, and Western Europe improved. Nixon's journey to Beijing in 1972 signified a new relationship. The Chinese remained concerned about the threat of encirclement from the Soviet Union although the intensity of hostile rhetoric occasionally ebbed as border talks periodically resumed. Over the next four years, Sino-American relations fluctuated while there was little sign of improvement in Sino-Soviet relations. The post-Mao era initially brought a sharp advance in Chinese relations with the United States and its allies, including full diplomatic relations with the United States and grandiose Chinese plans for economic assistance. With the Chinese invasion of Vietnam in 1979 in retaliation for Vietnam's occupation of Kampuchea, the Soviet invasion of Afghanistan, and the Chinese decision not to renew the 1950 Treaty of Friendship, the decade of the 1970s ended on a decidedly negative note.

The Reagan administration's initial position on Taiwan and insistent containment policies against the Soviet Union may have been one cause for the Chinese and the Soviets to reconsider their hostile relationship. In addition, the Chinese from 1979 were reconsidering the reform policies and ambitious economic ties that were first adopted in reaction against Maoism. Internally they were in most respects returning to the Soviet model. Their foreign policy was leaning less to the West and Japan as they tried to fashion an independent course with appeal to the Third World. De-Maoization had eliminated the basic source of the dispute. But the Chinese remained wary of Soviet military deployments on their border and of Soviet intolerance for a polycentric communist world. The Soviet conservatives continued their hostility to Chinese policies and warned against closer relations on terms that would be desired by the Chinese. Negotiations between the two countries began in late 1982; over the previous year a number of small steps had been taken to show each side's readiness to normalize relations.

Changing Soviet Images of China

There is no dearth of writings on the politics and polemics of Sino-Soviet relations from 1949 to the post-Mao era. The overview in the previous section offers a brief background for the discussion to follow. Many books provide a year-by-year, blow-by-blow account of the disputes that have marred the relationship of these countries.[63]

[63] G. F. Hudson, *The Sino-Soviet Dispute*; Donald S. Zagoria, *The Sino-Soviet Conflict, 1956-1961*; William E. Griffith, *The Sino-Soviet Rift*; Dennis J. Doolin, *Territorial Claims in the Sino-Soviet Conflict: Documents and Analysis*; William E. Griffith, *Sino-Soviet Relations, 1964-1965*; John Gittings, *Survey of the Sino-Soviet Dispute: A Commentary and Extracts from the Recent Polemics, 1963-1967*; O. Edmund Clubb, *China and Russia: The "Great Game"*; O. B. Borisov and B. T. Koloskov, *Sovetsko-kitaiskie otnosheniia 1945-1970: kratkii ocherk*; Kenneth R. Whiting, *Evolution of the Sino-Soviet Split: A Summary Account*; Harold C. Hinton, *The Sino-Soviet Confrontation: Implications for the Future*; Alfred D. Low, *The Sino-Soviet Dispute: An Analysis of the Polemics*; Morris Rothenberg, *Whither China: The View from the Kremlin*; George Ginsburgs and Carl F. Pinkele, *The Sino-Soviet Territorial Dispute, 1949-64*; Kenneth Lieberthal, *Sino-Soviet Conflict in the 1970's: Its Evolution and Implications for the Strategic Triangle*; Richard Wich, *Sino-Soviet Crisis Politics: A Study of Political Change and Communication*; Jonathan D. Pollack, *The Sino-Soviet Conflict in the 1980s: Its Dynamics and Policy Implications*; Herbert J. Ellison, ed., *The Sino-Soviet Conflict: A Global Perspective*; Douglas T. Stuart and William T. Tow, *China, the Soviet Union, and the West: Strategic and Political Dimensions in the 1980s*.

There also exists one scholarly analysis of how Soviet perceptions of China changed over this period. Entitled "Soviet Images of the People's Republic of China, 1949-1979," this 1981 doctoral dissertation at the University of Michigan by Gretchen Ann Sandles identifies five successive images (and a sixth competing image in the late 1960s and early 1970s). It shows that, as Sino-Soviet relations and internal policies in the PRC changed, new images of Chinese society were popularized. It probes beneath the short-term polemics to find the long-term patterns of interpretation.

Sandles's analysis summarizes the official Soviet response to the growing rift with China. When read together with some of the books on the history of Sino-Soviet relations, it makes intelligible variations by period in Soviet interpretations of China. Its period-by-period approach, however, must be supplemented by analysis of China's place in the Soviet worldview and a detailed examination of scholarly writings on distinct problems of China's social structure. Only from this broader perspective can we hope to comprehend the full significance of Soviet writings on China. At the general level that Sandles emphasizes and on topics such as foreign policy, leadership, and the political system, she is able to detect only short periods of open disagreement among Soviet specialists on China. Nevertheless, her work offers glimpses of substantial differences of opinion and of highly sensitive issues for Soviet citizens. It suggests the possibility of a topical analysis that draws on a wider range of sources,[64] including specialized scholarly studies, and stresses subjects on which uniform views are less likely. The nature of the Soviet worldview and of the dispute over the true path of socialism suggests the need for a sociological approach to examine the varied and informative writings on social classes.

How did Soviets interpret Chinese policies prior to the

[64] Gilbert Rozman, "Moscow's China-Watchers in the Post-Mao Era: The Response to a Changing China," *The China Quarterly* (June 1983), pp. 220-22.

breakdown in relations during 1960? For the most part, they applauded China's achievements and overlooked its problems. The unanimous judgment was that China was successfully making the transition to socialism. As the pace of institutional change in the PRC quickened from 1955, Soviet specialists wrote favorably of the accelerated transition. They approved the collectivization of 1955-1956; the antirightist campaign of 1957-1958, which was considered to be a decisive blow in the struggle against bourgeois ideology; the nationalization of industry and related policies to organize and benefit workers; and the general course of economic development and political transformation. During the second half of 1958, "the predominant Soviet image of the P.R.C. reflected enthusiasm for the policies of the Great Leap Forward."[65] Even initial Soviet reactions to the people's communes indicate the continued momentum of positive evaluations.

There were also early signs of a more troubled situation for Soviet China-watching in the 1950s. Not only was there tremendous growth in the field, there were repeated reorganizations of China specialists and high-level criticisms of shortcomings in scholarship.[66] Blame was variously placed on the legacy of Sinology as a field, which paid little attention to contemporary questions; on Stalin's cult of personality, which led to dogmatism or mechanically carrying over Stalin's position on the Russian Revolution onto Chinese soil;[67] and eventually on the Chinese, whose sensitivity to criticism and opposition to the establishment in 1956 of a separate institute on China contributed to the tendentious appraisals in Soviet writings. Soviet authors were eventually to look back to try to explain why they had overlooked serious problems in China during the 1950s.

[65] Gretchen Ann Sandles, "Soviet Images of the People's Republic of China, 1949-1979," p. 96.

[66] Gilbert Rozman, "Background," in Rozman, ed., *Soviet Studies of Premodern China: Assessments of Recent Scholarship*, p. 640.

[67] Sandles, "Soviet Images of the People's Republic of China, 1949-1979," p. 77.

Within three years of the announced de-Stalinization of the field after 1956, Chinese studies in the Soviet Union received a new jolt from the deterioration of official relations with China. Just as it was expanding rapidly and shedding some of the deleterious ideological controls of Stalinism, the field became the object of new accusations. "Beginning in early 1959, the work of the Institute of Chinese Studies drew criticism, the volume of publications on the PRC declined considerably and the tone of the articles published changed dramatically."[68] Leading Sinologists were held accountable for failing to provide a scientific assessment of China, and especially for praising unduly China's Great Leap Forward, which was now regarded as a sharp departure from socialism. The new institute was closed; its journal, *Sovetskoe kitaevedenie* (which had begun as recently as 1958) was suspended; and a new leadership for the field was soon selected, largely from the non-academic world. Although Soviet specialists now recall their private dissent from the rosy picture of Chinese society that was painted to 1959, the official record shows little evidence of it apart from some criticisms of economic problems, some comments about difficulties due to China's low level of development, and relative silence about some of the PRC's claims, including, in the first years after 1949, claims about Mao's original contributions to Marxist-Leninist theory.

The open rift between the two leading communist parties was revealed in articles published in April 1960, then in the July recall of Soviet technicians, and finally in an international meeting of communist parties in November. Relations continued to worsen through the 1960s. The initial response among specialists was silence. From 1960 to early 1964 (with the exception of a brief flurry of sharp attacks centered on foreign policy) no more than a handful of superficial observations were published on contemporary affairs in China. This quiet was broken by publication on April 3, 1964, of M. A. Suslov's report to the February

[68] Ibid., p. 116.

42

Plenum of the Central Committee of the CPSU. It warned the Chinese to avoid the mistakes that Stalin had made. The first serious public discussion of Chinese society ensued, but Khrushchev's ouster in October was followed by another period of silence. Only after 1967 was a concerted effort made to explain what had happened and was happening in the PRC.

Soviet explanations initially attributed China's failings to its superstructure, to the policies of Mao and his supporters, to the cult of Mao, to his ideological revisionism, and to China's military-bureaucratic dictatorship. The political system was at fault, and its failure became all the more apparent in the course of the Cultural Revolution. The Chinese were guilty of Great Han chauvinism (ethnic discrimination by the majority, Han Chinese), Sinicized Marxism, and other nationalistic manifestations. Because communist party congresses in China were rare (only three during the final thirty years of Mao's life) and the party was bypassed by Mao and other leaders and by the army in the Cultural Revolution, China was not being properly led. Policies that were voluntaristic, antiscientific, and disruptive of central planning signified that China was not benefiting by an understanding of the regularities of history. If China remained socialist—in most Soviet writings it was unclear whether China had receded to a pre-socialist stage—this was because its substructure, especially government ownership of property and China's class system, remained basically the same as in the previous period.

At the end of the 1960s Soviet Chinese studies reached their maturity. From this time to 1982 they would be marked by voluminous output, stable organization, and a consistent prevailing outlook on Chinese society. This outlook was an amplification of emerging views from the mid-1960s; so there was no fundamental change in thinking for about two decades under Brezhnev's and Suslov's leadership before 1982, when both leaders died and in the same year Sino-Soviet negotiations began.

Above all, Soviet writers stress China's backwardness. The

weakness of the modern sector, both in industry and agriculture, results in a disproportionate petty-bourgeois force in the social class system. Specialists trace this force to the legacy of the past—material, organizational, and ideological. They also devote a great deal of attention to policy mistakes since 1949 that can, in part, be explained by this pervasive petty-bourgeois heritage.

After Mao's death, there was a pause of about half a year before criticism of contemporary China resumed in force. Once the criticism began, the predominant approach until 1982 was that "Maoism without Mao" existed in China. But differences of opinion became evident as Chinese reforms repudiated major elements of the Maoist program. These differences revealed contrasting expectations about the forthcoming negotiations over Sino-Soviet relations, and they also indicated conflicting interpretations of the Soviet worldview and the nature of socialist society.

The Sino-Soviet split had made possible an extraordinary situation within Moscow's circles of social scientists. It had created a need for a creative, wide-ranging discussion of fundamental issues of socialism. The discussion began in secret; writing that appeared publicly in the late 1960s and early 1970s may have been a pale reflection of the sharp analyses written in the time of greatest indecision earlier in the 1960s. Suslov's warning in 1964 suggests that in the aftermath of the Twenty-second Party Congress of 1961, when Khrushchev most vigorously pursued de-Stalinization, direct comparisons of China and the Soviet Union were at the forefront of attention. There is no published material on Chinese society to support these suspicions, but the proximity to high officials of such reform-minded figures as L. P. Deliusin and Fedor Burlatsky was never greater. It is not unlikely that their forthright analyses of Chinese socialism in the early 1960s became the foundation for the reform-oriented critique of China discernible in the literature from the late 1960s to the early 1980s. Indirectly and intermittently, the proponents of this viewpoint kept the de-Stalinization perspective alive until they could articulate it more fully, if only in a Chinese context, in the post-Mao era. The field of Chinese studies harbored reform forces, who, while on the defensive through the 1970s, preserved a forum for reflection and continued analysis of the problems of socialism.

By the time Soviet leaders gave permission in 1966-1968 for a large-scale publication program on China, the tide had turned against the reform forces. The reins of power were placed firmly in the hands of an orthodox group who could be counted on to stifle challenges to the official worldview in this sensitive field. Despite the omnipresence of censorship organs, this task was not easy. The extraordinary shocks of the Cultural Revolution, the military skirmishes of 1969, the U.S.-China rapprochement, and the abrupt arrest of the "Gang of Four" produced a sharp jolt every three or four years. There was a continuous need to understand events in China in a new way and to mobilize public opinion in support of the official Soviet position. Specialists were separated by institutional affiliation, which offered an opportunity for personal bonds and protection. They found their own niches within the depths of China's wonderously rich history, at some distance from the most sensitive themes. The overall hostile viewpoint on Maoism set limits on diversity, but the fact that reform-oriented scholars articulated a negative position on Maoism that clearly supported the Soviet side in the Sino-Soviet dispute made them an elusive target. Their survival attests to support from elements of the Soviet leadership eager for historically informed judgments in a field that through the 1960s and much of the 1970s was considered not up to the task of providing the needed expertise.

In a 1983 article,[69] I suggested that the orthodox and reform groups have different outlooks on the possibility of improving Sino-Soviet relations as well as in their assessments of the post-Mao reforms. In the chapters that follow,

[69] Rozman, "Moscow's China-Watchers in the Post-Mao Era," pp. 215-41.

I draw attention to differences of opinion between orthodox and reform groups on a wide range of issues pertaining
to social classes. Nevertheless, it is important to emphasize
that both groups are working within (or close to) the confines of a single, official worldview and that they join together on the Soviet side of the Sino-Soviet dispute. In this
book I draw a general equation between Western criticisms
of the Soviet Union (labeled "anticommunist" by the Soviets) and Soviet criticisms of China from both the orthodox
and the reform perspectives. It would be a mistake to deny
the orthodox group's involvement in echoing "anticommunism." At the same time, I believe there is a separate
equation between certain especially deep Western criticisms
of the Soviet Union, reform-oriented Soviet criticisms of
China, and what I take to be implied internal criticism by
reformers aimed at Soviet society. Only by looking directly
at studies of social classes in China is it possible to move
beyond the general Soviet consensus evident in the first
equation to the internal split that excludes the orthodox
group from the second equation.

The Sino-Soviet rivalry accomplished what friendship in
the 1950s could not. It transformed Chinese studies in the
Soviet Union into a field where serious scholarship was
possible. In the process, it fostered an internal dispute over
how to assess Chinese society. A byproduct of the Sino-
Soviet dispute is the visible manifestation within Moscow's
community of China watchers of an internal orthodox-re-
form dispute.

The Sociology of China

Soviet images of China have been reenforced by the emergence of a new field within Chinese studies. Although it is
not formally part of the discipline of sociology, which was
revived only in 1956 after a quarter-century hiatus under
the repressive influence of Stalinism, the new field closely
parallels the emerging sociology of China in the United
States. It can be broadly portrayed as those studies of China

past and present that go beyond China's official ideology, leadership questions, technical economic problems, and foreign policy to examine the changing character of Chinese society. Because the Soviet worldview and the dispute with "anticommunism" center to a large extent on social change in the building' of socialism, sociology figures importantly in recent Soviet social science writings. As Soviet analysis of China was deepening in the 1960s with the search for the sources of the Maoist deviation, sociological writings became widespread in the field too.

From the late 1960s Soviet writers began to pay close attention to American and other Western publications on China. It is not simply a coincidence that the sociology of China should expand simultaneously in the two countries. Soviet bibliographies reveal a substantial acquaintance with Western sources, and a select group of Soviet specialists has visited American centers of Chinese studies. One justification for this close scrutiny is the leadership's demand that specialists intensify the ideological struggle against "bourgeois falsifications," but Soviets have also acknowledged that they were eager to learn from the superior China-watching results of the United States. They learned quickly, as their own publications on specialized aspects of Chinese life multiplied.

The Organization of Soviet Studies of China

Each party congress issues a message to specialists on how they should proceed over the next five years. The message to China specialists is often among the most pointed. At the Twentieth Party Congress in 1956, Soviet Orientalists were rebuked for slumbering while the entire East had been awakening. From that time studies of contemporary China expanded rapidly. Party congresses have also offered an assessment of the nature of Chinese society that specialists are expected to expand in their own writings. At the Twenty-sixth Party Congress in 1981, Brezhnev asserted, "The experience of the socioeconomic development of the PRC over the past two decades—is a grave lesson, having shown to what the distortion of the principles of socialism leads. . . . There are now occurring changes in the internal policies of China. Time will yet show their true meaning."[70] The apparent message to China specialists was to investigate changes inside China in order to determine their significance. Following each congress, articles have appeared in the leading publications of each field, including the journals *Problemy Dal'nego Vostoka* (translated as *Far Eastern Affairs*) and *Narody Azii i Afriki*, to designate the tasks that lie ahead.

Plenary meetings and major pronouncements of the Central Committee as well as significant speeches by Brezhnev have provided other occasions that give rise to articles and meetings to redefine the pursuits of the field. The July 14, 1963, Open Letter of the CPSU Central Committee to the party organizations and all communists of the Soviet Union, the resolutions of the February 1964 and the December 1966 plenary meetings of the Central Committee, Brezhnev's speech at the 1969 International Meeting of the Communist and Workers' Parties, and Brezhnev's March 1982 speech in Tashkent were developments of consequence for the field. In the intervals between these definitive assessments, specialists are guided by the authoritative articles written in *Pravda* under the pseudonym, I. Aleksandrov. A dozen or more articles by Aleksandrov during the crucial five years after Mao's death charted the official Soviet response—both skeptical and critical—to new developments. Following the Tashkent speech at which Brezhnev accepted the existence of socialism in China and offered warmer encouragement for negotiations with the Chinese than at any time since the mid-1960s, an Aleksandrov article on May 20, 1982, was even more optimistic, declaring "We are deeply convinced that there is a real

[70] "Iz doklada general'nogo sekretaria TsK KPSS tovarishcha L. I. Brezhneva 'Otchet tsentral'nogo komiteta KPSS XXVI s'ezdu Kommunisticheskoi Partii Sovetskogo Soiuza i ocherednye zadachi partii v oblasti vnutrennei i vneshnei politiki,' " *Opasnyi kurs* 11, p. 3.

possibility for improving Soviet-Chinese relations."[71] Other *Pravda* articles have also provided an immediate indication of the Soviet leadership's position on new developments.

Statements external to the field (I include the Aleksandrov column in this category although it is widely believed to have been written by someone in the field; prior to May 20, 1982, the author was alleged to be O. B. Rakhmanin) do not present many specifics about the nature of Chinese society. These specifics are worked out under the leadership within the field. Articles in the principal journals, which follow the Soviet party congresses, the major speeches by Soviet leaders, and also important events in China, identify the main problems in the field. For example, Rakhmanin, writing under the pseudonym, O. B. Borisov, interpreted the meaning of the Tashkent speech in his article "The position of the PRC and some problems of Soviet Chinese studies" (*Problemy Dal'nego Vostoka* 1982:2, pp. 3-14). From time to time general meetings of China specialists are also convened. In the aftermath of the Twenty-fourth and Twenty-sixth Party Congresses, the first two All-Union Conferences of China Specialists occurred. The January 25-27, 1982, second conference, which was organized by the Academy of Sciences' Scientific Council on Problems of the Foreign Far East, attracted about 400 of the approximately 1,000 Soviet China specialists representing all fields of the discipline.[72] Annual directives are read to the specialists in each department of each institute and a good deal of effort goes into regular reports by individual specialists, sectors, departments, and institutions on how they are fulfilling their annual plans.

Two principal institutes of the USSR Academy of Sciences are responsible for studies of China. The newer and larger center is the Institute of the Far East or Institut Dal'nego Vostoka (IDV). Established in 1966 after repeated

---

[71] *The Current Digest of the Soviet Press*, 34, no. 21 (June 23, 1982), p. 23.

[72] "Vtoraia Vsesoiuznaia konferentsiia kitaevedov," *Problemy Dal'nego Vostoka* 1982:2, pp. 183-89.

criticisms by Soviet officials of the state of Chinese studies in the Soviet Union, its mandate is to study the contemporary Far East and to advise leaders on this region. The older Institute of Oriental Studies or Institut Vostokovedeniia (IVAN) is the heir to the distinguished traditions of Sinology in prerevolutionary Russia. Despite repeated dislocation or deaths caused by the upheavals of revolution and Soviet reorganizations, the Stalinist purges, the siege of Leningrad in World War II, and the 1950 move from Leningrad to Moscow, eminent scholars such as V. M. Alekseev struggled to carry on these traditions. The primary division of labor is between the focus on premodern China of IVAN's Department of China (*otdel Kitaia*) and its other departments with small groups of China specialists, and the contemporary focus of IDV. There is not a firm division, however; at both institutes there are many specialists on the transitional decades to 1949 and a few members of the Department of China are also engaged in research on the PRC.

Senior figures, some of whom serve as department heads at IDV, were lured there in the late 1960s with the understanding that they would be working in a more policy-oriented, politicized environment. From its inception IDV reflected the orthodox position of the Brezhnev leadership—the crackdown on dissent following the Twenty-third Party Congress in 1966, the new Brezhnev doctrine that proclaimed the right to intervene in communist-led countries as demonstrated in 1968 in Czechoslovakia, and the tightened control in the social sciences after the Twenty-fourth Party Congress in 1971 as exemplified in the reorganization of the main institute of sociology. New personnel who were hired at this growing center of Chinese studies were often children of the Soviet elite or others who passed the tough screening procedures for entrants into sensitive fields in international affairs. Close oversight of IDV was vested in a committee that includes China specialists in the Central Committee's Department of Socialist Bloc Relations and at the Ministry of Foreign Affairs. On the whole, IDV has been staffed by people who appear to

approve of a tightly regulated environment in which creativity takes second place to orthodoxy. O. B. Rakhmanin
and others in leading positions work closely with supporters
at this institute. Together they constitute the dominant group
in the field.

The sociology of China has emerged within this controlled and hierarchical framework. Not surprisingly a small
group of individuals has been influential in shaping its development. Four powerful figures in the China field—
O. B. Rakhmanin, S. L. Tikhvinsky, M. S. Kapitsa, and
M. I. Sladkovsky—maintained a grip on Chinese studies that
was virtually unchallenged during the entire period of the
Sino-Soviet dispute. It is not coincidental that, following
the opening remarks by academician P. N. Fedoseev, a
nonspecialist representing the Academy of Sciences, at the
Second All-Union Conference of China Specialists in 1982,
the next speakers were Rakhmanin, first deputy director
of the Bloc Relations Department of the Central Committee
of the communist party; Sladkovsky, director of the Institute of the Far East where several hundred specialists are
employed; and Kapitsa (pseudonym M. S. Ukraintsev), director of the Far Eastern Department of the Ministry of
Foreign Affairs and from December 1982 deputy foreign
minister. Absent on this occasion was Tikhvinsky, who had
a prominent role at the First All-Union Conference, and
is the sole academician in the field, is the president of the
Diplomatic Academy under the Ministry of Foreign Affairs, and recently became the academic secretary in charge
of all institutes in the Academy of Sciences that emphasize
history.

The writings of these four men have guided the field.
Under their own names and pseudonyms, they published
an estimated 200 articles and books in the first six years of
the post-Mao era.[73] Rakhmanin's 1982 book, *The Internal
and External Policies of China in the 1970s* (Moscow: Politiz-

---

[73] Figures based on annual bibliographies for the number of publications by author (with pseudonyms identified) over three years can be
found in Rozman, "Moscow's China-Watchers in the Post-Mao Era," p.
222.

dat) brings together eleven of his evaluations of milestones in Chinese policies or Sino-Soviet relations, beginning with the Soviet Union's Twenty-fourth Party Congress in 1971 and ending with China's 1981 preparations for its Twelfth Party Congress. Kapitsa's 1979 book, *PRC: Three Decades— Three Policies* (Moscow: Politizdat) updates two of his previous works that assess the first decade, and then the first two decades of the PRC. Sladkovsky's 1978 book, *China: Basic Problems of History, Economics, Ideology* (Moscow: Mysl'), also focuses on the general course of China's development. Tikhvinsky's edited volume, *China and Neighbors: In Modern and Contemporary Times*, extends back to the seventeenth century and shows his broader historical range. Although the subjects treated by these four leaders overlap, one can discern a loose division of labor in their responsibilities: Rakhmanin has responsibility for ideology and politics, Kapitsa controls writings about Chinese foreign policy, Tikhvinsky provides the main evaluations of China's historical development and historical relations with its neighbors, and Sladkovsky administers the specialized departments in the Institute of the Far East that provide most of the detail on these subjects. All four write about Sino-Soviet relations and the anti-Soviet and antisocialist character of Chinese policies.

This Soviet group of four shares a great deal in common. They are the generalists in the field of Chinese studies. They are the principal defenders of the ideology, who insist that "it is necessary for Soviet specialists to be strictly governed by Marxist-Leninist methodology" and that it is essential, above all, "to see how in the Chinese specifics are present the general socioeconomic regularities of the development of human civilization."[74] It is they who proclaim the need for vigilant involvement in the ideological struggle against bourgeois falsifiers and Great Han chauvinists (a term used for Chinese who for nationalistic reasons have

---

[74] Borisov, "Polozhenie v KNR i nekotorye zadachi sovetskogo kitaevedeniia," p. 10.

strayed from the correct path of socialism). Their evaluations emphasize the tremendous accomplishments of the
field since the early 1960s. Thus their views represent a
defense of the status quo and of centralized control in the
field. In the 1982 debates over the prospects for improved
relations with the PRC, these leading participants in the
decision making were known as skeptics or hardliners, who
were reluctant to make serious concessions out of concern
for, among other things, the divisive impact on the international communist movement and the negative consequences for true communists both in China and the Soviet
Union.[75]

Although this group has presided over a rapidly expanding field, it has offered only mixed encouragement to
the areas associated with the sociology of China. On the
one hand, there has been an enormous proliferation of
specializations. At the 1982 All-Union Conference ten
branches of Chinese studies were represented: history, historiography, economics, internal policy, state structure, law
and tradition, foreign policy, ideology, literature and art,
linguistics.[76] Many of these branches can, in turn, be divided into numerous sub-specializations. The same conference referred to "the process of formation of a system
of historico-sociological research as a special, and moreover
a long-term direction of research in Soviet studies of China.
In connection with this the question arises of the necessity
of preparing cadres of China specialists—sociologists."[77] In
a period of fifteen years, the leaders in this field permitted
a manifold increase in the number of specialists on contemporary China and an expanded focus on sociological
problems.

On the other hand, the figures in this dominant group
have continually warned against overemphasizing the specifics of Chinese tradition. They set an example by fre-

[75] Rozman, "Moscow's China-Watchers in the Post-Mao Era."
[76] "Vtoraia Vsesoiuznaia konferentsiia kitaevedov," p. 183.
[77] Ibid., p. 187.

quently expressing their own views as deductions from ideological pronouncements, and they show little patience for the details and specialized knowledge essential to proper sociological analysis. Thus the topics of sociological research emerge under conditions in which the conclusions must not contradict the deductive or impressionistic views of leaders in the field. Although there are exceptions in the field of Chinese studies, the tight controls exercised by this group support a dogmatic defense of the Soviet worldview.

To circumvent the tight controls in their field, some China specialists have become more sociological in their orientation. Direct examination of similarities between China and the Soviet Union is, of course, taboo. Kapitsa's thorough oversight of proposed publications on foreign affairs excludes creative research in this area. There is little prospect of balanced scholarship on such sensitive issues as Mao's role in the history of the Chinese Communist Party. Under these conditions, there were not many places for serious scholars to turn, apart from retreating, if permitted, to join some of their distinguished colleagues who specialize in the history or literature of premodern China.

The circumstances of the 1960s offered one promising outlet for those who preferred not to retreat very far. The need to explain China's deviation encouraged research on the distinctive characteristics of traditional China and their consequences in modern times. It also justified an intensive investigation into the history of social thought in the first decades of the twentieth century in search of the impact of socialist and communist ideology on various social groups. Under the able leadership of L. P. Deliusin, the Department of China in the Institute of Oriental Studies became the center of a greatly expanded publication program in these areas. Annual conferences, from which approximately 100 papers are published in three volumes, began in 1970. Entitled "Society and State in China," these conferences have set a high standard for reporting research in progress. In direct contrast to the approach of the four dominant figures in Chinese studies and the Institute of the Far East, the spirit of these conferences embodies six principles appropriate to serious scholarship: 1) humility about how little is already known and how much remains to be learned, not confidence that Soviets already have the answers; 2) praise of diversity and encouragement for reports that are in disagreement with other views expressed in the field; 3) eagerness to learn from Western specialists, whose writing must be followed closely, rather than ideological struggle against them; 4) criticism of Soviet scholarly shortcomings, especially of deductive approaches that fail to take careful account of the facts of Chinese history; 5) stress on modern social science methods, including quantitative approaches; and 6) attention to historical continuities.[78] The papers presented at these conferences contained the seeds of articles and books that appeared in substantial numbers.

The Department of China at IVAN has sustained a more thriving intellectual community than IDV. Most of its staff began Chinese studies in the postwar decade of the late 1940s and early 1950s—a time when intellectual merit counted more heavily as a criterion for entrance into the field. Removed from pressing political issues, specialists have been largely concerned with problems that face all Sinologists—reading and interpreting primary sources, keeping up with the vast secondary literature from many countries around the world, and making original contributions to scholarship. Many at this institute take pride in preserving the heritage of Russian Sinology. It should not be surprising that this environment rather than IDV has nourished

---

[78] Beginning with the volumes from 1973 (the "fourth scientific conference"), a complete collection to 1983 of conference publications, *Obshchestvo i gosudarstvo v Kitae*, has been provided me through the American Council of Learned Societies–Academy of Sciences, USSR, Binational Commission on the Humanities and Social Sciences, Subcommission on East Asia. The goals of the conference are most fully articulated in the introduction to occasional books of longer articles taken from the conference proceedings. The first book, *Kitai: obshchestvo i gosudarstvo* was taken from the papers of 1970 and 1971. This was followed by *Gosudarstvo i obshchestvo v Kitae* and *Obshchestvo i gosudarstvo v Kitae*.

respect for scholarly standards. Around this core, specialists on China at several institutes have separately developed
a point of view about China that contrasts with that of the
orthodox group. On the basis of the evidence presented in
the following chapters, I label this a reform view.

In the post-Mao era, a second possibility along with research on traditional China emerged for serious scholars.
While the dominant group was minimizing the significance
of reforms in China as "Maoism without Mao," no fixed
position precluded detailed analyses of the course of social
change since 1949, perhaps as part of an assessment of
recent developments. The sector on China at the Institute
of the International Workers' Movement led by V. G. Gel'bras
formed the core of a growing effort to trace the changes
in social classes within the PRC. Many of its publications
convey an optimistic impression of brighter days for intellectuals and workers, sharply in contrast with the continued
pessimism expressed at the Institute of the Far East.[79] These
writings also show the importance of sociology to the struggle within the Soviet Union to explain what is happening
in China.

Both sides in this Soviet debate over China describe China
in terms that have been widely used in the West to describe
the Soviet Union. This is true even though they may have
different perspectives on aspects of the Soviet worldview,
on the nature of anticommunism, on the need for reforms
within the Soviet Union, and on the possibilities for improved relations between China and the Soviet Union. The
challengers in the field are not an organized force; they

[79] In 1978 the Institute of the International Workers' Movement (IMRD)
issued five pamphlets in editions of 100 copies each on Chinese social
structure: "Intelligentsia: mesto v obshchestve i politika rukovodstva KPK,"
"Problemy i protivorechiia v razvitii rabochego klassa KNR," "Rabochii
klass i polozhenie v profsoiuzakh KNR," "Sotsiologiia politiki: Problemy
issledovaniia," "Sotsial'nye problemy kitaiskogo obshchestva." In the following years books on Chinese social classes by specialists at IMRD began
to be issued, e.g., V. G. Gel'bras, *Sotsial'no-politicheskaia struktura KNR 50-
60-e gody*.

are small groups of specialists at institutes that are not directly under the control of the main figures in the field. In the following chapters the focus is on a general Soviet view of the social classes and groups in contemporary China, but a final section in each case seeks to distinguish the views of the dominant group of generalists from those of the challengers. Of course, it is somewhat of an oversimplification to pose a rigid dichotomy between the two groups of China specialists; the sections that do this should be taken as no more than a general indication of the contending views about Chinese society that are popular among specialists.

What we find in the voluminous Russian literature on China is a wide-ranging sociology of China. Although none of the authors treated is formally trained as a sociologist, many share with sociologists a basic concern for the analysis of separate social classes and the relations among them and the state. Because Soviets write from the long-established Marxist conviction that both the past and the future of a society can best be understood through the careful analysis of the structure and consciousness of its social classes, it should not be surprising that what they write adds a valuable dimension to the sociological study of China.

When they write about China, Soviet specialists understand that their sociological arguments will be interpreted in a larger context. Their leaders may refer to these arguments in deciding what steps to take to address the continued rift between the Soviet Union and China; this may be the main significance of deciding whether post-Mao reforms are turning Chinese society to the right on a bourgeois course or toward the Soviet Union on a socialist track. Analysts of China understand, too, the ideological sensitivity of their field, which from the time of the Chinese Revolution has been buffeted by criticisms of shortcomings from communist officials. Repeatedly urged to take an active role in the struggle against "anticommunism," they know that their criticisms of China tread a thin line between distinguishing China from the Soviet Union and reinforcing Western accusations of inherent shortcomings in communist-led societies. In the final analysis, the Soviet worldview must be sustained, not through idealized or one-sided interpretations of history, but through careful sociological analysis of actual conditions. Precisely because the genuine specialists on China are engaged in the rare enterprise of intensively analyzing the social relations in a communist-led country, their work has enormous importance for the Soviet worldview and for articulating the alternatives available for reform and orthodoxy at home as well as in China.

· 2 ·

PEASANTS

According to the Soviet worldview, the peasantry represents, on the whole, a positive force. In feudal and capitalist environments, especially under the extra burden of imperialism, peasants become an active revolutionary force. They resist exploitative landlords and despotic state officials. They struggle for a more equitable distribution of land and for various economic and political rights. Their violent struggle, along with the actions of the bourgeoisie, helps bring about the replacement of the feudal order. Years later peasants become active participants in the overthrow of the capitalist or semicapitalist order that brings the communists to power. The consolidation of power by the communist party also owes a lot to the peasantry's support, especially its enthusiastic backing for land reform. In alliance with the proletariat, the rural population continues to support the transition to socialism and the socialist policies that follow.

The Soviet worldview regards the peasantry, despite its largely supportive role, as a not wholly reliable ally. Well-to-do rural residents run the risk of being labeled class enemies—their distaste for greater equality may place them, at one time or another, in the camp of feudal landlords, rural capitalists, or violators of socialist laws. Whatever the circumstances, prosperity from private agricultural pursuits is viewed with distrust. A much larger number of peasants who are not so prosperous are seen as less dangerous, but still potential foes of collectivization and of restrictions on the private household economy. Due to ingrained traditions, insufficient education, and other factors, peasants are, it is recognized, slow to support the new order. Soviets warn that careful policies are needed to wean the peasants away from their private-ownership psychology. Of course, spokesmen insist that resistance can be decisively overcome; socialist policies will work because the basic structural determinants are on the side of a worker-peasant alliance, and the Marxist-Leninist science of society offers correct guidance about the strategy to be followed. It only remains for the communist party to apply these scientific principles in order to win continuous support from the peasants for each successive stage of its policies.

Evidence that agricultural and rural development policies have failed in the Soviet Union poses a serious challenge to this worldview. Spokesmen recognize some shortcomings; yet they concentrate on building a positive case and on defending it against alleged bourgeois falsifications. They are placed in a difficult position, however, when foreign accusations associate the shortcomings of rural policies in the PRC with those in the USSR. Their response has been to argue that China was exceptional, to try somehow to explain what has occurred in rural China without weakening the defense of the Soviet worldview and the refutation of "anticommunism." But this complex pursuit provides some leeway to a research scholar. For the creative specialist working in this environment there is opportunity in addressing specific problems of Chinese history to explain what can go wrong and what is needed to set things right again in a communist-led society.

The Russian literature on peasants in modern and contemporary China largely originates from four institutions, which, I believe, actually reflect two major groupings in Soviet scholarship. On the one side are specialists on rural society at IDV (the Institute of the Far East) such as P. B. Kapralov and L. A. Volkova. The viewpoint of this institute is presented mostly in yearbooks and collectively written overviews of agriculture in the PRC rather than in monographs. Associated with this viewpoint are the generalized interpretations of agriculture found in the writings of officials in the Central Committee, especially O. B. Rakhmanin. On the other side are the specialists on rural China at IVAN (the Institute of Oriental Studies), working in the

60

department headed by L. P. Deliusin. A. S. Kostiaeva, O. E. Nepomnin, G. D. Sukharchuk, and N. I. Tiapkina join Deliusin in publishing primarily about rural development in pre-1949 China. Specialists at two other institutes appear to be closely associated with this group: A. V. Meliksetov at the Moscow State Institute of International Relations (MGIMO) and V. G. Gel'bras and members of his sector at the Institute of the International Workers' Movement (IMRD). There are differences within these groupings and even within institutes but, period by period, contrasting viewpoints have persisted, each identifiable with one of the groupings identified here.

THE LEGACY OF THE PAST

In the past, little scholarly attention was paid in the USSR to China's prerevolutionary society. It was assumed that if communists were successful in revolution then conditions were also ripe for the transition to socialism. Despite the presumption in nineteenth-century Marxism that communist revolutions would occur in advanced capitalist societies, Soviet scholarship has, in fact, shown remarkably little interest in the problems that resulted from establishing socialism in Russia's relatively nonmodernized society. Given the even more glaring discrepancies between the original model and the state of Chinese society in 1949, it is also remarkable how long Soviets accepted without question China's readiness for socialism. Only when this point became a matter of debate did it become necessary to seek explanations rooted in history for what happened after 1949.

By the 1970s, according to V. G. Gel'bras, at least three points of view on the level of development in China toward the end of the 1940s could be found in Soviet writings.[1] The first has remained dominant since the 1950s and continued to be expressed in the 1970s by M. I. Sladkovsky

[1] Gel'bras, *Sotsial'no-politicheskaia struktura KNR 50-60-e gody*, pp. 22-24.

61

among others. It held that objective conditions—both material and otherwise—existed in China for the transition to socialism. Not only did this perspective permit ignorance about social conditions before the revolution, it also encouraged the belief that Soviet solutions could be transferred directly to China. As we might expect, this perspective was explicit or implicit in the writings of those who themselves paid little heed to the state of Chinese society before 1949. It is not an informed judgment based on comparative studies.

The second viewpoint became widespread after it was espoused by S. L. Tikhvinsky and L. P. Deliusin at a nationwide conference of Sinologists in 1971.[2] It holds that China remained a country of small-scale peasants (*melkokrest'-ianskaia strana*), which lacked the prerequisites for building socialism. The early advocates of this view were the two men who had served since the 1950s as administrators of the historians of China in the Institute of Oriental Studies within the Academy of Sciences. Apparently they were providing a rationale for the continued relevance of historical scholarship in the face of intermittent pressures to concentrate more resources on contemporary (post-1949) analysis. Perhaps it is no accident that Sladkovsky, the chief figure rejecting their approach, was the head of Moscow's rival Institute of the Far East established within the Academy of Sciences in 1966 to provide a contemporary orientation.

The third viewpoint is intermediate between the other two because it concludes that material preconditions existed for socialism, especially heavy industrial production, but that they were severely limited by region and sector. The second and third approaches share a negative appraisal of the readiness of the Chinese village for socialism. In addition to Deliusin, who has written on the agrarian question

[2] S. L. Tikhvinsky and L. P. Deliusin, "Nekotorye problemy izucheniia istorii Kitaia," in *Problemy sovetskogo kitaevedeniia*, pp. 21-47.

in the policies of the CCP during the 1920s,[3] a number of other advocates of the second or third approach, e.g. A. S. Mugruzin, I. I. Naumov, and O. E. Nepomnin, are specialists on the rural sector. Their writings on the pronouncements and policies of the CCP stress its failure to appreciate the true character of rural society.[4]

Many voices have joined in the verdict that rural China was backward. Tikhvinsky had drawn this conclusion for the Qing period (1644-1911) as early as 1966 (his long introduction was reprinted in 1975) in his book which onesidedly expounds the oppressive nature of Manchu rule.[5] Nepomnin supported this view in three books (1966, 1974, 1980) that provide a sequential study of China's rural economy over approximately a century to 1914.[6] A. V. Meliksetov (1977 and 1978) takes exception to Nepomnin's direct transfer to China of Russian categories for the rural population, but draws on evidence from the 1920s-1940s to substantiate the conclusion of rural backwardness.[7] Other noteworthy contributors are Mugruzin in his 1970 book on landholdings in the 1920s-1940s, A. S. Kostiaeva in her 1978 book on peasant associations of the 1920s, and N. I. Tiapkina in articles (1978, 1979) on village organization and lineages in the first half of this century.[8]

What were the signs of rural backwardness? Gel'bras

[3] L. P. Deliusin, *Agrarno-krest'ianskii vopros v politike KPK (1921-1928)*.

[4] See, for example, A. S. Mugruzin, *Agrarnye otnosheniia v Kitae v 20-40-kh godakh XX v.*

[5] S. L. Tikhvinsky, *Man'chzhurskoe vladychestvo v Kitae*; and *Istoriia Kitaia i sovremennost'*.

[6] O. E. Nepomnin, *Genezis kapitalizma v Kitae; Ekonomicheskaia istoriia Kitaia 1864-1894 gg.*; and *Sotsial'no-ekonomicheskaia istoriia Kitaia 1894-1914*.

[7] A. V. Meliksetov, *Sotsial'no-ekonomicheskaia politika Gomin'dana 1927-1949 gg.*, and "K voprosu o genezise kapitalizma v Kitae," in *Gosudarstvo i obshchestvo v Kitae*, pp. 158-89.

[8] Mugruzin, *Agrarnye otnosheniia v Kitae v 20-40-kh godakh XX v.*; A. S. Kostiaeva, *Krest'ianskie soiuzy v Kitae*; and N. I. Tiapkina, "O traditsionnoi sotsial'noi organizatsii kitaiskoi derevni v pervoi polovine XX v.," in *Gosudarstvo i obshchestvo v Kitae*, pp. 207-28, and "O klanovoi organizatsii v kitaiskoi derevne pervoi poloviny XX v.," in *Sotsial'naia i sotsial'no-ekonomicheskaia istoriia Kitaia*.

summarizes the conclusions in the field, noting the low level of development of productive forces, agrarian overpopulation (*perenaselenie*), the entrenched position of precapitalist elements, and the undeveloped state of the division of labor and of commercial-monetary relations.[9] He notes that "feudal-patriarchal relations enmeshed the entire Chinese society."[10] He contrasts prerevolutionary Russia, where capitalism was the predominant mode of production despite the persistence of many remnants of the precapitalist order based on serfdom, to the backwardness of China's primarily natural and seminatural economy. Gel'bras joins A. V. Meliksetov in rejecting the long accepted division of China's landowning population into landlord (*pomeshchik*), rich peasant (*kulak*), and middle peasant (*seredniak*) as an inaccurate reflection of the real character of economic relations in China to 1949. Despite their adoption by China's leaders, Russian terms do not apply well to rural relations in China, Gel'bras insists, adding "It is not coincidental that there is no expression in Chinese for the designation of village exploiters as a class, and a wide gamut of terms (*shenshi, tuhao, lieshen*, etc.) of narrower meaning is used."[11] Both its backwardness and its distinctiveness made China less prepared for socialism than Russia had been in 1917.

One line of criticism is directed against Chinese efforts to find an early and indigenous start for capitalism—what are called "sprouts of capitalism"—in the late Ming to mid-Qing, or the claim that spontaneous domestic sources of capitalism had formed but were repressed or distorted first by the Manchu takeover and then by the imperialist presence. This viewpoint is seen as exaggerating the level of development in China and its independent accomplishments.[12] Soviet writers such as Nepomnin who were ac-

[9] Gel'bras, *Sotsial'no-politicheskaia struktura KNR 50-60-e gody*, p. 25.
[10] Ibid., p. 26.
[11] Ibid., p. 30.
[12] G. D. Sukharchuk, "Tsiui Tsiu-bo ob osobennostiakh razvitiia kapitalizma v Kitae," in *Gosudarstvo i obshchestvo v Kitae*, p. 246.

cused of having been taken in by these views in the 1960s
have reconsidered how far development had gone. Nepomnin's recent writing emphasizes the "weakness of internal capitalist potential." He refers to the "primitive starting level and the low tempo of growth of rural capitalism"
and concludes that the "deformation of the traditional social structure at the beginning of the twentieth century did
not lead to all-around progress."[13]

Increasingly a consensus has been shaping that holds
that, in addition to its relative backwardness, China by the
1930s had a distinctive rural social structure with some
elements of capitalism. A 1978 review article by Meliksetov
on the genesis of capitalism in nineteenth- and twentieth-
century China notes the rapid advance in Soviet historiography of this key subject in recent years after a long period
in which no adequate base of socioeconomic research existed, but the article also points to difficulties of interpretation that still must be overcome.[14] Meliksetov indicates
the lack of clarity that prevails concerning the structure of
the ruling class and takes exception to Nepomnin's analysis
of the relations between landlords (*dizhi*, which he translates
with the neutral term of *zemlevladel'tsy*) and peasants. Indeed, Meliksetov's arguments that most land was held by
the peasants and that no prevailing tendency of concentration existed contradict views frequently espoused in the
Soviet literature.[15] Drawing on Nepomnin's evidence (but
not necessarily his conclusions) and on other Soviet and
Western writings, Meliksetov suggests that the state was the
primary exploiter. He concludes that five features in China
prior to its "opening" distinguish it from Western Europe:
1) the significant socioeconomic role of the despotic state;
2) the predominant role of taxes and rents as forms of
exploitation, historically the most flexible and adaptable to
various social conditions; 3) the absence of class limitations

[13] O. E. Nepomnin, "Krizis kitaiskogo obshchestva nachala XX v.: istoki
i osobennosti," in *Gosudarstvo i obshchestvo v Kitae*, pp. 142, 148, 155.

[14] Meliksetov, "K voprosu o genezise kapitalizma v Kitae," pp. 160-68.

[15] Ibid., p. 161.

in the possession of private property for the overwhelming majority of the population, and significant development for a precapitalist society of market ties, a consequence of which was the economic fluidity of representatives of the ruling class; 4) the enormous socioeconomic role of commercial-money-lending capital and also the extent of its unity with capital in land and agricultural production; and 5) the presence of a free labor force and free use of money sufficient at least for the manufacturing stage of the development of capitalism.[16] On the whole, he finds China in the early twentieth century predominantly a feudal or semifeudal society with many distinctive conditions and great complexity.

Recently specialists at the Institute of the Far East have also given some attention to the structure of the rural population before the Chinese Revolution. Although L. A. Volkova's 1972 book, *Change of the Socioeconomic Structure of the Chinese Village, 1949-1970*, totally ignored rural conditions before the land reform, the chapter on the peasantry that she contributed to a 1982 book, *Classes and Class Structure in the PRC*, begins with a 14-page overview of the earlier rural structure.[17] She notes that feudal relations predominated between landlords (*pomeshchiki*) and peasants, including noneconomic coercion of a patriarchal character when the landlord was simultaneously the head of the lineage. Volkova accepts the existence of a kulak group credited with owning about 20 percent of landholdings, treating the situation as a transitional mix of capitalist and feudal features, which complicates a precise designation of its class nature. Thus, she concedes, it is difficult to draw the line between the kulaks and the petty landlords on the one hand and the kulaks and the rich middle peasants on the other. Above all, Volkova finds that the wrong class contradictions were more pronounced than those (especially between

---

[16] Ibid., pp. 167-68.

[17] L. A. Volkova, *Izmenenie sotsial'no-ekonomicheskoi struktury kitaiskoi derevni 1949-1970 gg.*; and *Klassy i klassovaia struktura v KNR*, pp. 76-90.

landlords and other peasants) that should have prevailed in a society approaching a socialist land reform. In the complex picture of class and social relations in the Chinese village, the contradiction between landlords and peasants characteristic of a feudal society played a role. "However, the latter, almost to a man illiterate, crushed by need, ignorant, superstitious, had only begun to realize themselves as a social force, to realize their fundamental class interests. Therefore often, most visibly, contradictions of another sense appeared—between the propertied and propertyless part of the rural population."[18] All landed individuals were lumped together as enemies, not just the landlords. This kind of social contradiction was dangerous for the future development of rural areas.

Many of the conditions associated with the Asiatic mode of production appear clearly in these descriptions of the Chinese peasantry, although earlier suggestions that state or communal property was widespread are no longer repeated.[19] Although disagreement can be found on some points, a consensus exists that China's villages were backward, that the division of labor was weakly developed, and that class relations and struggle were distorted. Just as Western evaluations of Russian peasants in the early twentieth century stress their backwardness and lack of sharp class antagonisms and consider these factors important in the Soviet period, Soviet evaluations of China emphasize the serious limitations due to these same conditions in the PRC.

THE CHALLENGE OF REVOLUTION

One of the primary concerns of specialists on China has been the peasant movement of the first half of the twentieth

---

[18] *Klassy i klassovaia struktura v KNR*, p. 89.

[19] Deliusin, *Agrarno-krest'ianskii vopros v politike KPK (1921-1928)*, p. 421, notes the positive result in 1929 of the Sixth Party Congress of the Comintern, which rejected the Asiatic mode of production as not reflecting Chinese reality.

century and its role in the Chinese Revolution. Separate studies have focused on each period of peasant activism, from the Boxer movement at the turn of the century to the victorious revolution five decades later. Kostiaeva's writings analyze the nature of the struggle during the first decade of the century, when the rural population was involved in the overthrow of the Qing dynasty. She finds that the struggle at this time was of a traditional nature, i.e. directed against taxes and extortion by the local administration, and included the upper ranks of village society. "The Chinese village to a significant extent still acted as a single, monolithic mass and acted not against the landlord, but against the official. The explanation for this can be found in the social structure of the society, in the peculiarities of exploitation of the main producers, in the weak class differentiation of the peasantry, and from this—the weak class consciousness, and finally, in the position of the village gentry [shenshi], their role and influence."[20]

Much debate centers on the historical significance of the 1911 revolution. Reviewing this debate, Meliksetov concludes that Soviet authors have tended to exaggerate the possibilities of this revolution and thus to treat it as if it were a failure.[21] In fact, bourgeois revolution was not possible at this time. The nature of peasant society as well as the state of the urban bourgeoisie establishes that China was not ready for a new stage of development.

Even greater interest concentrates on the revolutionary movement of the 1920s and early 1930s. Here, too, recent assessments are critical of earlier exaggerations of the level of development of the workers' and especially the peasants' movement.[22] Deliusin observes that Chinese communists

[20] A. S. Kostiaeva "Rol' shen'shi v krest'ianskikh dvizheniiakh nakanune sin'khaiskoi revoliutsii," in *Agrarnye otnosheniia i krest'ianskoe dvizhenie v Kitae*, p. 243.

[21] A. V. Meliksetov, "Istoricheskoe znachenie sin'khaiskoi revoliutsii v Kitae," in *Kitai v novoe i noveishee vremia*, p. 95.

[22] A. S. Kostiaeva, "Osnovnye problemy revoliutsii 1925-1927 gg. v Kitae," in *Revoliutsiia 1925-1927 gg. v Kitae*, p. 14.

lacked a clear scientific conception of the socioeconomic contents of agrarian relations. Their program was based on the incorrect assumption that the revolutionary peasantry would strive to replace private ownership of land.[23] The party was correct, however, in emphasizing the importance of alliance with middle peasants and rejection of forced redistribution of lands that went against their interests. It reserved for itself the right to criticize the demand for equalization of land as "an illusion of petty-bourgeois socialism."[24]

Meliksetov presents the most general appraisal of the Chinese peasantry in the period of revolutionary activism. He stresses the delayed process of bourgeois class differentiation in the village, and the factors rooted in traditional society that prevented a horizontal division of society and that preserved vertical social ties.[25] The exploiters in the village did not reach the point of creating class organizations to protect their interests. There were no sharp social barriers in the village, and class struggle was dulled.

In 1973 there was an exchange of views on rural China by A. S. Mugruzin and Gel'bras. Mugruzin presented an overview concerning how "the classes of the society of Tsarist Russia noticeably differed in character from the classes of old China."[26] He found that China's rural population was a larger percentage of the total than was Russia's; it experienced pauperization rather than differentiation under the influence of capitalism and the gigantic scale of this "deformed" society. In a companion article, Gel'bras noted that in 1967, in response to O. E. Nepomnin's book, *The Genesis of Capitalism in the Agriculture of China*, Soviet scholars

[23] L. P. Deliusin, *Agrarno-krest'ianskii vopros v politike KPK (1921-1928)*, p. 126.

[24] Ibid., p. 434.

[25] Meliksetov, *Sotsial'no-ekonomicheskaia politika Gomin'dana 1927-1949 gg.*, p. 27.

[26] A. S. Mugruzin, "K voprosu o spetsifike klassovogo sostava sel'skogo naseleniia v Kitae nakanune pobedy revoiutsii," in *Kitai: obshchestvo i gosudarstvo*, pp. 313-15.

had demonstrated their disagreement with the conception that prerevolutionary Chinese society was becoming capitalist and began to demonstrate the nature of China's rural backwardness. However, new attempts to depict Chinese society as an archaic Asiatic mode of production without contemporary classes or economically independent classes, Gel'bras asserted, could not be supported by concrete research.[27] Taking exception to Mugruzin's criteria for designating social classes and to some negative comparative judgments that followed, Gel'bras nevertheless agreed with Mugruzin and Meliksetov that the Chinese village remained largely precapitalist.

Less is written about the methods that enabled China's communists to win over many of the peasantry in the 1930s and 1940s. It is readily accepted that the party gained support by limiting feudal exploitation and establishing a more progressive system of land use in its base areas than existed in Kuomintang areas, but little attention has been given to the methods of mobilization and their implications for the future. Whatever the reasons for the peasants' support of the revolutionary movement, Soviets take for granted that the peasants were not a dependable force for leading China to socialism. Deliusin writes, "The experience of the peasant movement in the Soviet districts of China testifies not so much to the spontaneous revolutionary activity of the peasants as to their passivity, political apathy, and inability to wage an independent political struggle."[28]

Biographies of Mao Zedong stress his exaggerated view of the peasantry as the leading force in the building of socialism. Soviet writers contend that Mao's failure to understand Marxist principles about social class relations led to repeated mistakes in rural policies. In the best Soviet biography of Mao, Fedor Burlatsky explains, "In China, leadership of the peasantry by the working class is of par-

---

[27] V. G. Gel'bras, "O klassovo-sotsial'noi strukture naseleniia Kitaia v kanun pobedy revoliutsii," in *Kitai: obshchestvo i gosudarstvo*, pp. 328-29.

[28] L. P. Delyusin [Deliusin], *The Socio-Political Essence of Maoism*, p. 22.

ticularly great significance because the Chinese peasants have not gone through the experience of capitalist development. That accounts for not only their petty-bourgeois inclinations but also their semifeudal features, ideas, and morals."[29]

LAND REFORM

The agrarian transformation that took place in most areas of China following the reform law of June 1950 is considered by the Soviets to have been a necessary step toward socialism. They applaud its goals of liquidating feudal-landlord holdings, dividing equally among the peasantry the lands of religious establishments, preserving the holdings that rich peasants farmed themselves, and maintaining intact the holdings of middle peasants. They note, however, that in practice some provisions of the agrarian reform were far from fully observed.[30] In local areas, excesses were often committed.

After the reform, even more than before, the Chinese village was an ocean of minute peasant units, such that most peasants lacked the possibility of marketing their products. In the next few years the situation grew dangerous; the amount of accumulation from so many small-scale units was insufficient for industrialization. Complicating the situation in China was the distinctive role of kulaks, who combined capitalist and feudal features. It was thus difficult to draw a clear line between them and other types of peasants, and many of them suffered from the anti-feudal direction of the land reform.[31] Many Soviets seem to agree that the primary problem was insufficient capitalism, not too much of it. There was little danger of capitalism developing quickly because the level of inequality was not high and middle peasants had few resources to transform themselves into

[29] Fedor Burlatsky, *Mao Tse-tung: An Ideological and Psychological Portrait*, pp. 88-89.

[30] G. A. Ganshin, *Ocherk ekonomiki sovremennogo Kitaia*, p. 47.

[31] *Klassy i klassovaia struktura v KNR*, p. 81.

kulaks.[32] Even for the level of inequality, there was weak differentiation into class relations. Agrarian reform freed China's peasantry from feudal exploitation, but it could not become a basis for much improvement in production, supplies to industrialization, or living standards.

The period of transition from land reform to collectivization requires a careful balancing act in which the private economy expands as state controls are tightened, i.e. socialism gains despite capitalism's growth in the rural sector. The Soviets do not give the Chinese particularly high marks for handling this complex transition. Part of the problem was the serious shortage of land for China's immense rural population. As a result, the majority of middle peasants were scarcely distinguishable from poor peasants even though they had a little more land and farm implements. Neither group had much inclination to produce in quantity for the market. A further hindrance to commercialization was the fact that severe land shortages in many localities caused provisions of the law to be ignored in order to redistribute a significant share of land belonging to kulaks.[33] In addition, the middle peasants were not sufficiently reassured to invest heavily in production. Although the rural economy was rapidly restored by the generally positive consequences of the agrarian reform and middle peasants gained at the expense of the extremes, further agricultural growth, and especially marketing, lagged seriously.

Gel'bras offers perhaps the sharpest attack on the consequences of land reform. He sees the CCP as failing in its proclaimed aim to preserve the kulaks and to guarantee the interests of the middle peasants and he argues that, in reality, land reform struck a severe blow against practically all well-to-do segments of the rural population, leaving the poorest part of the rural population as the winners. In the conditions of the destruction of traditional rural associations and forms of personal dependency, the appearance

---

[32] Ibid., pp. 97-98.
[33] *Sotsial'no-ekonomicheskii stroi i ekonomicheskaia politika KNR*, p. 77.

of more than 100 million tiny, independent peasant holdings served as a powerful impulse for the strengthening of central authority and its extreme independence in relation to society. Gel'bras links the land reform to the excessive centralization of power and to the tremendous influence of poor peasants on the CCP in favor of equalization and in search of material guarantees from hunger. To the extent that China lacked almost any democratic traditions and institutions, pressure from the poor peasants was a powerful stimulus in the CCP for excessive egalitarianism.[34]

More frequently Soviets have written in positive terms about the process of land reform and cooperatization to the middle of 1955. They make little mention of the vast numbers of the rural elite who were killed during land reform, and they rarely criticize the violent methods employed. (One exception is Burlatsky, who refers to Western estimates of millions executed in 1951 and wonders if brutality was not "becoming part and parcel of the new state.")[35] In general, Soviets credit the Chinese with patient adherence to a gradual plan for developing cooperatives on the basis of voluntary participation.[36] And they do not worry, as Gel'bras does, that inequalities were not sufficiently developed to cause a decisive breakdown in traditional, patriarchal, lineage relations and in the commonality of basic interests of peasants, which were determined by the narrow world of kin relations and the natural economy. For instance *Classes and Class Structure in the PRC* (1982) refers to the successful carrying out of the land reform as a big victory of the CCP, which opened the way for progressive development of the village.[37] It welcomes the new land distribution as answering the basic interests of the wide mass of working peasants and heightening their interest in

[34] Gel'bras, *Sotsial'no-ekonomicheskaia struktura KNR 50-60-e gody*, pp. 56, 62.

[35] Burlatsky, *Mao Tse-tung: An Ideological and Psychological Portrait*, p. 102.

[36] *Sel'skoe khoziaistvo KNR 1949-1974*, p. 31.

[37] *Klassy i klassovaia struktura v KNR*, p. 95.

expanding production and bettering their material position. This view expresses no concern about the absence of much capitalist development and, indeed, appears to contain a certain degree of approval for the Chinese success in keeping capitalism so well in check. At the same time, the authors recognize that the agrarian reform could not be an adequate base for the development of productive forces, the supply of the needs of industrialization, and a significant improvement in the lives of the rural population. If this perspective appears to support the need for rapid collectivization, the authors caution that the peasants must first be persuaded of the superiority of the collective economy, and, as Lenin once observed, this must be done more slowly, carefully, and systematically in a country that is more peasant than Russia.[38]

Another trend of thought can also be discerned in writings about rural society in the early 1950s. This view contrasts sharply with the notion that a mass of almost undifferentiated, poor peasants creates a base for excessive centralization. As expressed by V. I. Lazarev in his 1982 book, *Class Struggle in the PRC* (issued as a hardback in the extraordinary quantity of 100,000 copies), this viewpoint holds that after the land reform the Chinese peasantry was more petty-bourgeois than before.[39] Drawing on Lenin's appraisal of the situation in Russia following its land reform, Lazarev asserts that China's peasants retained the potential for activism under bourgeois influence.

COLLECTIVIZATION

Soviet charges that collectivization was bungled in China are reminiscent of Western criticisms of Soviet collectivization, which had occurred a quarter century earlier. This was not the initial Soviet reaction in the late 1950s, when relations with China remained close; it was the response a

[38] Ibid., p. 103.
[39] V. I. Lazarev, *Klassovaia bor'ba v KNR*, pp. 19-21.

decade later when the search for what had gone wrong in the development of Chinese socialism was already intense. Even then for a time the collectivization of 1955-1956 did not come in for unmitigated criticism. In 1972 Volkova concluded that, even in the unmechanized conditions of Chinese agriculture, cooperativization had a progressive character.[40] She observes, nonetheless, that the technology was too backward to permit a qualitatively new level of productivity, and the majority of the peasantry, who had dreamed for centuries of owning their own land and at last had been given it, did not realize the necessity of combining their holdings. Whereas the tempo and character of cooperatization up to the second half of 1955 was on the whole according to the principle of voluntarism, the events of 1957 when peasants rushed to leave their cooperatives demonstrate that a significant portion of the peasantry was not morally prepared. This was forced cooperatization.[41] Somehow overlooking the contradictions in her argument, Volkova offers the justification that industrial development was being held up because insufficient agricultural goods were reaching the market, and that the reorganization of 1955-1956 increased marketable goods by decreasing peasant consumption.

The indictment of Chinese collectivization became a constant refrain in Soviet studies of China. They criticized the way in which the decision was made at Mao's initiative and later approved by an enlarged Central Committee plenum at which the members and alternate members were outnumbered by others who were invited.[42] Soviets claimed that conditions were not ripe for collectivization: 1) the material-technical base was too weak; 2) traditional attitudes and illiteracy were too strong; and 3) cadres were too few and too inexperienced. And Soviets have pointed to

[40] L. A. Volkova, *Izmenenie sotsial'no-ekonomicheskoi struktury kitaiskoi derevni 1949-1970 gg.*, pp. 27-29.

[41] Ibid., p. 36.

[42] Burlatsky, *Mao Tse-tung: An Ideological and Psychological Portrait*, p. 102.

negative consequences resulting from collectivization: 1) no new single category of cooperative peasants was formed because social contradictions in the village were preserved; 2) the peasants reacted negatively (one manifestation was a mass migration to the cities, another was the slaughter of domestic livestock, and a third was uprisings in several regions; 3) the standard of living was lowered; 4) prices and the flow of funds were inimical to peasant interests; 5) the state became responsible for areas unable to meet their own needs; and 6) the production figures in 1957 were poor due to forced cooperativization.[43] Of course, Soviet writers do not conclude that the problem was collectivization in general. Rather they insist it was the particular timing and methods of collectivization in China. Concrete conditions had been ignored.

Even though the Chinese had made a mistake in rushing into collectivization, various Soviet writers have suggested that the situation could have been salvaged. Indeed, they applaud the reevaluation that took place in late 1956 and 1957, which began an essential, but massive and painstaking effort to strengthen the cooperative system. If state financial and material aid had been substantial, if qualified cadres and workers had been sent in large numbers to serve in the villages, if a cultural revolution had ensued, and if private plots had been much enlarged, the peasants could have been gradually persuaded of the advantages of the collective economy.[44] Gel'bras notes approvingly that market forces and material incentives based on small-scale group forms of organizing production were recommended by the Central Committee of the CCP to be accompanied by lightened financial and tax burdens, but what concrete measures followed were short-lived.[45]

If collectivization in 1955-1956 was a mistake, the establishment of communes in 1958 was regarded by the Soviets

[43] See for example, *Sel'skoe khoziaistvo KNR 1949-1974*, pp. 37-41.

[44] *Sotsial'no-ekonomicheskii stroi i ekonomicheskaia politika KNR*, p. 107.

[45] Gel'bras, *Sotsial'no-politicheskaia struktura KNR 50-60-e gody*, pp. 64-65.

as a disaster. First, there was the problem of inconsistency. Gel'bras observes that the sharp shifts in the foundations of the economy almost every year over the duration 1955-1965 showed the peasantry that land in fact was under the control of the state.[46] Second, the communes demonstrated conclusively that the state was most concerned about the mobilization and centralized use of rural resources based not on market forces but on coercive or administrative measures. Third, the system of rewards switched to the principle of "to each according to his needs"—a serious blow to incentives. Under these conditions the peasantry became disillusioned.

As people's communes took over local administration, the government could directly participate in the organization of production and in the distribution of income. The centralization of control was carried to an extreme. Soviets point to an excessive rate of accumulation, as the peasants' standard of living fell sharply and peasants felt helpless before higher authorities.

Although Soviets place the turning point in the agricultural policies of the PRC in 1957-1958 rather than 1955-1956 and the policies of communization are much more severely condemned, the conclusions about both periods of rural reorganization resemble Western criticism of Soviet collectivization. In each case critics charge that leaders forced change upon hostile peasants, reduced their incentives, and caused problems in production. Corrective measures born out of economic necessity over the next years permitted some amelioration, but it would be decades before substantial improvements would raise the peasants above their conditions of life on the eve of collectivization.

After the Great Leap Forward, under relaxed controls, socialism lost additional ground. For a time the Chinese tolerated a greatly expanded household economy. In these circumstances, lineages and other kin groups and secret

[46] Ibid., p. 128.

societies "got their second wind."[47] Poor peasants looked
to the collectives as their protectors and were soon encouraged to do so by China's leaders. No authentic collectives could emerge since peasants could not achieve mutual
awareness of their common interests. The poor peasants
pushed for payment according to need, and households
perceived the private sector as the only path to improvements in their livelihood.

THE CULTURAL REVOLUTION

Studies of rural China find the impact of policies associated
with the Cultural Revolution, the Dazhai model that was
held up as the ideal for self-reliant collectives, and Mao's
last years of life overwhelmingly negative. The Cultural
Revolution disrupted management and planning by undermining the system of leadership in production brigades
and communes and again reducing the labor incentives of
the peasants.[48] Supplies from the industrial sector were
interrupted, and rural areas became more vulnerable to
natural disasters. Self-reliance meant the state could not be
counted on for assistance.

Above all, a policy of class struggle characterized these
years. Artificial divisions into social classes and strata preceded this period and operated from the time of land reform as a barrier to a correct understanding of rural society. In the Socialist Education Movement from 1962 these
categories took on a more threatening form with Mao's
contention that class contradictions and struggle still existed and that there was a danger from spontaneous capitalist tendencies. An authors' collective at the Institute of
the Far East acknowledges that the broad masses were discontent, but it does not consider this to be adequate justification for the enormous scale and severity of the class
struggle in the village or the inclusion as targets of all who

[47] Ibid., p. 129.
[48] *Sel'skoe khoziaistvo KNR 1966-1973*, p. 11.

disagreed with Maoist measures.[49] Mao lacked a Marxist understanding of social classes. Revisionism came to mean the demand to improve the living standard and material incentives. Anyone who was critical of the periodic forced reorganization of rural life in ways harmful to incentives could become a target of class struggle; Mao sought to get even with his critics.[50]

Soviet writers regard the rural conditions that prevailed until the late 1970s as exploitative. Chinese leaders kept peasants on the verge of hunger. The state invested little in the rural areas, using the principle of self-reliance to curtail expenses even in the areas of education and health care, which localities had to fund. The state was motivated by the goal of concentrating as much money as possible on the military and industry. "The strategic aim of the agrarian policies of the Beijing leadership is to use agriculture as a source of the means for the rapid build-up of the military-industrial complex through minimal expenses on the part of the state in the development needs of the village."[51] A number of Soviet sources contend that the well-being of the working people is the key aim of collective ownership and the essential indicator of its socialist character.[52] By this standard, they judge collective ownership in China not to have been truly socialist. The state, extracting resources "on a scale that exceeded the economic possibilities of the village, prevented any improvement in the well-being of the peasants."[53]

State policies gave peasants little say in important decisions. Analysts criticize the Chinese leaders for denying the peasants an active political life and participation in the management of production and for harsh control, e.g. in birth

[49] *Sel'skoe khoziaistvo KNR 1949-1974*, p. 61.

[50] *Kitaiskaia Narodnaia Respublika 1973*, p. 158.

[51] *Sel'skoe khoziaistvo KNR 1949-1974*, p. 346.

[52] See for example Volkova, *Izmenenie sotsial'no-ekonomicheskoi struktury kitaiskoi derevni 1949-1970 gg.*, p. 115.

[53] *Klassy i klassovaia struktura v KNR*, p. 126.

control policies.[54] Peasants responded with low productivity. Just as Americans often point to the far greater number of farm workers required to produce a unit of output in the USSR than in the United States as an indication of that system's failure, Soviets note the much higher ratio of labor per unit output in China as a similar indication.[55] Peasants preferred their private-sector activities and perceived these as sharply in conflict with the collective sector. They were unconcerned about collective property, and in 1976, Soviet sources report, it was revealed that a sizable black market existed.

Another theme in Soviet assessments is the poor quality of rural management. From the late 1950s China lacked a scientifically based economic program. Villagers reeled from political campaign to political campaign without any opportunity for careful planning. Moreover, the insecurity and low quality of their leaders added to the structural problems that the ordinary villagers faced.

THE RESPONSIBILITY SYSTEM

How socialist was rural China in the late 1970s? P. B. Kapralov addresses this question in *Rural Regions of the PRC in the 1970s*. He sees China as still floundering in the transition to socialism that had begun with land reform. Repeating the prevailing assessment of collectivization, Kapralov concludes that the speed-up organized under Mao's leadership actually only complicated the situation in the villages. Then the communes set the villages back not just in economic output but also in organizational relations to the level of 1953-1954 and in many respects even to the early 1950s. The five years of hasty transformation from 1956 to 1960 were followed by years of "significantly more small-scale and compromise forms spontaneously adapted

---

[54] *Sel'skoe khoziaistvo KNR 1949-1974*, pp. 346, 350; and *Kitaiskaia Narodnaia Respublika 1974*, p. 19.

[55] *Sel'skoe khoziaistvo KNR 1949-1974*, p. 348.

to the backward agrarian system."[56] The production team that evolved was a mixture of the lower type of cooperative common in 1955 and the higher type that had followed, the former in the team's relatively small size and the latter in the team's collective property and functions. Chinese agriculture remained little mechanized. It is an axiom of Soviet writers that, in the USSR, industrialization preceded collectivization and that in China, where the same sequence should have occurred, it did not. China continued to lack the mechanization needed for collective farming. The agricultural reforms following Mao's death did not lead China to socialism. Rather they represented a step back to the mutual help groups of the early 1950s or even to earlier household economies in the immediate aftermath of land reform.[57] After three decades of transition, China was still far fom socialism.

Was the responsibility system from 1979 with its elements of decollectivization—especially the distribution of land to individual households and to small groups who are permitted to keep the earnings from additional production— a necessary response to the revival in the 1960s and 1970s of traditional village relations and the psychology of the private economy or was it a rightist step taken by a post-Mao leadership unconcerned about safeguarding socialism? This question appears to divide Soviet observers. The answer proposed by high Central Committee official Rakhmanin (writing under the pseudonym O. B. Borisov) is that at the end of the 1970s and the beginning of the 1980s China turned to the right, one sign of which was the retreat from cooperatives in the village.[58] The articles selected for reprinting in the annual publication, *Opasnyi kurs*, adhere to this viewpoint. For example, Iu. Semenov's 1981 article, "Intrapolitical and Social Problems of China," indicates that,

[56] P. B. Kapralov, *Sel'skie raiony KNR v 70-e gody: tendentsii sotsial'no-ekonomicheskogo razvitiia*, p. 7.

[57] Ibid., pp. 9-10.

[58] Borisov, "Polozhenie v KNR i nekotorye zadachi sovetskogo kitae-vedeniia," pp. 11-21.

despite the people's lack of support for the rebirth of the private sector, Chinese leadership is proceeding in this direction and is supporting the rich peasants.[59] Other writers concede that the new policies have the aim of stabilizing the situation in the village, but add that social problems actually become exacerbated and that the new policies do not solve the cardinal problems of increasing central capital investments in agriculture and interesting peasants in the development of production within the collective sector.[60]

Negative reactions to the responsibility system have appeared in the publications of the Institute of the Far East. For instance, in its yearbook, *Kitaiskaia Narodnaia Respublika 1979*, observers find no basic positive changes in agriculture. To them, the new measures reflect an absence of a scientifically based program and a continued tendency to exploit agriculture for the forced development of the military-industrial potential of the country.[61]

Elsewhere, there appears to be a more cautious, balanced reaction. G. A. Ganshin writes of the dual results of the new decentralization in the organization of agriculture. On the one hand, the material interest of peasants is raised, which contributes to increased production and income for a portion of the rural population. If this tactic will be temporary, Ganshin says, it can be considered justified. On the other hand, the system inevitably widens inequalities and damages the collective economy.[62] It strengthens petty-bourgeois psychology among a significant part of the peasantry. China's official recognition in 1979 that it could not mechanize as once planned in the heady days of 1977 is pointed to by Ganshin as evidence that modernization of agriculture is far off. He concludes that, even after prices and budgets were adjusted in favor of agriculture, the level of state assistance remained small.[63]

[59] Iu. Semenov, "Vnutripoliticheskie i sotsial'nye problemy Kitaia," *Opasnyi kurs* 11, pp. 98-99.

[60] *Klassy i klassovaia struktura v KNR*, pp. 155-57.

[61] *Kitaiskaia Narodnaia Respublika 1979*, p. 103.

[62] G. A. Ganshin, *Ocherk ekonomiki sovremennogo Kitaia*, pp. 192-93.

[63] Ibid., pp. 197-99.

A divergent view on the entire history of rural policies in China, including the reform measures of 1978-1980, can be found in the 1981 collective work, *The Working Class in the Socio-political System of the PRC*. The contributors are Gel'bras, two colleagues of his at the Institute of the International Workers' Movement, E. S. Kul'pin and A. V. Kholodkovskaia, and Deliusin. More than any other source, this book offers a viewpoint on rural China distinct from the prevailing interpretations at the Institute of the Far East. It poses the state as the enemy of the peasants.

Gel'bras and Kul'pin describe a bleak situation. The peasants lack democratic rights, they are close to starvation, they are forced to labor with little return, and they perceive the state as their exploiter. Part of the problem was the transformation of all rural cadres into government functionaries who are not elected and merely carry out orders from above.[64] Out of career interests, they sacrifice the interests of the peasantry to the demands of the state and suppress dissatisfaction through diverse means. Under conditions of minimal reward and equal distribution, peasants lack incentives for collective work and save their energies for private production. The authorities respond with militarized methods of organizing labor, by taking away from the peasants private plots and markets or by depriving them of the right to use their free time as they wished. Above all, low prices and high quotas for agricultural goods keep peasants in a desperate situation. The price increases in 1979 were not of much help; increases many times larger are needed.[65]

According to this perspective, the central problem at the beginning of the 1980s was not the rightist threat from an expanded household economy. It was instead the persisting problem of state exploitation of the peasantry. This problem even antedated collectivization. In the first years after 1949 the urban sector had little to provide the villages. In

[64] *Rabochii klass v sotsial'no-politicheskoi sisteme KNR*, p. 115.

[65] Ibid., pp. 118-19, 188; and E. S. Kul'pin, *Tekhniko-ekonomicheskaia politika rukovodstva KNR i rabochii klass Kitaia*, pp. 73-78.

1953-1955 it had more, but the state preferred to extract increasing amounts of rural production without adequate compensation. It "forced a significant part, sometimes a majority, of peasant families to lead a half-starved existence. Such a situation did not correspond to the class interests of the peasants."[66] They were not compensated for their labor. Collectivization did not solve this problem. Indeed Kul'pin goes so far as to say, "The transition to more progressive forms of production was impossible without a change in the economic relations of the state and the peasantry."[67] Peasant agitation was evidence of their opposition. Suppressing or ignoring this hostility, the state turned its attention to the problem of low agricultural productivity only in the 1970s, when it had become a more serious brake on economic growth in other sectors. The small-scale industries that spread in the early 1970s offered some benefits, although for rural development there is no alternative to direct dependence on large-scale urban industry. Greater inequality of incomes is seen by Kul'pin as an unavoidable consequence of higher prices paid to the rural producers.[68] In short, increased inequality is not to be feared because, rather than leading China to the right, it will reduce exploitation by the state and create reasonable incentives.

The danger in the post-Mao rural reforms, Kul'pin observes, is the continued role of cadres eager to protect their own power and privileges. "The absence of rights and the persecution of peasants, the uncontrolled behavior and omnipotence of the cadres were one of the most important conditions for the overgrown misuse of power by the latter in the direct exploitation of the peasants."[69] The officials have extraordinary powers they can use completely without control from below.[70] Misuse of power has brought about a national misfortune. The state exploits the peasantry,

[66] *Rabochii klass v sotsial'no-politicheskoi sisteme KNR*, p. 182.
[67] Ibid., p. 184.
[68] Ibid., p. 83.
[69] Ibid., p. 123.
[70] Ibid., pp. 125-26.

whose means of production have been taken away. These are the perceptions of present-day China to which one group of Soviet specialists draws attention.

CONCLUSIONS

Western criticisms of Soviet and Chinese rural policies have much in common with Soviet criticism of rural China. There are at least four essential accusations of error in these criticisms: ignorance, coercion, disincentives, and dependency.

First, there is the criticism of leaders who are poorly informed by the social sciences; they misunderstand the nature of the prerevolutionary rural society and act on this misleading analysis. Western critics see this ignorance as inherent in communist ideology. Although Soviets insist that the ideology is in no way at fault, they do criticize dogmatism, including the failure to see variations in actual conditions, and some Sinologists have criticized the blind transfer from the Russian experience of categories for differentiating the rural population without proper historical concern for the distinguishing features of China's rural society. Leaders stand accused of failing to understand the social class structure and the patterns of association of enormous numbers of people whose life circumstances they are prepared to alter. Ignorance, in turn, breeds mistakes, such as the undue repression of "rich" peasants (kulaks), which Soviet critiques of China also note.

Second, Western critics of both the Soviet Union and China charge that communist leaders force the peasants against their will to reorganize and change their manner of work and life in general, with long-term negative consequences for personal motivation. Similar Soviet accusations against the Chinese center on hasty, "voluntaristic" actions by leaders without regard for the readiness of the masses to follow their guidance. In other words, Chinese leaders are criticized for coercion, for measures imposed against the will of the vast majority of villagers, including, above all, the forced collectivization of agriculture.

Third, both types of critics charge that peasants are not offered a fair return for their labor. They are victimized by the low prices paid for goods they are obliged to sell and the high prices demanded for goods originating elsewhere and by the unavailability of much of what they desire. Peasants lack incentives. Private plots and household sideline activities are severely restricted. Rural living standards are low. Perhaps as much as anything else, this factor is seen as the cause of widespread hopelessness.

Fourth, Western observers consider the rural residents of the Soviet Union and China to be essentially helpless pawns, controlled to such an extent that they are powerless in their own villages to do what is necessary to ensure a better future for themselves. Peasants lack independence. Outsiders are appointed to run rural organizations, largely to satisfy the demands of central authorities. In the final analysis, there is little local input or flexibility in policies imposed from outside the villages that radically transform daily life. This view is also found in Soviet studies of rural China.

Against this array of criticisms levied against Soviet policies, the published response in the Soviet Union is that these are bourgeois falsifications. Soviets claim that communist ideology offers a scientific understanding of rural conditions at all stages of development and that the party has been guided by scientific laws not by ignorance. They argue that the majority of peasants favored collectivization and that, except in the early period for a minority of exploiters, policies have been based not on coercion but on the will of the rural population. The policies of the CPSU are alleged to have been based on the material interests of the peasants, who found in them incentives to produce and responsibility to control their own destinies. On all four counts, the criticisms by outsiders are labeled distortions of Soviet history. Errors have been committed, but nothing anywhere near as serious as these fabrications allege. However in the case of China, Soviet critics are in the forefront in raising such charges.

Soviet writers do not question that collectivization is a positive development. They do not suggest any shortcomings in Marxist-Leninist writings about rural policies in the transition to socialism. Nevertheless, their critique of the rural policies of the PRC repeats the fundamental criticisms found in Western evaluations of Soviet rural policies. They attack misinformed leaders who lack a concrete understanding of rural conditions. Soviets blame coercive methods that were bitterly resisted by the majority of peasants. They find fault with decades of inadequate incentives. They point to the abuse of authority by the state and local cadres; those who controlled property had great power to do as they pleased with the lives of rural inhabitants. There is essential agreement with Western sources on what happened in Chinese villages after 1949 and there is essential agreement on what was bad about it. At this general level, there exists a Soviet consensus.

Disagreements among Soviet critics of China are more in evidence with regard to why these negative consequences occurred and what alternatives were available. The general Soviet viewpoint is that if the Chinese had been more patient and had adhered to their original plan for a gradual and voluntary transition from lower small-scale cooperatives with payments to peasants for their land and tools to higher-order collectives with payment only for labor over a 15-year period they would have succeeded in collectivization. Yet, a number of arguments in the Soviet analysis suggest that this conclusion is not easy to sustain. First, if the legacy of village society was not conducive to socialist development and there were a great many features clearly and importantly distinct from the Russian case, why should collectivization have succeeded even in the 1960s? Second, if land reform left China with a very weak base for capitalist development in the countryside and the state desperately needed a large outflow of resources into the cities, how could a gradual transition to collectivization have been achieved? Weren't Chinese peasants being squeezed by low prices and high quotas in a manner that would guarantee their continued hostility?

Kul'pin takes up this question in a speculative discussion of three possible routes to further economic development.[71] The first would be through mechanization and other material improvements to create conditions for rapid growth in the productivity of peasant labor. But she rules this out due to China's weak industrial base. The second would be through an exchange of industrial goods so beneficial to the peasant that he would be willing to go hungry for a time in order to work harder and sell more farm goods to procure industrial goods. This would require a lively market economy. The third possibility would be forced seizure of the peasant's surplus, and more, although it would block any increase in labor productivity. If a powerful industrial base could be built up quickly, it could serve both for defense against imperialist aggression and the eventual development of agriculture accompanied by the formation of "normal relations" between the working class and the peasantry. The peasants should see their sacrifice as temporary, a kind of credit that would be repaid in the long run. Kul'pin finds that China took the third route without offering any prospects of repaying the peasants in the future.[72]

Along with Kul'pin and Gel'bras, Meliksetov, Burlatsky, and Deliusin have espoused a reform view of Chinese peasants. On the other side are Rakhmanin (Borisov), Lazarev, and, to a large degree, the researchers at the Institute of the Far East. From their point of view, the Chinese peasantry remains a stronghold of petty-bourgeois attitudes and a threat to socialism. The menace from the right gains sustenance largely from the rural population of China, whose striving for land and profit has now been encouraged by the post-Mao leadership. The lines between these two viewpoints are sharply drawn.

[71] Ibid., pp. 180-81.
[72] Ibid., pp. 184, 185.

In an essay entitled "The Classes and Social Groups Whose Interests Maoism Expresses," included in his 1976 English-language book, Deliusin disagrees with the assumptions underlying the interpretation of China as petty-bourgeois and the peasantry as a source of support for the right. He writes, "There are some who hold that Maoism is a bourgeois ideology or something close to it and that Mao Tse-tung expresses the interests of the national bourgeoisie of China. This view represents a misconception of Maoism and the national bourgeoisie of China for it completely ignores the anti-capitalist tenor of the Maoist views and is contradicted by facts. Maoism as an ideology that is opposed to scientific communism took final shape after the tasks of a bourgeois-democratic revolution had been accomplished and the political and some of the social conditions had been prepared for the gradual establishment of the economic basis of a socialist society. Chinese society consists of two principal classes, the working class and the peasantry. Landlords were abolished as a class in the course of the agrarian transformations in the early 1950's. Kulaks, an insignificant part of the rural population even before the people's revolution, ceased to exist as a social group after the establishment of co-operatives. . . . Ownership of the means of production by the exploiter classes was eliminated once and for all . . . since the revolution the position of the peasantry has changed appreciably. It has gone over from individual to collective forms of farming."[73] Deliusin goes on to argue that it is the poor peasants and certain middle peasants whose standards of living are low (and who prefer equal distribution and have nothing to do with the market) who are the rural social base of the Maoists.[74] Clearly policies aimed at strengthening market forces and rewarding hard-working peasants—the policies of the responsibility system—do not strengthen this social base. The notion that Maoism was a petty-bourgeois threat from the right and

[73] Delyusin [Deliusin], *The Socio-Political Essence of Maoism*, pp. 78-79.
[74] Ibid., p. 81.

that the danger from the right is intensifying is refuted directly by Deliusin and other Soviets who find the real culprit to be excessive state power and the role of officials.

The challenge to the orthodox camp comes from detailed, sociological analysis of the peasantry in China. In place of the unsupported deduction that conditions were ripe for the transition to socialism, historical research on rural society builds a case for the absence of prerequisites. Rather than uncritically transferring social class categories from Russian history, specialists argue for the need to find categories appropriate to Chinese conditions. Critics of previous writings also point to the negative consequences of taking for granted conclusions (both Chinese and Soviet) that were earlier accepted instead of drawing new conclusions from the available facts.

In addition to criticizing other Soviet writers, the reform group faults the Chinese Communist Party for its inadequate sociological understanding of China. From the 1920s the party's policies were based on incorrect assumptions about the attitudes of the peasantry. The CCP was repeatedly mistaken about peasant reactions to its reforms and in predicting how they would be implemented. Ignorance about rural society led the party to neglect incentives for those who would produce more. At least some Soviets apparently conclude that the result was a brutalization of rural life and a reliance on uneducated, poor peasants, whose main interest was to gain security through redistribution, not to work hard for greater reward. Having little insight into rural conditions, China's leadership was generally satisfied with this situation because it enabled a large-scale mobilization of resources and highly centralized control over what mattered most to the state.

The reform argument voiced by Deliusin accepts the view that there was no danger from the right in China. It suggests that, if peasants had been given ample opportunities to produce for the market and to raise their living standards, a more favorable base for genuine socialism would have emerged. The balance should have shifted from ignorant officials to sociologically informed experts, from controls within a centralized system to democratic participation within a decentralized system, from equality to incentives. Without directly questioning the principles of collectivization or the leadership of the communist party, the reformers manage to convey a sweeping indictment of what can go wrong in a society that is already socialist and to suggest a broad program of fundamental reforms to set things right.

The consensus between the orthodox and reform viewpoints on rural China recapitulates the essence of what Soviets call "anticommunist" criticisms against Soviet rural policies. It calls for specialized knowledge to overcome policies based on ignorance. Although the two sides disagree on the proper balance between the applicability of general laws and the need for detailed investigations, both recognize that leaders claiming to be communists acted from ignorance and committed mistakes that should have been averted. Both Soviet groups point to unjustified policies, including collectivization in 1955-1956, that were imposed on the peasants against their will. They recognize the danger of coercion by the state in a communist-led system. Furthermore, there is a consensus that Chinese leaders failed to offer adequate motivation for residents of villages to work hard. The peasants were not given high enough prices or access to sufficient material benefits to induce them to give genuine support to the system. Finally, Soviets concur that peasants were not in charge of their own fates. They were helpless. They were repressed.

This range of arguments about rural China testifies to the basic similarity between Western criticisms of communist-led systems and Soviet criticisms about China. Clearly the agreement runs deeper between the views of reform-minded Soviets and the precise explanations offered by Westerners of what is at fault. But this fact should not divert us from recognizing that a more widespread convergence of views exists.

Their reactions to China's post-Mao responsibility system

reveal the true inclinations of Soviet writers. This far-reaching reform revitalized agriculture in the PRC—in many respects reviving the family farm as the basic unit for making production decisions, allocating labor, and reaping the benefits of increased production. This initiative occurred in China just as the Soviet Union was experiencing a series of severe harvest shortfalls and was discussing (through the appointment of a commission and circumspect commentaries in the press on possible options) agricultural reform and decentralization. To the likely chagrin of many Soviet citizens, the new steps announced in the Soviet food program and other pronouncements of the early 1980s did not represent substantial decentralization, although the emphasis on collective contracts in 1983 under Andropov may indicate that more is to come. In this context of obvious parallels between the shortcomings of agriculture in the two communist-led countries, the orthodox group vigorously rejects China's reforms as a rightist retreat from socialism. This group conceals the facts of rural change in China (the responsibility system has not been the subject of detailed studies) and prevents comparison with the Soviet Union. Of course, the reformers cannot directly comment on the relevance of China's recent experience, but obliquely they appear to be saying that decentralization of agriculture—especially by removing officials from the backs of the peasantry—is compatible with and even necessary for socialism.

· 3 ·

WORKERS

The contrasts in the histories of communist party relations
with workers in China and the Soviet Union are striking
and well-known. The workers of China were much less
involved in the revolutionary movement that brought the
party to power. Their numbers and benefits did not expand
as rapidly in the decades after the revolution. And they
were not credited with as primary a role in the ideology
that the Chinese leaders developed. Clearly grounds exist
for sharp distinctions between the policies of the two countries, especially by Soviet writers who are intent on showing
what went wrong in China.

There are also similarities in the experiences of the two
countries that complicate the task of criticism and open the
way to interpretations of China with direct relevance to
Soviet events. For example, both countries adopted methods that gave low priority to increases in labor productivity.
By the early 1980s, new leaderships were struggling with
the legacy of these methods, with the stifling of local initiative by rigid central planning in the industrial sector, and
with the dearth of individual incentives in a system that
virtually guarantees job security. Reforms were constrained
by the entrenched positions of state bureaucrats and also
by the engrained expectations of the workers who benefited
most. Parallels can also be identified in the way communist
leaders initially mobilized armies of laborers in large-scale
enterprises.

In recent years a new literature has appeared, mainly
under the auspices of the Institute of the International
Workers' Movement (IMRD), on the transformation of
workers under communist party leadership. This literature
reflects on the structure, organization, cultural level, and
psychological state of the working class. These are all issues

that are also raised in Western criticisms of Soviet and Chinese policies. Independent of their writings on China, the Soviets are developing a generalized approach to the transformation of the working class in a socialist system. A brief review of this approach should establish the context for the materials on China.

Perhaps the most thorough presentation of this general approach is in a 1982 book that compares workers in five countries: the USSR, Bulgaria, Hungary, East Germany, and Czechoslovakia. This book was written collectively by members of the Soviet leadership (including K. U. Chernenko and B. N. Ponomarev in the Politburo and P. N. Fedoseev, vice-president of the Academy of Sciences), leaders and academics in East European countries, and specialists at IMRD. Entitled *The Development of the Working Class in a Socialist Society*, this volume sets forth the requirements for transforming workers and suggests, at least implicitly, the dangers that might stand in the way of a successful transformation.

What conditions are necessary for socialism to develop? According to this 1982 book, first, socialism rests on a structural requirement. There must be enough workers and they must be sufficiently concentrated. Moreover, continued advances in the building and strengthening of socialism require increases in the number of workers. "One of the most important objective preconditions for strengthening the leading role of the working class in a socialist society is its significant and, in many socialist countries, its very rapid quantitative increase."[1] As the numbers increase, the workers also are more and more concentrated at large industrial enterprises. Where the work force at an enterprise is large, preferably in the thousands, conditions are superior for an organized, collectivist, and disciplined environment. Both in the revolutionary movement against capitalism and in the later process of building socialism and communism, workers benefit from this sort of environment. By impli-

---

[1] *Razvitie rabochego klassa v sotsialisticheskom obshchestve*, p. 7.

94

cation, the book indicates that a genuine proletariat is not likely to arise, even in conditions of wage labor and manufacturing, in small-scale enterprises scattered within a society that lacks an impersonal labor market.

Second, in addition to the quantity and concentration of the workers, the quality of the workers needs to be taken into account. "The most important precondition for strengthening the role of the working class as the main producing force and the leading sociopolitical force of the socialist society is also the continuous and genuine increase of the general cultural level of the workers."[2] The interests of socialism are served by a more experienced force with better education and higher skills. A mature work force accustomed to disciplined labor and informed through education becomes the leading element in society and the basis of the communist party. State policies matter in creating conditions that affect the cultural level of the workers.

Another determinant of the cultural level is the degree to which the working class is hereditary. Are workers familiar with machine technology and the routines of factory life? If they are not, then deficiencies will occur in discipline, collectivism, and class consciousness. Indeed, the book makes clear that, even under the intensive industrialization in countries guided by communist parties, the large influx of nonworkers creates conditions in which for a time the working masses become less proletarian than before.[3] Village habits bring patriarchal-peasant traditions inimical to a disciplined work environment. If the country has only recently realized socialism, the immaturity of the work force is compounded. The consequences can be serious. "A certain weakening of the tradition of mature workers' collectivism and a lowering of the level of conscious discipline, practically unavoidable in the face of a 'lesser proletarian' composition of the working class, complicates the development of socialist democracy and gives birth to the danger

[2] Ibid., p. 8.
[3] Ibid., pp. 404-405.

(and the possibility) of an attempt to replace it with a bureaucratic administration. As is known, in some circumstances this danger acquires quite real forms."[4]

Third, the development of the working class depends on
material rewards. Wage differentials must be scientifically
determined in accordance with the value of the work performed. This widely repeated principle is qualified in two
ways. It is alleged that gains in the overall material well-
being may be delayed for good reasons, e.g. due to the
need for a time to devote enormous resources to the basic
restructuring of the economy on a socialist basis when a
weak material foundation was inherited from the past, or
due to sharp class conflicts inside the country and on the
international arena.[5] Alternatively, there is the possibility
of narrowing wage differentials too much when wide dis-
parities in productivity remain; labor is insufficiently homogeneous to warrant such equal treatment. If this occurs,
wages lose their effectiveness as a stimulus to work; this
violates the socialist principle of distribution according to
one's work.[6] Clearly remuneration policies are seen as steer-
ing the workers toward a more socialist outlook.

Western criticisms of Soviet and Chinese policies stress
this last theme, exposing both the inadequacy of actual
material rewards and the inefficiency for productivity of
the existing inequalities in distribution. Critics argue that
increases in the labor effort of individual workers are not
well reflected in improvements in their material positions.
Westerners also contend that the communist authorities are
concerned with workers as producers, not consumers;
workers are dissatisfied or, at best, passive. Do Soviet writings on China contain these same critiques?

Other Western criticisms focus on the workers' inadequate access to decision making under conditions of heavy-
handed and inefficient management and organization of
labor. They portray workers as pawns rather than masters

[4] Ibid., p. 405. This reform view is expressed by L. A. Gordon and
E. V. Klopov of IMRD.
[5] Ibid., p. 429.
[6] Ibid., p. 433.

of their own fate. Neither the communist party nor the trade unions are regarded as primarily concerned with defending the workers' interests. The critics also point to the lack of application of scientific principles to management. Are these views shared by Soviet critics of China?

Yes, as we see below, all of these criticisms can be found in Soviet writings on China. While proclaiming that politically, ideologically, and materially, the workers have been the main beneficiaries of the Bolshevik Revolution, Soviet writers see the workers as having made some early gains after the Chinese Revolution and then having been among the losers. The aftermath of the Chinese Revolution has failed to serve the interests of the working class. In the Soviet perspective, the fate of the workers—more than that of the peasants—has determined and will continue to determine the course of socialist development in China.

On the subject of workers we can identify the same two groupings of specialists on China that appeared in Chapter 2. Specialized studies of the historical roots of the contemporary working class produced by T. N. Akatova and others in Deliusin's department at IVAN as well as by Meliksetov give a reform viewpoint. As one might expect, the bulk of the specialized scholarship is by Gel'bras, A. V. Kholodkovskaia, and others at IMRD—the institute dedicated to the study of the working class. The reform perspective of this institute is notable especially in the treatment of Chinese workers. On this subject, the orthodox view is less visible. Nonetheless it is sufficiently in evidence to identify an interpretation divergent from that of IMRD for the problems encountered by workers in China. Collective publications from IDV, supplemented by the writings of V. I. Lazarev and others whose views are widely disseminated in *Opasnyi kurs*, present this orthodox viewpoint.

THE LEGACY OF THE PAST

The condition of the working class in China prior to 1949 is a matter of no small importance to Soviet analysts. Their negative assessments of the revolutionary potential of this class figure into discussions of all the major events in this century. One of the tasks researchers have set is to measure the developing potential of the working class to determine the course of China's history; once that point is reached, it is argued, China will return to the path of socialism. But it is the failures of the working class that have been at the center of attention.

The Soviet view of the early history of workers can be summarized as follows. Even before the beginnings of modern factory production following China's defeat in the Opium War, the traditions of the country were not conducive to the development of a proletariat. In their historical studies of late imperial China, E. P. Stuzhina and N. I. Fomina present detailed evidence on the state of cities, guilds, and merchant associations, giving support to the oft repeated Soviet position that the development of the bourgeoisie and of freely hired labor was slowed or blocked in China.[7] The reasons for this can be found in the activities of government, guided by the conservative Confucian ideology, and in the structure of existing organizations that kept merchants and others in their embrace. Under these circumstances, the social psychology of the various strata of traditional society was similar in many respects.[8] This means that the process of class formation—class consciousness and consolidation—occurred slowly in China. O. E. Nepomnin describes three centuries of relative stagnation under the Confucian system, which before the mid-nineteenth century stood in the way of the development of early forms of capitalism.[9]

With the introduction of factory production by foreigners, a working class and a workers' movement emerged in the late nineteenth and early twentieth centuries. Until World

[7] E. P. Stuzhina, *Kitaiskii gorod XI-XIII vv.: ekonomicheskaia i sotsial'naia zhizn'*; E. P. Stuzhina, *Kitaiskoe remeslo v XVI-XVIII vv.*; and N. I. Fomina, "Kupechestvo v sotsial'noi strukture srednevekovogo Kitaia," in *Sotsial'nye organizatsii v Kitae*, pp. 67-99.

[8] *Istoriia Kitaia s drevneishikh vremen do nashikh dnei*, p. 107.

[9] Nepomnin, *Sotsial'no-ekonomicheskaia istoriia Kitaia 1894-1914*, p. 268.

War I, however, the movement remained little developed. The workers first began to be involved in political struggle in the 1911 revolution, but they were not a major force and were motivated by nationalism rather than class consciousness.[10] Following the rapid expansion of factory production at the time of World War I, the zenith of the workers' movement in China was reached in the 1920s. Soviets have given considerable attention to this decade, from the May Fourth Movement of 1919, when workers became major participants in the political struggle, to the end of the 1920s and the beginning of the 1930s, when the primary arena of political confrontation shifted to the rural areas. Specialists have examined both the debates within the CCP and the history of the working class in an effort to explain why a bourgeoning workers' movement was subdued.

Studies of the first decade of the CCP illuminate the divergent views about class relations among Chinese activists. Above all, they point to the meager sociological understanding of the actual conditions in Chinese society. For example, analyzing articles published in 1919-1920, L. P. Deliusin writes, "It is necessary to recognize that the supporters of Marxism had a very weak notion of the class structure of Chinese society. . . . They did not yet distinguish the proletariat from the entire mass of the indigent."[11] This theme reappears in writings on the CCP in all periods to the present and, of course, in the prolific literature on Mao Zedong's understanding of social classes.[12]

[10] A. V. Meliksetov, "Nekotorye osobennosti formirovaniia rabochego klassa Kitaia k nachalu noveishego vremeni," *Obshchestvo i gosudarstvo v Kitae* 9:3 (1978), p. 8.

[11] L. P. Deliusin, *Spor o sotsializme v Kitae*, p. 138.

[12] A. P. Bulkin, *Iadro maoistskoi "sotsiologii"*; L. P. Deliusin, *Agrarno-krest'ianskii vopros v politike KPK (1921-1928)*; A. M. Grigor'ev, *Revoliutsionnoe dvizhenie v Kitae 1927-1931 gg.*; *Ideino-politicheskaia sushchnost' Maoizma*; *Kritika teoreticheskikh osnov Maoizma*; V. A. Krivtsov and V. A. Krasnova, *Li Da-chzhao: ot revoliutsionnogo demokratizma k Marksizmu-Leninizmu*; Burlatsky, *The True Face of Maoism*, and *Mao Tse-tung: An Ideological and Psychological Portrait*; O. Vladimirov and V. Ryazantsev, *Mao Tse-tung: A Political Portrait*.

It makes clear that the failure of communist policies was due not only to the actual conditions in China but also to the inadequate understanding of Marxist-Leninist thought and of the sociology of class relations.

Soviet analyses of shortcomings in the working class in the 1920s repeat themes that can be found in other Soviet writings on the state of the proletariat at the time of the communist victory in 1949. For the most part, they seek to answer the question, why was the working class not a strong force in China. This question was long neglected, according to T. N. Akatova, who, along with V. I. Khor'kov, is the major Soviet authority on workers of the 1920s.[13] Akatova criticizes early Soviet commentators on the events in China and Soviet historians who right up to the end of the 1960s exaggerated the class character of the 1925-1927 revolution and the political maturity of the proletariat.[14] Acknowledging that class struggle was a factor and thus disassociating herself from Kuomintang ideologues who, she insists, ignore it altogether, Akatova places primary emphasis on the role of nationalism and anti-imperialism in the revolutionary movement of the 1920s. She concludes that the existence of the national liberation movement strengthened the impact of bourgeois ideology within the working class.[15] Khor'kov takes up the following period when the workers' class struggle had quieted. He attributes the effectiveness of government measures not only to the devastating blows inflicted on activists by the brutal methods used in the northern march of the Kuomintang and its subsequent repressive control but also to the influence of the Kuomintang's ideology of social reform, to anti-imperialist concerns, to the struggle for labor legislation, and to the persistence of traditional views and interpersonal rela-

[13] T. N. Akatova, "Rol' natsional'nogo faktora v rabochem dvizhenii Kitaia 1919-1927 gg.," in *Revoliutsiia 1925-1927 gg. v. Kitae*; and V. I. Khor'kov, *Nankinskii Gomin'dan i rabochii vopros 1927-1932*.

[14] T. N. Akatova, "K otsenke klassovoi bor'by kitaiskikh rabochikh," *Obshchestvo i gosudarstvo v Kitae* 9:3 (1978), p. 30.

[15] Ibid., p. 35.

tions.[16] Together these two specialists on workers present a chronology of a movement's rise and fall.

The issue of leadership is at the forefront of Soviet explanations for the condition of the workers' movement. The existence of a national liberation movement in which the working class participated differed from the revolutionary experience in Russia. In these conditions, there was an increased need for independent class struggle by the industrial proletariat; however for twenty years this potentially active force was cut off from the CCP and fell under the influence of the Kuomintang. Moreover, Mao and his supporters underestimated the importance of party work in this sphere and by 1949 had recruited only 4 percent of party members from among those who had been workers.[17] Even though, according to some Soviets, the workers' movement from 1945-1949 reemerged as a decisive factor in the struggle for power, Mao's group is alleged to have continued to distrust the working class.[18] In short, there was a failure of leadership in the decades before 1949 with enduring consequences for the development of socialism thereafter.

Even more negative than Akatova's criticism of previous Soviet interpretations of the role of workers in pre-1949 China is Meliksetov's dismissal of the way the concept of the working class has figured in Soviet writings on China. Meliksetov insists that the concept needs to be differentiated into groups or strata and argues that only the real factory proletariat can be the bearers of the ideas of Marxism-Leninism, not the much larger total of 2.5–3 million workers who are widely considered to have formed China's working class in the 1920s. He criticizes Akatova and the main textbook on contemporary China issued by IDV for

[16] V. I. Khor'kov, *Nankinskii Gomin'dan i rabochii vopros 1927-1932*, p. 142.

[17] *Rabochii klass Kitaia (1949-1974)*, pp. 13-14.

[18] M. Iu. Spirina, "Rabochii klass Kitaia v bor'be protiv gomin'-danovskogo rezhima i agressii SShA (1945-1949 gg.)," *Obshchestvo i gosudarstvo v Kitae* 10:3 (1979), p. 125.

committing the error of transposing to China the concept of a unified working class, which is adequate only for capitalist countries.[19]

The structural conditions to which Meliksetov refers are also mentioned in V. G. Gel'bras's examination of workers.[20] The list of conditions identified by these two that limited differentiation in the working class of pre-1949 China includes at least 23 points:

1) the small size of the factory proletariat;
2) the geographical concentration of workers in a small number of cities and regions;
3) the small scale of enterprises;
4) the predominance of light industry with a weak technological base;
5) the significant role of foreign capital;
6) the large ratio of bourgeois exploiters to exploited workers;[21]
7) the undeveloped division of labor between urban and rural;
8) the high rate of labor turnover;
9) the predominance of first-generation workers;
10) the youthful ages of the adult workers;
11) the large number of women and children in factory labor;
12) the presence of many short-term and seasonal workers concerned with earning money to buy land;
13) the dearth of experienced worker cadres;
14) the narrow limits of geographical mobility;

[19] Meliksetov, "Nekotorye osobennosti formirovaniia rabochego klassa Kitaia k nachalu noveishego vremeni," pp. 8, 3.

[20] Meliksetov, *Sotsial'no-ekonomicheskaia politika Gomin'dana 1927-1949 gg.*, pp. 6-44; and Gel'bras, *Sotsial'no-politicheskaia struktura KNR 50-60-e gody*, pp. 22-49.

[21] Gel'bras argues that the share of exploiters in China in 1949 was three times larger than in Russia at the end of the last century and that of the proletariat and semi-proletariat was three times smaller; consequently there was not as clear a class differentiation of Chinese society. Ibid., p. 35.

15) the living arrangements in barracks under strict supervision;
16) the hiring and conduct of labor relations through intermediaries who kept workers in a dependent relationship;
17) the absence of a general labor market;
18) the weakness of worker organizations;
19) the minimal level of worker rights already won;
20) the lack of class solidarity or realization of the nature of their exploitation;
21) the low level of literacy;
22) the low standard of living; and
23) the existence of a large reserve army of labor under conditions of overpopulation, including coolies, ricksha drivers, day laborers, and numerous semi-employed members of the *lumpen* proletariat.

All of these conditions, identified on the basis of implicit or explicit comparisons, slowed the development of a genuine working class.

Gel'bras, Meliksetov, and other Soviets trace these structural limitations back to several historical causes. Perhaps most attention is given to persisting precapitalist relations between workers and their bosses in small-scale manufacturing enterprises. One source refers to the persistence of feudal-patriarchal relations.[22] Workers often sided with the owners or regarded the new groups of factory laborers as competitors. Traditional bonds endured not just in villages and small-scale shops but even in large enterprises. A related explanation centers on the traditional psychology of workers, including the persistence of egalitarian ideals expressed in peasant uprisings that were not conducive to the formation of a united proletarian ideology. Unlike Europe, there was no tradition of the independent individual who was a member with full rights in the society—a concept that developed in conditions of free capitalist competition and along with bourgeois freedoms based on citizenship in the

[22] *Rabochii klass Kitaia (1949-1974 gg.)*, p. 9.

society.[23] The bourgeoisie failed to consolidate in China, and the proletariat was thereby weakened. By the twentieth century, China's status as a semicolony contributed to that condition, with the imposition of higher forms of capitalism from abroad. Imperialism divided the bourgeoisie, as one source claims, and created a proletariat before there was a national industrial bourgeoisie.[24] Without a strong bourgeoisie, the proletariat was limited in its development.

Another explanation for the workers' plight stresses problems of leadership in the decades leading up to the 1949 revolution. It was difficult to build up a new leadership because of the severe losses of worker activists in 1927 and the destruction of factories during the years of war with Japan and Civil War. In the absence of CCP leadership, students and others with little experience took charge.[25] Whatever structural problems existed were compounded by problems of leadership.

Some Soviet analyses are less gloomy in their depiction of conditions on the eve of the 1949 victory. Two different approaches are evident. First there are discussions of the special role of Manchuria, which, following the defeat of Japan there by Soviet troops, became the bastion of the communist forces. On the basis of the heavy industry in this region and the help of the Soviet Union, the People's Democratic Administration and the People's Liberation Army set up there became the decisive forces in the revolution.[26] This view appeared as part of the expanded effort in the 1970s to accentuate the importance of Soviet assistance and the Manchurian base area in the Chinese Revolution.[27] In addition to reasserting the significance of the proletariat in the revolution, this view also is consistent with the conclu-

[23] Gel'bras, *Sotsial'no-politicheskaia struktura KNR 50-60-e gody*, pp. 43, 44.

[24] *Klassy i klassovaia struktura v KNR*, p. 8.

[25] S. A. Gorbunova, "K kharakteristike rabochego klassa Ukhania (osen' 1926-leto 1927 gg.)," *Obshchestvo i gosudarstvo v Kitae* 9:3 (1978), pp. 23-29.

[26] *Problemy i protivorechiia industrial'nogo razvitiia KNR*, pp. 6-7.

[27] Borisov, *Sovetskii Soiuz i Man'chzhurskaia revoliutsionnaia baza.*

sion that an industrial foundation adequate for moving ahead to socialism was present in China. A book prepared under Sladkovsky's direction at IDV compares statistics on industrial production in Russia in 1913 and China in the 1930s and concludes that, although China was well behind and required a longer transitional period, it "had all the conditions for the achievement of the socialist revolution and the gradual building of the new society."[28]

Meliksetov takes a different approach to the development of the working class. His optimism is based not only on industrial statistics but also on his positive assessment of the modern sector's development under the Kuomintang. Taking aim at Chinese communist writings on the noncapitalist character of bureaucratic capital and on previous Soviet acceptance of this negative view, he offers a positive appraisal of capitalist gains in the 1920s and 1930s. Meliksetov concludes that there was a greatly increased economic role for the state and a substantial acceleration and deepening of the capitalist evolution of China.[29] It is not difficult to take this argument a step further and to give major credit to the Kuomintang for making possible the rapid development of modern industry and the working class in the years immediately following 1949.

Evidence of the importance Soviets attach to understanding the workers' movement in China is found in a Russian-language bibliography published in 1982. Entitled *The Workers' Movement in China 1917-1949, Part I, Directory of Sources and Literature*, it gives 3,104 titles under 1,830 listings in Russian, Chinese, and Western European languages published from 1917 to 1978.[30] The first 397 listings, which are primarily in Russian, and to a lesser extent in Chinese, appear under four main headings: I. V. I. Lenin on the working class and the workers' movement in China; II. The

---

[28] *Sotsial'no-ekonomicheskii stroi i ekonomicheskaia politika KNR*, pp. 4-5.

[29] Meliksetov, *Sotsial'no-ekonomicheskaia politika Gomin'dana 1927-1949 gg.*, pp. 299-303, 97-100.

[30] *Rabochee dvizhenie v Kitae 1917-1949, chast' 1, ukazatel' istochnikov i literatury.*

Communist International and the CPSU and the workers' movement in China; III. The communist party of China and the workers' movement in China; and IV. International workers' organizations and the workers' movement in China. This array of materials clearly provides an extensive basis for research on the international dimensions of the workers' movement by scholars who know Russian. There are as many as 660 listings under the next heading, V. The working class and its socioeconomic position. The numerous subheadings indicate separate bibliographies for such topics as the work day, the living standard, the position of transport workers, and child labor. The remainder of the listings are under the headings: VI. The working class and problems of social policy; and VII. The workers' movement in China. This final heading comprises materials on the various trade unions and associations of workers. As the Soviet analyses reviewed in this section make clear, research continues to draw on many of the sources identified in this bibliography to interpret the place of the workers and their organizations in Chinese society up to 1949.

The Path to Nationalization

A consensus exists in the Soviet Union that the period from 1949 to 1957 was mostly favorable for the development of the working class in China. Soviets agree that although the situation of this class at the time of the Chinese Revolution was far from adequate for the transition to socialism, a great deal of progress was made in the years of reconstruction and the first five-year plan. Even so, much more remained to be accomplished. A careful reading of Soviet sources indicates that disagreements exist about how much more was required and, consequently, how serious were the mistakes in policies concerning the workers during the first eight years of the PRC. The disagreements as well as the general consensus are informative about what Soviets deem necessary for the transition to socialism.

In 1949 the immediate need in China was to complete

106

the bourgeois-democratic stage of the revolution. In the cities this was accomplished through the nationalization of foreign capital, the confiscation of property belonging to the enemies of the Chinese people (this term is used by writers from the Institute of the Far East, much as in the PRC, to refer to those labeled bureaucratic capitalists, counterrevolutionaries, and war criminals), the buildup of the state sector, and the restoration of the economy.[31] Successful realization of these goals set the working class on the path to socialism. Furthermore, this made it possible to limit the exploitation of workers by the national bourgeoisie and to create conditions for fully eliminating relations based on exploitation.[32]

The Chinese made major advances in transforming the working class in the years 1949 to 1957. The size of this class expanded threefold. More rapid increases, which were registered by those employed in the sector of heavy industry, helped to improve the structure and the level of concentration of the working class. Gradually a nucleus of workers formed, possessing specialized skills associated with contemporary production.[33] Nationalization and the formation of cooperatives ended the exploitation of workers by private owners of the means of production. Campaigns to combat illiteracy helped raise the educational level of workers. In addition to structural and cultural changes in the work force, organizational factors were important. The activism of workers was encouraged through the formation of the new unions, the recruitment of workers into the CCP, and other organizational changes. Workers now had a role in management and took part in socialist competitions among units and enterprises. "In new China the productive activity and labor enthusiasm of the workers rose sharply."[34]

Soviet authors also report favorably on improvements in material conditions of workers. One book notes that the

---

[31] *Problemy i protivorechiia industrial'nogo razvitiia KNR*, pp. 130-31.

[32] *Klassy i klassovaia struktura v KNR*, p. 13.

[33] Ibid., pp. 16-17, 30.

[34] *Problemy i protivorechiia industrial'nogo razvitiia KNR*, p. 136.

average yearly wage of workers and employees was 42.8 percent higher in 1957 than in 1952, and, in addition, there were growing expenditures on the social needs of workers including health insurance. Unemployment was virtually eliminated.[35] The overall assessment clearly depicts a qualitative improvement in conditions of life and work. The workers were major beneficiaries of the new order in China.

Despite these positive evaluations, Soviets recognize that serious problems continued to exist for the working class. They appear to agree on the main structural problems that persisted in this period. The number of workers remained small relative to the population. Their locations were insufficiently concentrated. Many of the workers had only recently entered the industrial work force.[36] There were few second- and third-generation workers. Along with their problematic social class origins, most workers carried with them a nonproletarian ideology. There were too few skilled workers and experienced leaders from these ranks.[37] Understandably the legacy of the pre-1949 society could not be quickly overcome and the rapid buildup of a new industrial force bore with it some additional problems for the working class. In 1957 there was still no large, experienced, and dependable proletariat in China.

While structural inadequacies were largely unavoidable, other problems resulted from CCP errors. The development of China's people's democratic revolution into a socialist revolution required close ties between the CCP and the working class. The Soviets criticize Mao Zedong's failure to appreciate this need and the mistakes committed from 1950 to 1957 that reflect an inadequate understanding of the worker question. In 1949 the CCP "was not purely proletarian, not in its ideological bases, not in its social composition, not in its norms of party building." The successes of the early 1950s were due in large part to im-

---

[35] *Sotsial'no-ekonomicheskii stroi i ekonomicheskaia politika KNR*, pp. 96-97.

[36] *Rabochii klass Kitaia (1949-1974 gg.)*, pp. 42-44.

[37] *Klassy i klassovaia struktura v KNR*, pp. 35-39.

proved ties with the working class, including the establishment of party cells in factories.[38] The CCP in both policy and structure moved closer to the working class. But these ties were insufficient, and serious problems resulted from the failure to give priority to the needs of workers.

According to Soviet analysts, the essence of the transition to socialism is the establishment of a workers' state. In the urban sector, Chinese leaders during the first eight years of the PRC moved expeditiously to build the material foundation for this. Soviet assistance and the Soviet experience were vital. China's successes at this stage are attributed to the leadership of elements in the CCP with a genuine working-class interest, especially, before they were purged in 1955, to Gao Gang and Rao Shushi, the leaders of the northeast revolutionary base who had experience organizing the workers, and to trade union leaders who were continually active in opposing Mao's views through the mid-1950s.[39] An intraparty struggle continued in which viewpoints characteristic of diverse classes and strata were represented. Successes were undermined by Mao's views, which did not represent the working class and, indeed, were based on distrust of the workers.

As a result of the Maoist line, the CCP did not formulate a program on the worker question or a set of concrete steps that had to be taken to give meaning to the declaration that workers comprise the ruling class.[40] Pronouncements failed to show concern about the danger of the *lumpen* proletariat and the semiproletariat elements within the CCP and the PLA. Personnel policies were in error. At first, a shortage of personnel necessitated temporary reliance on the PLA, but the continued reliance on the army for the recruitment of cadres to government, party, and mass organizations indicates Mao's underevaluation of the political role of the working class.[41]

[38] Gel'bras, *Sotsial'no-politicheskaia struktura KNR 50-60-e gody*, pp. 53, 58.
[39] *Rabochii klass Kitaia (1949-1974 gg.)*, pp. 22 and 37.
[40] Ibid., p. 32.
[41] Ibid., p. 36.

The social psychology of the working class suffered, in particular, from three leadership shortcomings analyzed in the writings of the Institute of the International Workers' Movement: 1) continuous shortcomings in the socialization of workers; 2) inadequate defense of workers' interests by China's trade unions; and 3) mistakes associated with the forced speed-up of industrialization in 1956. The first of these shortcomings was especially serious because the backward technology and structural conditions of China's working class made it even more imperative than in Soviet Russia that the party and the state expend enormous energies in encouraging the correct attitudes.[42] Yet, the CCP gave insufficient attention to this, and even when programs were formulated local organizations did not necessarily carry them out as intended. In addition the workers were not guaranteed adequate rights, e.g. the electoral system gave rights to the urban population as a whole, more than half of which was nonproletarian.[43] Workers were troubled by inadequate material rewards and harsh conditions of work. There were often obligatory savings of part of the workers' salaries.[44] Wages rose much slower than productivity, falling below the planned ratio of 1:2. Fines in the workplace were widespread and excessive. Work hours were extended without regard to existing laws.[45] Too few workers were entitled to social benefits.[46] A one-sided approach favored increased production at the expense of rewards to the workers who brought it about. The frequent compulsory meetings and study sessions were an example of bureaucratic extremes. Forced attendance at endless political meetings helped drive the workers to exhaustion.[47] Workers justifiably demanded increased participation in the management of enterprises

---

[42] Ibid., p. 44.
[43] Gel'bras, *Sotsial'no-politicheskaia struktura KNR 50-60-e gody*, pp. 97-98.
[44] *Rabochii klass Kitaia (1949-1974 gg.)*, p. 48.
[45] A. P. Davydov, *Profsoiuzy KNR 1953-1958*, pp. 31-32, 37.
[46] Gel'bras, *Sotsial'no-politicheskaia struktura KNR 50-60-e gody*, p. 100.
[47] *Rabochii klass Kitaia (1949-1974 gg.)*, p. 48.

and economic planning, but their proposals and criticisms were slighted.[48]

Repeatedly during the first years of the PRC, Mao's charges against "economism" clashed with the basic interests of the working class. While Mao was hostile to material incentives, a proper socialist policy would be to appeal to the workers' material interests in accord with the principle, "to each according to his work."[49] Groups of workers were labeled backward for pressing concerns about wages and work conditions. Because these were usually the older, more qualified, and experienced workers, these labels created suspicions against those who should have been the leaders in the workers' movement. Negative labels were also unjustly pinned on workers striving to improve their qualifications, to change their specialization, or to avoid a transfer. Mao sought to maximize labor inputs in order to speed development at all cost.[50] This was a serious error. As Gel'bras writes, "When small-scale forms of production predominate in a country, the hegemony of large-scale production and the working class can be formed and strengthened only as a result of the development of a subtle system of political and economic relations that have interested and attracted all classes and strata in the building of socialism. However the tendency that began to show in the 1950s for the government to apply methods of brute force and constraint in relations with all classes and strata of the population not only interfered with the development of the political role of the working class, but even undermined the class–social basis of the new order."[51]

A. P. Davydov's studies of trade unions in this period criticize in detail Mao's policies against so-called "economism." One article focuses on the initial period from 1949-1952 when unions were reorganized and extended to reach

[48] *Klassy i klassovaia struktura v KNR*, p. 47.

[49] *Rabochii klass Kitaia (1949-1974 gg.)*, p. 21; and A. P. Davydov, *Prof-soiuzy KNR 1953-1958*, pp. 36-37.

[50] *Rabochii klass Kitaia (1949-1974 gg.)*, pp. 49, 52.

[51] Ibid., p. 57.

large numbers of workers. In it Davydov provides a rare look at the role of Soviet assistance, naming the main advisers and adding up the number of hours they lectured on various subjects. At the same time that he counters charges that this assistance made China politically dependent on the Soviet Union, Davydov concludes that "Soviet unions made no small contribution in the matter of the formation and development of the working class and the unions of the PRC."[52] His monograph on the period 1953-1958 criticizes bourgeois literature on China for ignoring the problem of unions due to an underestimation of the role of the working class and its organizations and to the mistaken view that these years were a quiet period for the unions.[53] He finds instead that the unions were a major battleground where the opposition to Mao was intense. On the one side was Mao's bureaucratic style with its dual goals of intensifying labor and holding down the income of workers. On the other side were the interests of workers and many union leaders to increase worker participation in decision making, to stimulate increased qualifications and interest in work, and to improve material and cultural conditions. Not only were the opinions of workers ignored, many unions at the enterprise level dealt harshly with those who complained. The unions' neglect of worker interests under the force of Maoist policies and warnings is evident in the greatly increased number of occupational injuries.[54] This neglect along with the other shortcomings in union work contributed to worker dissatisfaction. The same result was perhaps, above all, a reflection of improper or unjust remuneration policies that left the workers doubting that the unions were interested in their material well-being and that wages were a true reflection of labor input. The 1955-1956 wage reform

[52] A. P. Davydov, "Iz istorii sovetsko-kitaiskikh profsoiuznykh sviazei i organizatsii profsoiuznogo stroitel'stva v KNR (1949-1952 gg.)," *Rabochii klass i polozhenie v profsoiuzakh KNR*, pp. 41-62.

[53] Davydov, *Profsouizy KNR 1953-1958*, pp. 5-7.

[54] Ibid., pp. 27-33, 37-38, 52-53.

was an exception, for it addressed these problems and showed, along with the speeches of union leaders, that efforts were being made to defend the workers. Davydov also concludes that the role of unions in the PRC was too circumscribed; they were insufficiently involved in matters other than production.[55]

During the first eight years of the PRC one period stands out, according to Soviet analysts, for policies inimical to the interests of workers. This was the time of the forced tempo of industrialization in 1956. Writers at the Institute of the Far East, who generally find less than others to criticize in the worker policies of 1949-1955, stress the imbalances that resulted from the errors of 1956. They argue that the necessary economic base was missing and the principle of gradual socialist transformation was violated.[56] But they see corrective measures in 1956 and 1957 as bringing a large degree of stability. Gel'bras and his fellow analysts at IMRD do not make as sharp a distinction between what happened in 1955-1956 and the policies of the entire eight-year period. And they expose more shortcomings in the treatment of workers, for example in 1956 the reduction of participation in management and of selection of cadres from the ranks of workers.[57] Because they incited dissatisfaction among the workers, Gel'bras criticizes such policies as transferring large numbers without their families, maintaining the earlier wages after transfer to a new place of work, and lengthy apprenticeship service. Furthermore he attributes organized worker opposition to mistaken policies. He writes, "It is precisely the strikes of the first [factory workers] in 1956-1957 that demonstrated the trouble in the relations of the party and government with the working class."[58]

[55] Ibid., pp. 30-33, 66-67.

[56] *Sotsial'no-ekonomicheskii stroi i ekonomicheskaia politika KNR*, pp. 97-98, 128.

[57] *Rabochii klass Kitaia (1949-1974 gg.)*, p. 57.

[58] Gel'bras, *Sotsial'no-politicheskaia struktura KNR 50-60-e gody*, pp. 103, 101.

DISUNITY IN THE WORKING CLASS

The turning point in Chinese policies toward the working class came in 1957. It was manifested in a number of ways, primarily in the decisions of the Third Plenum of the Central Committee of the CCP in September. This meeting rejected the approach, taken at the Eighth Congress a year earlier and deemed by Soviets basic to Marxism-Leninism, that pay should be commensurate to the value of the work performed. It froze wages, established a lengthy period of apprenticeship, and set payments for new workers of rural origin in terms of prevailing peasant incomes. Even prior to 1957, seasonal and temporary workers had been common. "However, up to 1957 there did not exist clearcut normative acts dividing workers into separate groups and strata. From the time of the Third Plenum of the CCP Central Committee the situation radically changed."[59] The leaders of China were promoting disunity in the working class.

Both Davydov's book on trade unions and the sections on Mao's ideology in *The Working Class of China, 1949-1974* analyze the background and aftermath of the Third Plenum. Davydov reviews the sharp criticisms at the end of 1956 and early 1957 leveled against the union leadership, showing that they revealed the strong Maoist opposition to the 1956 reforms of wages, living conditions, and work conditions.

First the unions were stripped of some of their financial authority; then in the campaign against "rightist elements" in the summer of 1957, the trade union and worker ranks were purged (mainly of communists with long party service who were held in great respect by party organizations). Later in the spring and summer of 1958 this purge was referred to in the Chinese press as neither deep nor full, and a further campaign unfolded for the "final liquidation of opposition in the unions." The fate of the unions was mirrored in the deteriorating position of the working class.

[59] Ibid., p. 105.

Davydov makes it clear that the trade unions ought to have been organized more independently of the party in order properly to serve the workers; in the purges they lost even this degree of independence as they succumbed to "political terror."[60] He traces the Chinese press's legitimate concern with improving the ties between the unions and the masses before this theme disappeared at the time of the 1957 purge. From that time the trade unions of China largely failed to represent the interests of the workers.

The 1957 turnabout is linked in the analysis by the Institute of the International Workers' Movement to the continuous search throughout the 1950s for a path to minimize the negative influence of the village on the tempo of industrial growth. In contrast to the history of the Soviet Union, where heavy industry is seen as having been dominant in the economy by the time of the victory of the socialist revolution, in China in 1957 this dominance was still some distance away. Supplies from the rural sector were insufficient. An additional complication was that the number of handicraft workers decreased sharply during the process of collectivization, thus damaging the agrarian economy.[61] Action was required to meet the needs of the village for industrial products. This was one of the urgent problems in 1957 that encouraged changes in policy toward the working class, but Soviets claim that the changes that came had nothing in common with Marxism-Leninism.

Mao failed to understand the need for the working class to have the leading role in relations with the peasantry. Whereas the Eighth Congress had correctly concluded that, in the struggle between socialism and capitalism, the basic question of distribution had already been resolved, Mao declared that class struggle had not ended. It persisted mainly between the proletariat and the bourgeoisie. Mao misidentified each of these groups; he included illiterate poor peasants as part of the proletariat and semiproletariat,

[60] Davydov, *Profsoiuzy KNR 1953-1958*, pp. 93, 96-97, 98.
[61] *Rabochii klass Kitaia (1949-1974 gg.)*, pp. 67, 69, 73-74.

and equated the bourgeoisie with "enemies of the people," i.e. those who thought differently from Mao. With this perspective, Mao placed whomever he wished in the bourgeoisie, even the intelligentsia and the so-called "worker aristocracy" consisting of experienced, skilled, and well-paid workers.[62] Emphasizing attitudes, Mao substituted the discipline of political ideology for political economics as the basis for analyzing society. This subjective approach became dominant in policy making circles in 1957 and 1958.

In the Great Leap Forward, the situation of workers deteriorated rapidly. A. V. Kholodkovskaia is typical of Soviet observers in concluding, "The Maoist policies of the 'Great Leap' exerted an enormous negative socioeconomic and sociopsychological influence on the working class."[63] The number of workers rapidly expanded, but this was due to the forced establishment of numerous unproductive small enterprises and the severalfold expansion of the unskilled work force in many large enterprises.[64] The structure of the working class was damaged by the tremendous influx of peasants who lacked the educational or cultural prerequisites of experienced workers. With their arrival, the working class became less experienced, less disciplined in outlook, and of inferior origins. The barracks existence and semimilitary organization that greeted these new entrants did little to raise their proletarian consciousness. At the same time, many skilled workers were sent out of the major industrial complexes to the countryside, where they became dissatisfied and came under the influence of the peasant environment. This struck a blow against the nucleus of working class leaders. In short, structural changes in 1958-1959 seriously weakened the Chinese working class.

The new entrants to the working class of 1958-1960 formed the second contingent of recruits in the PRC, following the contingent that entered the labor force in the years 1949-

[62] Ibid., pp. 70, 80, 97, 124.
[63] A. V. Kholodkovskaia, *Rabochii klass Kitaia v period "uregulirovaniia" (1961-1965)*, p. 5.
[64] *Klassy i klassovaia struktura v KNR*, p. 52.

1957 and preceding, after a hiatus caused by negative or slow recruitment, the third contingent of 1968-1976.[65] The experiences as well as the structure of this contingent were distinctive. These recruits were paid badly and had little chance of advancement as they acquired new work skills and experience. They received little in the way of social benefits. These workers were not only underpaid, they were without rights. Along with all workers during the Great Leap Forward, they were made to labor almost without rest. Exhausted by that grueling experience, they then experienced the years of hunger and, for many, relocation in villages. The Great Leap Forward was characterized by reduced worker participation in management, wages that provided little incentive to diligent work, unconcern about the well-being of workers, and an erroneous ideology about the nature of the working class. Due to inadequate attention to conditions of work and exhaustive use of men and machines, the rate of accidents sharply increased. All of these factors led to growing dissatisfaction and passivity.[66] Even those members of this huge contingent of workers who remained in the urban work force were not well prepared to acquire a socialist outlook on life. In the years that followed, the second contingent remained less proletarian than the first.

After the extreme conditions of the Great Leap Forward, the circumstances of workers improved, but not quickly and not for long. "The extreme physical and moral fatigue, apathy, disappointment, and dissatisfaction little by little disappeared." By 1962 nearly 25 million people had been resettled in the countryside, leaving a trimmer, more proletarian working class—however, one that was deeply scarred. The gradual increase of the working class in the years that followed brought in better educated youths; in this period only about one-quarter of high school graduates were ad-

[65] *Rabochii klass v sotsial'no-politicheskoi sisteme KNR*, pp. 92-94.

[66] Kholodkovskaia, *Rabochii klass Kitaia v period "uregulirovaniia" (1961-1965)*, p. 27, 22.

mitted into higher education. Part-time study for workers expanded greatly, although this was accompanied by a sharp drop in the quality of education. On the whole, the structure and the education of the working class partially recovered from the low point a few years earlier. Kholodkovskaia's book examines many areas where recovery occurred, and discerns a "positive effect" in the policies of the early 1960s. But the book also points to a reversal following the Tenth Plenum of September 1962 and especially in 1964 after Mao's "Socialist Education" campaign spread from the countryside to industry and transport.[67] The late 1950s' attacks against material incentives and unions were revived after only a short respite in the new offensive identified as the class struggle. The situation of the working class had taken another downturn, and the cumulative experiences of 1957-1966 weighed heavily on the consciousness of workers on the eve of the Cultural Revolution.

Behind the cities and units held up as models in the first half of the 1960s, Soviets detect contrasting views of the role of the working class in China. The Ma-an-shan statutes of the early 1960s favored one-man management, material motivation, and a heightened role of specialists, while omitting mention of the damaging slogan of politics in command, mass movements, and physical labor for officials and specialists. The slogan "learn from Shanghai" appeared for a time in support of the experience of the city where the strongest elements in the working class lived. In contrast, the An-shan statutes were held up by the Maoists in opposition to a sharp division of labor, personal responsibility for work performed, and material stimuli for each worker.[68] By 1963-1965 the campaigns to "Learn from the PLA" and "Learn from Daqing" (the model community that combined urban and rural functions) were being pushed vigorously. Their negative consequences were responsible for

[67] Ibid., pp. 40, 44-45, 50, 52, 90-91.
[68] *Rabochii klass Kitaia (1949-1974 gg.)*, pp. 117-29.

118

reversing some of the short-lived concessions of the early 1960s.

A central theme of Soviet critiques is the increasing heterogeneity of the Chinese working class. Under the mistaken policies of China's leaders, separate generations of workers from different backgrounds and subject to different conditions of work could not form a unified class. The core of the proletariat was not built up to absorb increasing numbers, but was allowed to atrophy. The powerful force of peasant influence was not narrowly constricted, but actually drew support from policies of the Great Leap Forward and some of the policies of the following period as well. Peasant influences spread through the mass influx of peasants into the work force in the Great Leap Forward, through the forced resettlement of workers in the countryside, and through heavy reliance on the army, which mainly consisted of peasants and supplied many of the leading officials among the working class. Beginning in 1957-1958, China's leaders divided the workers against each other and deceived themselves about the consequences of their actions. Impressionable youth were taken in by the cult of the infallible leader Mao; uneducated older workers resented better educated young workers who were promoted ahead of them in the 1950s and even refused to divulge the secrets of their work.[69] Workers with very different rights and rewards labored side by side. In these circumstances, it is no wonder that they perceived themselves in conflict with one another.

One of the most serious threats to the unity of the working class in the mid-1960s was the expanding system of "both worker and peasant." By 1966-1967 there were already millions in this category and there existed dozens of forms this type of temporary or seasonal labor could take. Soviet writers observed that all types were marked by heightened state control over the population, not by a labor

[69] Kholodkovskaia, *Rabochii klass Kitaia v period "uregulirovaniia" (1961-1965)*, pp. 53-54, 68, 100; *Klassy i klassovaia struktura v KNR*, p. 53.

market in which individuals with equal rights participated as full members of the society and enjoyed a free choice of place of residence and work. "Both peasants and workers" were denied the right to bring their families with them, to establish residence, to receive a normal worker's share of the benefits, and to receive equal pay for equal work. They were personal dependents of their brigades or communes, which received part of their salary. In essence, this was a form of forced labor. In the mid-1960s, this system was one factor that led to "a loss of belief in the party, the state, socialism." The system was to expand in the first half of the 1970s.[70]

Writings on this period stress the exclusion of workers from power and the rejection of democratic procedures. As a rule, entrance to the CCP is one indicator of the level of political organization of workers. In the decade after 1956 there was essentially no increase in the representation of workers in the party. In contrast, in 1965 alone hundreds of thousands of soldiers from the PLA were admitted. The Chinese failed to work out the meaning of the concept of the dictatorship of the proletariat. The minor role of workers in the party and the government made it easier for Mao's group. Workers were promised participation in management in the early 1960s, but the reality was characterized by Soviet critics as a form of "social demagoguery that was directed at the creation of illusions in the working class." According to another source, although there were positive developments in the early 1960s, participation was very modest and occurred only at the lowest level with little possibility of influencing the enterprise plan. Official propaganda was contradicted by reality.[71]

The Soviets also accused the Chinese of rejecting the democratic character of the unions in favor of methods of

---

[70] Gel'bras, *Sotsial'no-politicheskaia struktura KNR 50-60-e gody*, pp. 108, 109, 116; Kholodkovskaia, *Rabochii klass Kitaia v period "uregulirovaniia" (1961-1965)*, p. 110.

[71] Kholodkovskaia, *Rabochii klass Kitaia v period "uregulirovaniia" (1961-1965)*, pp. 70-71, 85-89; *Klassy i klassovaia struktura v KNR*, p. 57.

raw force. "The unions helped the Maoists to organize the labor of workers by means of ideological pressure, the introduction of army-barracks procedures." Further evidence of the absence of democratic procedures is found in the reduced opportunities of Soviet delegations to China to visit industrial enterprises and, in those rare cases when they were able to converse directly with workers, the officials of the unions who were present "unceremoniously interfered in the conversation."[72] As opponents of Mao pointed out, the unions had the "character of the 'apparatus.' "[73] Their primary concern had shifted in 1963-1965 to propagating the "ideas of Mao Zedong."

The whole range of Soviet criticisms of Chinese policies adds up to harsh condemnation of a system that forced workers to exhaust themselves and gave them little in return. The workers were inadequately represented. When they protested, they were persecuted. There was great waste. "Production for the sake of production never was and never will be the moving force stimulating a rise of revolutionary activity." Maoists ignored the "union of science and work." They disregarded the well-being of the workers. Although in the first half of the 1960s the priority of agriculture and light industry was proclaimed, "precisely then enormous material, financial, technical and scientific resources were thrown at military needs. . . . In 1965 direct military expenses exceeded by almost twice the scale of capital investment in industry."[74] This greatly reduced the funds available for the important needs of Chinese society. This is the message that one finds in the writings on China of the Institute of the International Workers' Movement. The writings of the Institute of the Far East scarcely treat the themes in this section; so it is not possible to specify an

---

[72] Davydov, *Profsoiuzy KNR 1953-1958*, p. 110, and *Profsoiuzy Kitaia: istoriia i sovremennost' (1949-1980 gody)*, pp. 74, 97.

[73] Kholodkovskaia, *Rabochii klass Kitaia v period "uregulirovaniia" (1961-1965)*, p. 107.

[74] *Rabochii klass Kitaia (1949-1974 gg.)*, pp. 103, 118.

alternative approach of the more orthodox group in the Soviet Union.

THE CULTURAL REVOLUTION

There is complete Soviet agreement on the obvious: "The Maoist 'Cultural Revolution' inflicted a heavy blow on the Chinese working class." The workers lost materially, through lower incomes and lower standards of living, the elimination of bonuses and piece work, the widespread practice of forced savings, and severe cutbacks on benefits. Their work conditions worsened; military control over enterprises and restructuring along the lines of army units subjected them to forced labor while onerous working hours and disregard for safety threatened their well-being. Proletarian elements experienced a structural loss too, as the number of workers stagnated for a few years and leadership roles were assumed by less educated and less qualified individuals. In this environment, workers were deprived of their organizations and their political rights. "Mass terror" spread through the country.[75]

What was the reaction to this "frontal assault on the economic and political interests of the working class, on the material conditions of life, on its political organization, and also on its class ideology"? The surviving nucleus of this class acted to defend its interest but, in the face of the long duration of mutual opposition among separate groups of workers and the weakness of party cells in the factories, was unable to unite the entire working class. Both structural and organizational weaknesses blocked such efforts. As a result, soldiers assumed the leading role in the newly created revolutionary committees, which in function and structure were directed against the interests of the working class.[76] Workers showed their dissatisfaction in various ways.

[75] Ibid., p. 158.

[76] *Klassy i klassovaia struktura v KNR*, pp. 60, 62; *Rabochii klass Kitaia (1949-1974 gg.)*, p. 153.

There were strikes and other forms of protest, but, in the absence of an adequate organized expression of their interests, the most widespread responses were forms of passive resistance such as a decline of discipline and resistance to orders.[77] When the most able representatives of the workers became targets of the Cultural Revolution, the struggle was carried on by inexperienced younger workers and others in the contingent that had come from the countryside in 1958-1960 and were relegated to inferior status.[78] Even if they had some success in mobilizing these workers, the Maoists were unable to build reliable and stable organizations from little educated and unskilled workers of nonproletarian backgrounds. In 1969-1970 the Maoists were forced to restore earlier work norms, to rehabilitate former enterprise leaders, and to abandon plans for the creation of new worker associations comprising those workers who had supported Mao.[79] The attempt to organize the least proletarian of the workers against the true interests of the working class failed.

In the aftermath of the Cultural Revolution, the situation of workers improved somewhat. By 1970 the separation into two economic systems, central and local, was becoming more and more pronounced. Those in the central system benefited from a revival of methods intended to raise labor productivity and worker discipline. The leadership, however, did not aim at returning the country to the socialist path of development; it continued to impose military control and to carry out reforms in the interest of Great Han chauvinism rather than the working class. Existing material incentives were limited by the allotment of minimal resources. Wages remained unchanged from the level of 15 years earlier. A six-day, 48-hour week persisted with no vacation except for seven holidays and visitation periods for those workers who lived apart from their families. Many

[77] Gel'bras, *Kitai: krizis prodolzhaetsia*, p. 103.
[78] V. I. Lazarev, *Klassovaia bor'ba v KNR*, p. 166.
[79] *Rabochii klass Kitaia (1949-1974 gg.)*, pp. 161-62.

123

did not have the right to a pension. There was little housing construction, and large numbers of workers lived without modern amenities such as heating and water pipes. Soviets make clear that the workers were deeply dissatisfied with these inadequate conditions.[80]

In a jointly authored book under the direction of Gel'bras, A. N. Anisimov attempts to quantify the worsening of the material position of workers and employees. He argues that between 1957 and 1972 the goal of production changed to "production for the sake of production." An unduly high figure of over 80 percent of factory workers labored for heavy industry. A substantial intensification of labor (and increase in the value of industrial output) was not accompanied by improvements in living conditions. Indeed, conditions deteriorated. For example, all possible limits were placed on the use of electricity for personal needs. Pollution became severe. Medical care and education were decidedly worse in the early 1970s than a decade before. Rationing severely limited access to important items. Incomes of some families had risen somewhat by the mid-1970s as women and youngsters fortunate to stay in the city entered the labor force, but there was no corresponding increase in the products available for household purchase.[81]

While material incentives improved after their low point in the Cultural Revolution, the structure of the working class was deteriorating. A. V. Ostrovskii identifies five respects in which deterioration occurred: 1) the educational level in positions requiring high skills was lowered by the practice of promoting workers on the basis of insufficient study in the so-called July 21 universities (where part-time training prevailed) to the rank of engineering-technical personnel; 2) the skill level and income of many workers was held down by the failure to advance workers who became more qualified, and sometimes political criteria led to the denial of a promotion; 3) from the end of the 1960s

[80] *Sotsial'no-ekonomicheskii stroi i ekonomicheskaia politika KNR*, pp. 219, 221, 226-27.

[81] *Rabochii klass Kitaia (1949-1974 gg.)*, pp. 192, 194-97.

the rapid influx of young workers into enterprises began to reduce the percentage of skilled workers; 4) the quality of education of the new workers and thus the qualifications of workers declined; and 5) the process of matching the skills of the workers to the requirements of the job further deteriorated.[82] Gel'bras also comments on the structural changes that were undermining the formation of a working class. He points to the localization of social processes as individuals lost the freedom to move; thus their field of vision narrowed to the confines of separate enterprises and cities. Gel'bras observes, "In the PRC in the 1960s and 1970s a paradoxical situation took shape: the number of industrial workers rose, their influence on the economic life of the country became enormous, however the possibilities of their political influence on the life of society sharply decreased." The state as represented by local organs of power, the enterprises, and the communes (production brigades) was the owner of labor. Forced labor occurred as workers were deprived of elementary rights of citizenship. They could not through their own initiative enter into labor agreements or search for superior conditions of work and pay. Estates were forming characterized by insurmountable social barriers. These differences within the working class were manipulated by Maoists in the Cultural Revolution in their own interests and continued in the 1970s to deform proletarian psychology.[83]

From 1973 to 1975 there was a struggle in China over the reestablishment of trade unions. Through an analysis of Chinese press coverage of this struggle, A. V. Kholodkovskaia adds to the far-reaching research on Chinese workers under Gel'bras at the Institute of the International Workers' Movement. She argues that the unions were created from the top down and "the democratic foundations of the election of the leading organs of the unions was fully

---

[82] A. V. Ostrovskii, "Nekotorye aspekty issledovaniia vnutrennei sotsial'noi struktury rabochego klassa KNR," in *Problemy i protivorechiia v razvitii rabochego klassa KNR*, pp. 65-81.

[83] Gel'bras, "Problemy razvitiia rabochego klassa i rabochego dvizheniia v KNR," in ibid., pp. 29-31, 42.

consigned to oblivion."[84] Activists of the Cultural Revolution became the delegates to union congresses. In the intense struggle before the Tenth Party Congress, the Chinese leadership forced the creation of mass organizations of the working class. Over the next three years the leaders tried to focus the unions' attention on "class struggle" and on pitting one group of workers against another as a weapon in the political struggle. Study classes absorbed tremendous amounts of time. According to G. F. Saltykov, in 1974-1976 the struggle for worker support became intense, involving threats, physical force, and frequent killings as well as slowdowns, passivity, refusal to go to work, and sabotage.[85] Factional conflict in the working class was the Maoist legacy. Attacks on the principle of material incentives in the course of the 1975 campaign for the study of the theory of the dictatorship of the proletariat showed that the new unions refrained from any defense of the rights and interests of workers.[86]

In 1981-1982 two Soviet monographs were published that are primarily concerned with a broad interpretation of the consequences of the Cultural Revolution for the working class of China. One by V. I. Lazarev, entitled *Class Struggle in the PRC*, stresses the petty-bourgeois influences on this class. The other by G. F. Saltykov, entitled *Sociopsychological Factors in the Political Life of the Working Class of the PRC in the 1970s*, focuses on workers' attitudes and their informal associations. Although the themes of the two books have a good deal in common, the differences in their approach and conclusions point to important divisions within the Soviet Union in interpreting the legacy of Maoism.[87]

[84] Kholodkovskaia, "Kampaniia 'uporiadocheniia i stroitel'stva profsoiuzov' i ee vliianie na rabochii klass (1973-1975 gg.)," in *Rabochii klass i polozhenie v profsoiuzakh KNR*, p. 17.

[85] G. F. Saltykov, *Sotsial'no-psikhologicheskie faktory v politicheskoi zhizni rabochego klassa KNR 70-kh godov*, pp. 82-83.

[86] Davydov, *Profsoiuzy Kitaia: istoriia i sovremennost'*, pp. 128, 132-33.

[87] Lazarev, *Klassovaia bor'ba v KNR*; Saltykov, *Sotsial'no-psikhologicheskie faktory v politicheskoi zhizni rabochego klassa KNR 70-kh godov*.

Until his death in 1982, Lazarev was a frequent contributor to *Voprosy istorii KPSS*, whose articles are republished in the orthodox compilation *Opasnyi kurs*,[88] and was associated with the dominant group in the field led by Rakhmanin. Lazarev advances the view that the events of the 1950s-1970s were in "a single process, bearing the features of a petty-bourgeois counterrevolution." The liquidation of the big exploiters created favorable conditions for small-scale owners. Even after collectivization deprived the class of small-scale owners of its economic base, it continued to exist as a social type with influence on social life, politics, and ideology, particularly to the extent that it could escape from under the influence and leadership of the proletariat. The weak position of the working class, the low level of technology, and deeply rooted national traditions gave this class its opportunity. According to Lazarev, the Maoists transferred power from the working class in 1966-1969, breaking up its organizations and disregarding its interests. He argues that all Chinese leaders including Deng Xiaoping were orthodox Maoists and were united in leading China away from socialism. A military-bureaucratic dictatorship formed, supported by brute force and by terror, while separatist and even anarchist tendencies spread. Lazarev finds in Maoist policies a reminder of Hitler's policies toward the German working class.[89]

This is a view of China as turning to the right, of a reactionary system in which the working class lost all influence.

Easy to reconcile with this conclusion is the comparison Rakhmanin (Borisov) draws between developments in 1961-1965 after the Great Leap Forward and in 1971-1975 after the Cultural Revolution. He finds a difference of principle between the two periods, with the former representing a

---

[88] Lazarev, "Antimaoistskaia tendentsiia v Kitae," *Opasnyi kurs* 9, pp. 240-62, and "Kompartiia Kitaia: proshloe i nastoiashchee (k 60-letiiu KPK)," *Opasnyi kurs* 11, pp. 210-31.

[89] Lazarev, *Klassovaia bor'ba v KNR*, pp. 12, 22-23, 38-41, 158-61, 197, 219.

return to socialist methods and the latter only drawing on certain socialist methods and forms for policies incompatible with socialism, namely to develop the economy in preparation for war and to firm up the military-bureaucratic regime. Rakhmanin accuses anticommunist and revisionist visitors to China of being silent about the fact that "workers receive a miserly wage, that more than 20 million persons are held in forced labor camps or in so-called reeducation schools (similar to 'May 7 schools')." He sees China as moving further from socialism.[90]

Saltykov shares the view that Maoism is an antiproletarian ideology; it seeks to destroy the specific sociopsychological characteristics of the proletariat and replace them with a *lumpen* proletarian psychology. One interesting feature of his book is his concern with traditional personality traits in China. He points to thrift as a feature of Chinese national character associated, for example, with the severe shortage of fuel, and he observes that in the 1970s "the cult of thriftiness reached an unprecedented scale in China" as "all expenses of the population were placed under the most severe control." Mao took advantage of traditional traits, especially in his methods to subject the individual to the group and to control behavior. In addition to studying the psychological heterogeneity of the working class, Saltykov examines the informal groups of the late 1960s and 1970s, claiming that they rather than the official organizations led the broad mass of workers. Whereas the formal organizations operating under tight control contradicted the interests of workers, the informal groups, influenced by tradition, reflected the genuine but divided concerns of the workers. He describes in considerable detail an ongoing struggle between the authorities and the informal small-scale groups with their narrow and personal interests, above all tied to wages and the provision of daily needs. Negative processes that intensified in the Cultural Revolution left a

[90] Borisov, *Vnutrennaia i vneshniaia politika Kitaia v 70-e gody*, pp. 141, 216-17.

deeply divided and heterogeneous working class in competition for a place to work and for the right to live in the
city. Fear and uncertainty about tomorrow left a strong
residue in the late 1970s. Saltykov describes an atmosphere
of mass repression and fear before the army and the police
in which workers lost their feeling of self-worth. In this
atmosphere, Chinese have lost their traditional love of work;
they have become a "society of idlers."[91]

The view that Maoism does not represent a turn to the
right, but a repressive state in which the army controls all
areas, is more directly expressed by Deliusin. He challenges
the notion that Maoism is somehow an expression of bourgeois ideology or interests. In contrast to Lazarev or Rakhmanin, he sees the social class system of socialism as remaining largely intact while state oppression of the workers
occurred on a large scale. The explanation given by Deliusin does not ignore the heterogeneity of the peasantry and
working class, but it places primary emphasis on the army
and on the officials, whom we will examine in Chapter 5.[92]

THE POST-MAO ERA

The prevailing Soviet view in the six years after Mao Zedong's death up to September 1982, the eve of the resumption of Sino-Soviet negotiations, was that workers benefited little from recent policy changes, and then only to
the extent that leaders were obliged to take action. The
leadership "needed the working class for the realization of
its aims for turning China into a first-rank power in economic and military relations." It had "to make some concessions to the workers . . . although the influence of the working class of the PRC on other classes and social groups is
of little importance."[93] After Mao's death, China is seen as
having turned sharply to the right, significantly retreating

---

[91] Saltykov, *Sotsial'no-psikhologicheskie faktory v politicheskoi zhizni rabochego klassa KNR 70-kh godov*, pp. 18, 43-44, 66, 104, 132-33.

[92] Delyusin [Deliusin], *The Socio-Political Essence of Maoism*, pp. 78-86.

[93] *Klassy i klassovaia struktura v KNR*, p. 75.

from positions already occupied by socialism. These conditions have created new socioeconomic difficulties, such as a rise in unemployment as well as popular skepticism that there will be improvement in the life of the workers.[94] Wage increases have been canceled out by rising inflation.

The writings of the Institute of the Far East and the group led by Rakhmanin reveal little optimism about recent changes in policies toward workers. The IDV yearbook for 1978 pointed to the continued small size of the working class (9-10 percent of the economically active population), of which half worked in small-scale county or commune enterprises and another 28 million persons in commune enterprises functioned as "both worker and peasant" in a system of temporary employment. It noted that in order to build an industrial base for its military potential, Chinese leadership turned to material incentives for large enterprises, where many new workers were placed through backdoor connections, while enterprises under local control did not raise wages. "Under the slogan 'strengthening work discipline,' 'observing order' actually occurs a process of intensifying the exploitation of Chinese workers as a result of the intensification of labor." Open protests against such policies were cruelly suppressed by the authorities. The leadership proposed that the workers further tighten their belts and offered no concrete measures for increasing living standards. The initial reaction to policies aimed at the four modernizations in agriculture, industry, defense, and science and technology, indicated that the authorities at IDV believed these would further split the working class.[95]

The 1979 yearbook maintained the same tone, especially deriding the treatment of young workers in the PRC. It noted that the severe unemployment problem among young people was being met by the creation of small-scale collective enterprises. In these places of work without modern technology it was difficult to raise one's qualifications, to

---

[94] V. Ia. Matiaev and V. P. Fetov, "Kitai: nekotorye aspekty vnutrennego razvitiia," *Problemy Dal'nego Vostoka* 42 (1982:2), pp. 40, 41.

[95] *Kitaiskaia Narodnaia Respublika 1978*, pp. 82-83.

improve one's social position, or to receive a decent wage. Workers there were regarded as second-class citizens. The low educational level of workers and the longstanding serious barriers against advancement for those with comparatively high skills also operated against a productive work force. The IDV authors conclude that China's leaders "fully ignored the interests of youth."[96] A 1980 conference paper by one of the authors of the yearbook sections on workers also mentions the divisive effects of the wage adjustment of November 1, 1979, which further separated older and younger workers. China's leadership thus sought to create a privileged part of the working class—older, with longer service, more qualified, and with higher wages. At the same time it ignored the interests of young workers, denying them the opportunity to improve their qualifications. Thus the post-Mao era has brought an even greater split between the core of the working class and others, leaving the peasants altogether excluded from the large-scale industrial sector.[97]

The 1982 book by Lazarev includes a long chapter on China after Mao which argues that "The basic direction of the development of China—the general aim and the methods of its attainments remained Maoist, they did not undergo cardinal changes after the death of Mao." In support of this proposition, Lazarev claims that Mao's heirs did nothing to raise the authority of the working class in society. Despite the convening in October 1978, after a twenty-one-year hiatus, of the all-China congress of trade unions, under cover of the struggle against "syndicalism" there were barriers to the development of the democratic rights of unions. In short, this Soviet viewpoint asserts that the counterrevolution continues to develop in the PRC to the detriment of the working class.[98]

An alternate perspective places the blame on the psy-

[96] *Kitaiskaia Narodnaia Respublika 1979*, pp. 76-78.

[97] Ostrovskii, "Problemy razvitiia rabochego klassa i programma 'chetyrekh modernizatsii,' " *Kharakter i osobennosti ekonomicheskogo i sotsial'nogo razvitiia KNR na sovremennom etape*, pp. 39-40.

[98] Lazarev, *Klassovaia bor'ba v KNR*, pp. 241, 251-53.

chological state persisting in the post-Mao working class. Crediting the post-Mao leadership with introducing the principle of material incentives that led to an upsurge of labor activity, Saltykov argues that the effect was limited because inflation ate up the wage increase. The new leadership also failed to redress the psychological distress of the workers because of policies aimed at every possible intensification of labor and thrift, while ignoring the need for safety measures. Due to these conditions, at the end of the 1970s the quality of production deteriorated further. At the same time, drinking, gambling, corruption, deceit, and other forms of immorality increased among Chinese workers. Continuing the process of the early 1970s workers became "much less proletarian."[99] In essence, this viewpoint holds that the problem was not a swing to the right but a persistent disregard by the state authorities for the well-being of the workers.

This view that workers were deeply dissatisfied due to the perpetuation of controls and poor material conditions is clearly articulated in the 1981 book on the working class by a group at the Institute of the International Workers' Movement. It states, "The workers of China, as before, are deprived of the basic democratic and civil rights; rights to change the place of residence, to select a profession, a place of work, conditions of work. Enterprises are deprived of the rights of independently deciding on questions of hiring, transferring to regular work, promotion, etc." On the positive side, this book notes a broadened range of discussion after Mao's death, followed by policy improvements in 1979 after the Third Plenum. On the negative side, the study downplays their significance, concluding, for example, that the principle of payment according to work and material incentives were introduced too slowly and inconsistently. It faults the antiworker essence of the decisions of the Ninth Congress of Trade Unions in October 1978. It notes that

[99] Saltykov, *Sotsial'no-psikhologicheskie faktory zhizni rabochego klassa KNR 70-kh godov*, pp. 135, 137, 154.

the rehabilitation of old workers in 1979 and the sharp change in the status of workers who had supported the Cultural Revolution added one more contradiction to the many that already divided worker collectives. Above all, it stresses for the most recent years the absence of democratization and the subordinate role of the trade unions as a political weapon of the Chinese leadership that did not reflect the true material interests of the working class. As before, the workers carry on their struggle through all organizations, mainly illegal and semilegal, and methods available. Associations of a traditional character play a major role and, in the analysis of the situation based on what is printed in the Chinese press, it is difficult to separate proletarian actions from the acts of declassé and criminal elements.[100] This Soviet perspective focuses on civil rights, material benefits, genuine union representation, and democratic participation as persisting problems that a repressive and exploitative state leadership has not remedied. In brief, de-Maoization has not been carried far enough because of the vested interests of power holders.

Conclusions

Soviet publications on China contain no hint that any of the shortcomings they observe in the treatment of the workers of China had precedents in Soviet history. By quoting Lenin repeatedly and alluding occasionally to positive developments in the USSR, these writings appear to equate the Soviet experience with the model transition to socialism. In many respects they agree on what that model comprises and the consequences of deviations from it. But there are also notable differences in what they idealize as the crucial elements in socialism and where they see the Chinese leaders going astray. The similarities indicate a shared viewpoint of the structural transformation of the working class

[100] *Rabochii klass v sotsial'no-politicheskoi sisteme KNR*, pp. 168, 173-78, 196-97.

through rapid growth, concentration in large enterprises, and education and a mutual acceptance of the need for planned, gradual transformation, material incentives, and worker representation in decision making. The differences show one Soviet group's greater concern with the rights, well-being, and genuine participation of the workers and a second group's primary concern with the effectiveness of central control and coordination.

The critics associated with the Institute of the International Workers' Movement hold China up to a model of socialism that could be perceived as a reform agenda for the Soviet Union as well. They insist on the need for unions that truly represent the concerns of workers, for improved wages and benefits, and for active participation in important decisions. They write about the dangers of worker apathy and dissatisfaction as manifested in low-quality products and informal associations that work at cross purposes with enterprise goals. The 1983 campaign against low productivity and lack of diligence in the Soviet workplace shows the relevance of these criticisms of Chinese conditions to Soviet reality.

As in Soviet studies of the peasantry, the reform view of the working class emphasizes the meager sociological understanding of China's communists. Leaders wanted to believe that the workers would support them in the 1925-1927 revolution and on crucial occasions over the next half-century, but they failed to understand the true nature of this class in the conditions of China. Not understanding the workers, the Maoists failed to lead them properly. Distrust bred centralized control and a disregard for democratic procedures.

Just as sociological analysis of the peasants would have shown China's leaders the special dangers of egalitarianism and centralization in that society, careful research on the working class would have warned the Chinese of the need to nurture this group in order to build up a large, experienced, and dependable proletariat. Experts rather than ex-army personnel should have assumed leadership roles.

They should have promoted democratic participation among the proletariat, especially through more independent trade unions that genuinely represented this class. Rewards should have been increased and distributed in such a way as to foster a social psychology of self-interest and hard work. It was a mistake to substitute brute force for benefits and procedures designed to attract workers and to encourage them to raise their qualifications and to strive for better conditions. The Soviet consensus on China's mistaken policies for workers accepts these points.

To the reformers, it is dangerously subjective for leaders to judge workers for their relations to the leaders' policies. What is needed is to strengthen the corps of experienced, skilled, and well-paid workers and to grant them an increasingly leading role in society. As in their approach to the peasantry, the Chinese failed to encourage a meritocracy. Erroneous policies resulted in growing dissatisfaction and passivity among the workers. Limitations on equal rights and freedom of choice along with disguised forms of forced labor severely undermined worker morale and even their belief in the communist party. Official propaganda may have deceived some, especially impressionable youths, but illusions are not easy to maintain when they are so clearly contradicted by reality.

Although Westerners are likely to find the sweeping indictment of Chinese policies toward workers by Soviet reformers particularly attuned to our own criticisms of socialism, even the writings of the orthodox camp have much in common with our criticisms. Again there is a call for policies based on expertise, material incentives aimed at individual motivation, and channels for participation and representation. The Soviet reform camp more fully shares the Western concern about the inherent dangers of centralization and control from above, but there appears to be a broad consensus in the Soviet Union on most of the criticisms that can be found in Western writings.

At the beginning of the 1980s the Solidarity movement in Poland brought the position of workers in socialist countries to the world's attention. Soviet leaders chose to condemn the rightist drift of this movement, but at the same time they showed an interest in exposing the policy errors in a socialist state that can alienate large numbers of workers. The writings from IMRD on China established a precedent for this task. It would not be surprising if Soviets with a reform orientation hoped through evaluations of mistaken policies elsewhere to increase the chances for improvement in the lot of workers inside their own country.

· 4 ·

THE INTELLIGENTSIA

There could hardly be a sharper contrast than that between the massive expansion of higher education and employment of specialists in the Soviet Union and the devastating contraction of advanced education and denigration of specialists in China during the last decade of Mao's life. The engineers, state planners and managers, doctors, scientists, and teachers of the Soviet Union formed a nucleus of specialists who led the modernization of their country. The dearth of specialists in China and the demoralization of those who were not permitted to apply their skills severely retarded modernization in that country.

In other respects, however, there are similarities in the position of educated people in China and the Soviet Union. These are identified in Western publications on each country that accentuate the controls placed on creative endeavors and scientific investigations. Writing about education, the arts, the mass media, management, and academic research, Western observers point to similar kinds of problems in the two countries. They describe censorship and heavy-handed bureaucratic methods. Soviet publications, on the one hand, vigorously reject the Western criticisms of the role of the intelligentsia in their country while, on the other hand, finding fault with China for many of the same shortcomings. Again we see Soviet writings performing a dual role. And again there is reason to construe the differences observable in their perceptions of China as a forum for opinions about what socialism should be and how it can go wrong.

The appraisal of what has gone well in Soviet history offers a model for how the intelligentsia is transformed in the transition to socialism and its aftermath. Along with nationalization of industry and collectivization of agriculture, Soviets identify a cultural revolution as the third basic transformation in the transition to socialism.[1] The cultural revolution has three major aspects. First, it must attract, control, and reeducate the bourgeois intellectuals who, if initially drawn to the exploiting classes, can be gradually reoriented. By the end of the transition period from capitalism to socialism, there should have formed a homogeneous stratum of the intelligentsia including the remnants of the prerevolutionary educated population. Second, the cultural revolution demands a broad-based upgrading of the knowledge of the masses, through campaigns against illiteracy and through compulsory primary education as well as through developing the mass media and the arts to raise the cultural level of the rural and urban masses. Third, large numbers of workers, peasants, women, and national minorities must be brought into the intelligentsia, some through promotion to leading posts, and others through training as specialists as the educational system develops. Soviets contend that great changes in the social composition of the intelligentsia are essential for success in the cultural revolution.[2]

All of these changes are made possible by the existence of the dictatorship of the proletariat and the expropriation of the means of propaganda so that the exploiting classes cannot shape social consciousness.[3] The state planners promote an enormous expansion of education. At the same time, their policies produce basic changes in the composition of the intelligentsia, increasing the rural intelligentsia, engineering and technical personnel, and specialists in professions associated with education, science, and culture. On the basis of changes in the size, composition, social origins, and organization of the intelligentsia, a socialist

[1] *Ot kapitalizma k sotsializmu: osnovnye problemy istorii perekhodnogo perioda v SSSR 1917-1937 gg.*, II, p. 265.

[2] L. M. Zak, V. S. Lel'chuk, and V. I. Pogudin, *Stroitel'stvo sotsializma v SSSR: istoriograficheskii ocherk*, pp. 76-88, 238-53.

[3] P. D. Pavlenok, *Formirovanie i razvitie sotsial'no-klassovoi struktury sotsialisticheskogo obshchestva*, p. 42.

society emerges and develops. Soviets contrast these achievements with what happened in China, where mistakes in policies concerning the most educated groups formed a firm barrier to the realization of socialism and its further development.

The appraisers are themselves intellectuals operating under a restrictive, communist-led system. They have experienced the way their own society and field have been buffeted by the cold winds of political intervention. The suffering and constraints on intellectuals under Stalinism were noted obliquely in the 1960s; otherwise there has been no public format to discuss this sensitive subject. What better situation could be found for transposing their concerns than the case of China, which Soviet specialists were called upon to criticize and where conflicts between officials and intellectuals were at the center of consciousness. How relevant must the Chinese tradition of arguing by illusion to another time or place have seemed!

The sensitivity of this subject may have made it difficult for reformers to approach it directly. The most pertinent book-length treatments to be discussed in this chapter—those by Markova, Antipovskii, Borevskaia, and Franchuk, and a collective from IDV—are not from the reform group. Nevertheless, in indirect ways, in obscure publications, or in the context of examining other topics, reform voices have been heard on this theme. On many criticisms of China, they share the standard, negative assessments of their Soviet colleagues, but their deep-seated explanations of failures suggest a more severe judgment of the contradictions between the Chinese state and its experts.

THE LEGACY OF THE PAST

At the end of the 1960s Soviet writers discovered the value of traditional Chinese society as an explanation for what had gone wrong in the evolution to socialism. This discovery was obviously influenced by their growing interest in Western writings on China. Western publications on traditional China concentrated heavily on the scholar-officials, Confucianism, and the gentry or those close to them and aspiring to join them. They gave primary attention to the attitudes of the elite—their worldview, their concerns about education, and their ambivalence between the demands of state service and the self-interest of serving kin and community. Soviets have been slow to focus on the traditions of the intelligentsia and have given this topic much less attention than the traditional carryovers of the peasants and the workers identified in Chapters 2 and 3. Nevertheless, in 1968 there was a symposium on the role of tradition in the history of China;[4] the book, *Cults, Religions, Traditions in China*, appeared in 1970;[5] and some authors have shown a deep interest in Western writings in this area, noting, for example, that the work of John K. Fairbank concludes that tradition defeated not only capitalism but communism in China.[6] To the extent that the attitudes of the old intelligentsia shaped the thinking of Maoists or were shared by other groups of Chinese, Soviets have recognized that they were consequential after 1949.[7]

Gel'bras presents a brief overview in his 1980 book of the pre-1949 Chinese intelligentsia. He observes that, over the course of a century, this group experienced deeper changes than any other group in the population. He also remarks that, "It is difficult to name even one other country like China where the intelligentsia historically was so limited by ethnocentrism and simultaneously so cut off from the people." Yet, he notes, too, this group's deep feeling of responsibility before society and state and its role as the only source of bureaucratic service. Gel'bras finds China exceptional for the persistence of "two directly opposed traditions: respect for literacy, knowledge, literature and art, esteem for great thinkers and 'just officials' and, si-

[4] *Rol' traditsii v istorii i kul'ture Kitaia.*

[5] L. S. Vasil'ev, *Kul'ty, religii, traditsii v Kitae.*

[6] A. V. Meliksetov, "Nekotorye aspekty istoricheskoi kontseptsii Dzhona Feirbenka," *Obshchestvo i gosudarstvo v Kitae* 6:3 (1975), pp. 611-16.

[7] *Sovremennyi Kitai v zarubezhnykh issledovaniiakh*, pp. 67-82.

multaneously, scorn, even hatred of knowledge, the intelligentsia, the officials." This tension was a starting point for the modern evolution of the intelligentsia. In the transition period after 1840 differing views emerged about Western thought; the intelligentsia divided into two camps—the traditionalists and Westernizers. In the 1920s another camp emerged—the revolutionary activists. Gel'bras highlights the divisions within the intelligentsia, but also its significant leadership and support for the forces of revolution and the fact that at the beginning of the 1950s, of five million in the intelligentsia as many as one million were party members—a level of representation no other class or stratum could match.[8] For reasons of tradition and in response to imperialism and the Bolshevik Revolution, the modern Chinese intelligentsia was substantially on the side of socialism. Soviet writings find fault with Mao and other Chinese leaders for failing to capitalize on the inclinations of the educated population.

It is not so much what the intelligentsia thought or did that interests most Soviet analysts, but how they managed, within the environment of imperial China, to transmit traditions that became deeply embedded in the lives of the ordinary people. Articles published in 1972 by Saltykov, Vasil'ev, and Zhelokhovtsev all make this point.[9] They attribute to tradition a decisive role in the fate of China, weakening class antagonisms and strengthening bureaucratic authority. Vasil'ev concludes that as long as most peasants remain poor and barely literate, old traditions will live on and nourish the restoration of elements typical of old China such as a strong central authority. Zhelokhovtsev develops this theme further, finding in what seemed new

[8] Gel'bras, *Sotsial'no-politicheskaia struktura KNR 50-60-e gody*, pp. 131, 132, 134.

[9] G. F. Saltykov, "Traditsiia, mekhanizm ee deistviia i nekotorye ee osobennosti v Kitae;" L. S. Vasil'ev, "Traditsiia i problema sotsial'nogo progressa v istorii Kitaia;" and A. N. Zhelokhovtsev, "Rol' traditsii v formirovanii stereotipov myshleniia i povedeniia v sovremennom Kitae," in *Rol' traditsii v istorii i kul'ture Kitae*, pp. 4-23, 24-60, 349-73.

during the years of the Cultural Revolution much that was rather a holdover of mass religious consciousness. He equates the dogmatism of Maoism with that of Confucianism and sees parallels in the demands on culture to illustrate doctrines and thus depart from realism. Rather than giving way to scientific socialism, the popular consciousness formed by Confucian ideology lived on as the Maoists attempted to take advantage of it. If some of the intelligentsia helped keep these traditions alive, analysts give primary blame to peasants and petty-bourgeois elements.

The ideas in these articles owe a lot to Western writings. Elsewhere Soviets, especially L. S. Kiuzadjan and his colleagues at the Institute of Scientific Information in the Social Sciences, make clear that they are summarizing the viewpoints of American specialists on China, e.g. the political culture studies that sought to identify the key to Maoist authority in traditional childhood socialization and national character. Kiuzadjan and T. N. Sorokina are careful to show how Western views of tradition in China clash and to expose shortcomings in the methods used.[10] Even so, and despite a lack of Soviet research on the mechanisms by which traditions are passed on, explanations centering on traditions are very much a part of Soviet writings.

In the absence of a strong bourgeoisie or proletariat, Soviets contend that the petty-bourgeoisie had an important role in the decades before 1949. According to one source, "The Chinese petty-bourgeoisie of all the classes of Chinese society (with the exception of the landlords) was the most closely tied with tradition."[11] It was both deeply dependent on the state bureaucracy and closely tied to the village, factors contributing to conservatism. To the Soviets, Maoism represents Great Han chauvinism, nationalism, and other petty-bourgeois traits. Although the staff of the Institute of the Far East and their associates, who are the

---

[10] L. S. Kiuzadjan and T. M. Sorokina, "Vliianie traditsii na Maoizm v otsenke zarubezhnogo kitaevedeniia," *Kitai: traditsii i sovremennost'*, pp. 279-319.

[11] *Ideino-politicheskaia sushchnost' Maoizma*, p. 39.

primary source of these criticisms about the petty-bourgeois (and conservative) essence of Maoism, write little about the impact of the old intelligentsia, they are, in some sense, charging it along with related petty-bourgeois forces with perpetuating traditional outlooks inimical to socialism in China. By implication, they are contending that more should have been done after 1949 to root out these conservative tendencies. This approach clashes with the apparent view of Gel'bras and others that the intelligentsia should have been dealt with more gently and trusted because it was largely a progressive force.

EDUCATION AND REEDUCATION, 1949-1957

It is, of course, agreed by all Soviets that China needed a genuine cultural revolution. As one writer asserts, "It is precisely the cultural level of the people and the rate of increase of this level which to a significant extent determine the rise of productive forces, scientific and technical progress, the socialist reconstruction of life—all that without which building a socialist society is impossible."[12] Although the attitude of the educated minority toward cultural revolution (in its Soviet meaning, not as redefined by Mao in the 1960s) was largely sympathetic, the Chinese leadership did not capitalize on it. The intelligentsia is regarded as having given China a headstart in this process following its revolution. Whereas in Russia a large part of the intelligentsia was hostile to the October Revolution, in China they were not, owing to the semifeudal and semicolonial position of the country which inevitably democratized the consciousness of the intelligentsia over the first half of the twentieth century.[13] This advantage was squandered by Mao's distrust and even disdain for people engaged in mental labor, already evident in 1942 in the Yanan period and essentially unchanged thereafter.

[12] S. D. Markova, *Maoizm i intelligentsiia*, p. 5.
[13] Ibid., pp. 7-9.

Accusations against Mao's erroneous views about intellectuals figure importantly in Soviet writings. One criticism is that Mao was obsessed with putting culture at the service of workers, peasants, and soldiers but objected to any mention of service to other strata as if it were the result of a tendency to serve the bourgeoisie. The obligation to orient artistic works to the level of the illiterate masses was combined with a rejection of Chinese classical intellectual and artistic traditions and all foreign culture. This isolated the Chinese people from all the achievements of world culture. It reduced the level of artistic works to a very low common denominator when more effort should have gone into achieving the highest standards and raising as many people as possible to benefit from them.

The Soviet literature frequently discusses the campaigns against intellectuals. Writers allege that, already in the first ideological reeducation campaigns after the revolution, Chinese leaders adopted methods damaging to the intelligentsia. S. D. Markova in her book *Maoism and the Intelligentsia* asserts that many intellectuals of the old generation considered themselves unprepared ideologically for full participation in the new society and willingly underwent reeducation. However, they were disappointed when they were subjected to Maoist methods, life in dormitories, public accusations and secret denunciations, daily meetings, and growing pressure. The 1951 campaign against the movie "The Life of Wu Xun" revealed Mao's ahistorical approach to a person long considered by Chinese historians to have been progressive and humanitarian. At that very time, Markova states, many intellectuals needed guidance to understand the agrarian reform and a campaign might have done some good. Yet the approach to this group was misdirected.[14]

The same perspective, more boldly asserted, is contained in Gel'bras' statement that the majority of the intelligentsia greeted the birth of the People's Republic with enthusiasm,

[14] Ibid., pp. 26-27, 28-29.

but in the early campaigns under the pressures of forceful class struggle this enthusiasm was diminished. Maoists demanded that the intelligentsia refrain from independently trying to find out the essence of social phenomena. They took the traditional view that "only the political authorities have the right to 'full' knowledge, interpretation and transmission of part of it to separate elements of society."[15] This appears to say that intellectuals were told to obey rather than to understand, to accept gaps in information rather than to strive for truth. While crediting the CCP with many achievements from 1949 to 1957, Gel'bras argues that the results in enlisting the intelligentsia in the building of socialism could have been much more substantial.

The fullest treatment of the campaigns of this period is given in L. S. Kiuzadjan, *Ideological Campaigns in the PRC 1949-1966*. Kiuzadjan finds fault with campaigns that concentrated on political study, especially study of Mao's work, and wasted thousands of hours for each person when the acquisition of knowledge needed for economic, technical, and cultural construction was so vital. The effect of these endless lessons and of the attempt to force the process of "thought reform," based on the misjudgment that reeducation was a comparatively simple matter, was to dampen the initial eagerness of the majority of the intelligentsia to respond to the call to study. Kiuzadjan identifies the second phase of mass ideological campaigns as beginning as early as 1950 with the campaign to condemn the United States. "The element of force already dominated over persuasion, and therefore the results of the campaign in many ways were negative." Kiuzadjan criticizes the excessively formal character of the campaigns, e.g. the prearranged confessions that did not actually mean that reeducation had taken place. He concludes that, despite the positive results of widely publicizing the classics of Marxism-Leninism and introducing the Soviet experience of cultural revolution, there were early signs of serious errors in China's excessive

---

[15] Gel'bras, *Sotsial'no-politicheskaia struktura KNR 50-60-e gody*, p. 137.

reliance on force toward the intelligentsia. Kiuzadjan even draws on the work by the American psychiatrist Robert Jay Lifton, which, on the basis of Hong Kong interviews, exposes the techniques of "brainwashing" in the PRC that attempted to cut an individual off from his past, his family, his entire internal spiritual world.[16] From this discussion, a position clearly emerges on how not to reeducate intellectuals.

An assessment of early PRC educational policies is given by a team of three authors in *Policies in the Area of Science and Education in the PRC 1949-1979*. In Chapter 1, N. E. Borevskaia recognizes problems caused by inexperience and lack of trained personnel, while giving credit to the measures that established a new system of education. Borevskaia notes serious shortcomings in early discussions about pedagogy and in the views expressed by Mao Zedong about education. She observes that the influence of American pragmatism on Mao led him to underestimate the role of theory and also that Mao's views showed excessive concern with utilitarian training while rejecting the cultural functions of education. Continual campaigns, excessive reliance on physical labor, and overloading students and teachers with activities other than their regular classwork interfered with professional training. Soviets suggest that leftist elements were in too great a rush to root out bourgeois ideology. N. V. Franchuk, the author of the chapter on higher education, argues that "Many educational figures mistakenly did not draw the line between bourgeois culture and the culture of bourgeois society." They rejected too much of contemporary culture and placed undue emphasis on Mao's works. Also in the pursuit of quantitative indicators, the selection of new students was done hastily, which caused a good deal of waste as some students lacked the ability to complete their work. Additional waste occurred, often due to political motives, in the failure to use graduates in their

[16] L. S. Kiuzadjan, *Ideologicheskie kampanii v KNR 1949-1966*, pp. 24-25, 26, 32-33.

specialty and in the inadequate organization of labor.[17] These were all problems of China's educational system during the early years of the PRC.

What was the essence of the problem in the early 1950s? Gel'bras lists many problems faced by the intelligentsia and then adds, "However in these years the intelligentsia collided with the harsh demands on themselves from the side of the completely culturally undeveloped forces of the revolution."[18] The reality of this clash became more evident in the new campaigns unfolding from late 1954. According to Markova, the criticism of Hu Shi, known for his views on the role of the individual in history and his admiration of American culture, played a constructive role in socialist reeducation. But it could have had a more positive effect if it had not widened into a rejection of all of his activities, leading to the attribution of a mass of sins to the entire intelligentsia. A simultaneous campaign was directed against Hu Feng, a man who understood the shortcomings of Maoist designs against the entire foreign literary and artistic heritage and against the concept of humanism, as well as tendencies to rely on coercive methods of administering culture. Many cultural figures suffered in this campaign, and it "thickened the atmosphere of suspicion and ill-will created by the preceding campaigns." According to Kiuzadjan, the campaigns in 1954 and 1955 went well beyond literature and touched the entire intelligentsia, including engineers. They were counterproductive, demonstrating the leadership's political distrust of the entire older generation of the intelligentsia and driving them to confess guilt only as a means of self-preservation.[19] In comparison with policies toward peasants and workers during the early years of the PRC, Soviets portray the policies toward the intelligentsia

[17] A. A. Antipovskii, N. E. Borevskaia, and N. V. Franchuk, *Politika v oblasti nauki i obrazovaniia v KNR 1949-1979 gg.*, pp. 18, 92, 102-103.

[18] Gel'bras, *Sotsial'no-politicheskaia struktura KNR 50-60-e gody*, pp. 141-42.

[19] Markova, *Maoizm i intelligentsiia*, pp. 32, 33, 35, 40.

147

as less consistent with the needs of the transition to socialism.

The "Hundred Flowers" period of 1956-1957 brought the policies toward this group to the fore. The Chinese leadership needed the intelligentsia and had to reconsider its approach; intimidation was not working. Against the advice of some, Mao launched the "Hundred Flowers" campaign calling for open criticism of shortcomings in Chinese society by the intellectuals. A tirade of critical commentaries ensued. When invited to speak out, the intelligentsia split into many class positions, according to Soviet analysts. But whatever their differences, the views of China's intellectuals coalesced in a demand for "the elimination of bureaucratism, the liquidation of the privileges of cadres, of administration by mere injunction, of methods of compulsion and force. This criticism reflected the real interests of a broad mass."[20] Of the more than 2 million critical statements issued by employees (not all intellectuals) of enterprises and institutions of Shanghai, more than 50 percent referred to the style of leadership. There was a widespread outcry in defense of the rights of man. Gel'bras emphasizes this outcry against heavy-handed control.

Recognizing the justness of many of the criticisms raised in 1956-1957, Markova, nonetheless, stresses the absence of a Marxist-Leninist outlook among the intellectuals and the failure of leaders to take immediate steps to point this out. She points to examples of petty-bourgeois ideology appearing at this time and even to the blossoming of genuine bourgeois, antisocialist flowers. In her view, this free exchange of views was a non-Marxist policy that struck a blow against socialism, especially in a country where socialism was only beginning to solidify its position. Elsewhere she refers to this period as providing fertile soil for bourgeois-idealistic conceptions.[21] Her emphasis on the danger

[20] Gel'bras, *Sotsial'no-politicheskaia struktura KNR 50-60-e gody*, p. 138.

[21] Markova, *Maoizm i intelligentsiia*, pp. 59, 75-76; *Sud'by kul'tury KNR (1949-1974)*, p. 77.

from intellectuals on the right contrasts with Gel'bras's concern about the heavy-handed state.

Markova's orthodox viewpoint also appears to be contradicted by another Soviet specialist. Kiuzadjan insists that China's leaders were out of touch with the true leanings of the intelligentsia, having erroneously assumed that earlier campaigns had brought great successes. Yet, he adds, Mao realized in the aftermath of the Twentieth Party Congress in the USSR that "the former style and methods of leadership, in particular ideological work, could not find support." In pursuit of his own self-aggrandizement and, following the Hungarian events of 1956, to demonstrate that he could quickly unite Chinese society, Mao tried to show that he was on the side of democratization. Referring to articles in the Chinese press, Kiuzadjan accurately summarizes the events of the "Hundred Flowers" period: the creation of a "free creative atmosphere," the criticisms of officials for forcibly driving peasants into collective farms, the opportunity to criticize articles in the *People's Daily* as not providing the last word on a policy question, and other developments of this short-lived period.[22] Here we again find what appears to be the Soviet reform perspective, highlighting the value of open expression.

THE ANTIRIGHTIST CAMPAIGN AND ITS AFTERMATH

For the intelligentsia of the PRC, the summer of 1957 was a turning point. Some Soviet sources strongly support the need for a crackdown in 1957. There had been "open slander of the CCP"; members of the democratic parties "began to pretend to a dominant role in the life of the state"; "the Chinese communists had to begin a struggle with the counterrevolutionaries." But these sources attack the actual crackdown for it centered not on real bourgeois rightist elements, but on party and nonparty workers in the area

[22] Kiuzadjan, *Ideologicheskie kampanii v KNR 1949-1966*, pp. 51-53, 60-76.

of culture, on Mao's opponents in aesthetic and other matters. Accusations against the intelligentsia unjustifiably focused not only on their critical remarks in the previous months but also on utterances overheard, on private letters, sometimes on fabrications. The blow to their morale was great.[23] Before this struggle died down, a further sharp decline in scholarship and artistic quality resulted. In place of professional art, there was regimentation and state-induced low quality amateur art.

Franchuk finds that higher education deteriorated as well. "The entire system of leadership of higher educational institutions was reckoned only on sending instructions down from above."[24] Teachers and scientific councils in schools had a very weak leadership role. Foreign scientific literature and periodicals frequently were inaccessible to teachers in the humanities, and it could take a year or longer to obtain literature from libraries. The individual inclinations of young people were often ignored in the choice of school, career, and place of work. Mao's concept of the "new man" was to be realized by narrowing the amount of knowledge acquired. As education was greatly restructured in 1958, its quality both at the elite and the mass level declined. Advocates of nationalism and chauvinism (also described as traditionalists who believed in a Chinese path) took charge, as supporters of Western, bourgeois, and Soviet proletarian culture were attacked.[25]

To achieve economic recovery after the Great Leap, China's leaders had to seek the participation of the intelligentsia. A portion of those condemned as rightists in 1957 were rehabilitated; Gel'bras is careful to point out that those who benefited came from the liberal and petty-bourgeois intelligentsia.[26] The rate of growth in the number of teachers and medical personnel was disproportionately slow in

---

[23] *Sud'by kul'tury KNR (1949-1974)*, pp. 89-90, 95, 96.

[24] A. A. Antipovskii, N. E. Borevskaia, and N. V. Franchuk, *Politika v oblasti nauki i obrazovaniia v KNR 1949-1979 gg.*, p. 107.

[25] Gel'bras, *Sotsial'no-politicheskaia struktura KNR 50-60-e gody*, p. 140.

[26] Ibid., p. 141.

comparison with that of engineers and scientists, and the traditional intelligentsia continued to weigh heavily in the former professions and in the arts world. The intelligentsia, the petty-bourgeoisie, and the exploiting strata in general also remained the principal sources of entrants to higher education. These factors contributed to the persistence of a wide cultural gap between the intelligentsia and the people.

In the early 1960s, conditions were not as favorable for this class as before 1957. For example, the network of health institutions, clubs, and palaces of culture expanded very little. Gel'bras mentions these relatively minor matters as an indication of general conditions. In this environment, intellectuals were isolated. Their social activism had fallen sharply. Gel'bras considers it important that the Chinese did not bring about a systematic increase in the cultural level of succeeding generations. The number of new specialists was only a small fraction of those needed by society, and the quality of their preparation had declined. Without the support of the most educated part of the Chinese people, the party "doomed itself, the society, and the state to serious failures in all areas of life."[27]

Markova takes exception to the Maoist view of the dominant role of the masses in literature and art, philosophy, and economics. She argues that the rejection of professionalism in the arts and sciences contributed to the dissatisfaction of the Chinese intelligentsia. This was also the effect of the further enlargement of Mao's cult of personality, the regimentation and militarization of life spurred by the campaign to "learn from the PLA," and the spreading "Socialist Education Movement" with its purges first in the countryside and then in the city. In 1964 and 1965 new attacks on bourgeois views in literature and art led writers and artists to shy away from depicting real contradictions and complexities of life; countless primitive productions ensued, filled with the slogans of the moment and citations

[27] Ibid., pp. 144, 148.

from the works of Mao Zedong.[28] All creativity was stifled under the pretext of eliminating bourgeois manifestations.

Summarizing the fate of China's intellectuals even before the Cultural Revolution and especially in the antirightist campaign of 1957 and the class struggle movement in the mid-1960s, Kiuzadjan uses strong language. He writes that: "lies and sham became the norm"; punishment occurred on an enormous scale "without trial or investigation"; from a judicial point of view "the coarsest violation of human rights that had been fixed in the Constitution of the PRC pursued the aim of debasing man, morally breaking him"; the Chinese leadership "tried to suppress all views of culture except its own conceptions."[29]

In an unusual comparison, Markova points out that organizations in Soviet history had tried, in the name of the future, to burn Raphael, to destroy museums, to dispense with Tschaikovsky, and to criticize Pushkin for working on *Evgenii Onegin* for years without devoting a minute to the lives of miners. But, she adds, the Soviet leadership took all possible measures to fight these tendencies and to preserve for the people the cultural achievements of the past, while it was precisely the Chinese leadership that inspired destructive acts of this sort in their country.[30]

THE CULTURAL REVOLUTION AND ITS AFTERMATH

There has never been any doubt expressed in Soviet sources about the devastating consequences of the Cultural Revolution. As Deliusin asserts, it was inspired by Mao's hatred for enlightenment and education and his goal of establishing the eternal dominance of his own ideas. It "began with the closing of schools and institutes, with a pogrom of teachers, professors, writers, and all people of mental labor, with the destruction of works of literature and art, not meeting

---

[28] Markova, *Maoizm i intelligentsia*, pp. 117, 121-22, 130.

[29] Kiuzadjan, *Ideologicheskie kampanii v KNR 1949-1966*, pp. 192, 222.

[30] *Sud'by kul'tury KNR (1949-1974)*, p. 130.

the ideas of the 'great helmsman.' " These actions delivered an enormous and irreparable blow to Chinese society. Control over culture tightened to such an extent that Deliusin refers to a muzzle being placed over the Chinese intelligentsia.[31] Sober people remaining in the leadership tried more than once to restore education, to rehabilitate a part of the battered and humiliated intelligentsia, but each time they ran up against the opposition of Mao's forces. As a result, the losses to the intelligentsia and to the education, scientific achievement, and artistic heritage of the Chinese were enormous.

In a 1981 publication, Deliusin expands on his more optimistic assessment of developments after Mao's death. He asserts, "The view of the place of the intelligentsia in Chinese society and on its role in the building of socialism has radically changed." "Professors, scientific workers have today become in China almost heroes of the day." "Not only are scholars experiencing joyous days after a decade of gloom. Authors and painters, composers and artists live with bright hopes."[32] In this section of a book written mainly by Gel'bras and his colleagues at IMRD, Deliusin elucidates his views of the importance of the intelligentsia under socialism. He observes that, "The sociopolitical 'climate' defining the life of workers in the PRC, in many ways depends on the character of relations between the state and other classes and strata of society, in the first place the intelligentsia and the peasants." He draws attention to recent Chinese statements that the vast majority of the intelligentsia belong to the working class, that persons in this category brought up in conditions of building socialism differ from workers only by possessing more knowledge and culture, and thus that the intelligentsia is the progressive, better part of the working class. Rather than condemning the Maoists, as other Soviets do, for condoning

[31] L. P. Deliusin, "Sud'by intelligentsii v Kitae," in *Intelligentsiia: mesto v obshchestve i politika rukovodstva KPK*, pp. 7, 9.

[32] *Rabochii klass v sotsial'no-politicheskoi sisteme KNR*, pp. 99, 108, 110.

the expression of a wide range of opinions in 1956-1957, Deliusin points out that as a result of the right of "freedom of opinion some representatives of the intelligentsia began to express their thoughts openly and to make critical remarks concerning shortcomings, mistakes of one or the other department or ministry, abuse of power of individual leaders."[33] This is an unabashed defense of the intelligentsia as the knowledgeable force that can keep the society on a course of justice and progress, even when leaders let power and ignorance go to their heads.

One of Mao's responses to criticism in the Cultural Revolution was to announce a rule, the essence of which was: "Only nonspecialists can lead specialists."[34] Subsequently a main criterion for evaluating students in admissions to higher education and during the course of study was their political behavior. These are the degradations of scholarly standards to which Deliusin draws attention. His views stand in stark contrast to the prevailing Soviet approach to the intelligentsia. The Maoist treatment of educated people, which Deliusin equates with fascist terror, set China back many years. But this was not, in Deliusin's view, because China drifted to the right. What he leaves unsaid is that the villain was the state and its officials who misused their tremendous power. The situation could not be easily remedied, even when new leaders recognized that they desperately needed a large and competent class of specialists. Several years after Mao's death, there was still the need to bolster the intelligentsia in many ways: to raise their pay, to improve their conditions of work, and even to eliminate continued hostile treatment still found in many localities. With these stipulations, Deliusin makes an unqualified case for respect for mental labor in a socialist setting.

One of the first books on the Cultural Revolution was I. M. Nadeev, *"The Cultural Revolution" and the Fate of Chinese Literature* (1969). Nadeev discusses the cruel repression,

[33] Ibid., pp. 99, 113-14, 101.
[34] Ibid., p. 101.

154

psychological pressure, physical punishment, and falsifications of this period. Most of all, he points to Mao's cult of personality. All energies went into glorifying Mao's role as theorist, organizer, and leader, to present Mao as the infallible leader. While there had been previous campaigns against the creative intelligentsia, none could compare to the scale of destructiveness of the Cultural Revolution.[35] Perhaps because the parallels with Stalin, even if unstated, were so obvious, the repeated emphasis on the cult of personality and on Mao's self-glorification did not figure so prominently in subsequent Soviet publications. A decade later, A. N. Zhelokhovtsev wrote a more broadly oriented monograph on literature in the PRC in which he charged that foreign Sinologists (specifically Simon Leys) were trying to identify Mao's ideas with Marxism-Leninism while consciously ignoring the resistance to these ideas in the CCP. Zhelokhovtsev regards Mao's theories as reactionary and harmful to the cultural growth of the people. They bore "the darkest legacy of the past: tyranny, ignorance, want of culture, national isolation, xenophobia."[36]

Markova is one of many who finds fault with Mao's broad interpretation of the concept of the intelligentsia. She notes that at the end of the 1960s all young people who had received education before the Cultural Revolution, regardless of their class origin, were branded bourgeois. Among the errors of this period, she mentions the attempts to reeducate the elderly and the sick by imposing severe conditions of labor and life and the use of physical labor as a form of punishment. Further she notes that the suppression of all good feelings and ordinary human desires in young people was one of the main principles of reeducation. Although recognizing many correctives in cultural life that occurred in 1971-1973, she concludes that the changes were not basic. Policies remained repressive. In the final

---

[35] I. N. Nadeev, "Kul'turnaia revoliutsiia" i sud'ba kitaiskoi literatury, p. 10.
[36] A. N. Zhelokhovtsev, Literaturnaia teoriia i politicheskaia bor'ba v KNR, pp. 188-89.

analysis, the intelligentsia was important far beyond its numbers; it recognized its duty before country and people and resisted the ideals of "barracks communism" (mass mobilization on the basis of minimal survival) and Mao's aims to erase the cultural experiences of the people. In turn, it bore the brunt of Mao's wrath. But, Markova optimistically concluded in 1975, it was not broken and at the slightest opportunity would seek to return to China the best cultural achievements of the past and present.[37]

One of the most unusual Soviet books because of its juxtaposition of ancient thought and contemporary events is L. S. Perelomov, *Confucianism and Legalism in the Political History of China*. Perelomov generalizes that, in periods of relative stability of authority or temporary consolidation of forces, history has a limited role in policy debates, while in periods of a crisis of authority, the sphere of history greatly widens. The peak of historical discussion within China occurred from mid-1973 to late 1976 and is examined closely in Perelomov's book. The author's view of the enduring force of tradition is unmistakable. He asserts that there is no doubt of the influence of Confucianism and Legalism, especially early Confucianism (6th-3rd centuries B.C.), on China in the present and in the centuries to come.[38]

Perelomov attributes to Lin Biao opposition to closer relations to the United States and to worsening relations with the Soviet Union. In the quotations from Confucius found in Lin's diary, Perelomov finds Lin contrasting Mao's tyranny to the force of Confucian humanity. He argues that, when Mao learned about these writings after the murder of Lin at the end of 1971, he decided once and for all to root out Confucianism from the consciousness of the Chinese people. Mao had long been alarmed by the strength of family ties. To Perelomov, who is half-Chinese, obedience to parents and respect for elders are among the best fea-

---

[37] Markova, *Maoizm i intelligentsiia*, pp. 201, 223, 238.
[38] L. S. Perelomov, *Konfutsiantsvo i legizm v politicheskoi istorii Kitaia*, pp. 3, 11.

tures of Chinese national character. While recognizing the progressive character of the anti-Confucian tradition in the first half of this century, Perelomov praises Confucianism's positive effects in recent times. "With the support of Confucianism, the Chinese family, following long established traditions, preserved its well-known autonomy from authority and freedom of internal spiritual life. In conditions of the Maoist regime, which was trying to disrupt the traditional family ties, the norms of relations, and to subject man spiritually only to the leader, national stereotypes of behavior came to interfere with the 'upbringing' of the new generation."[39]

Perelomov recounts the debates over the beginning of feudalism in China, arguing that it was necessary for Mao to place Confucius in the slaveholding period and the Legalists in the feudal period. In the 1950s this early periodization had also been a matter of concern. Perelomov brings up the case of Tong Xue, who in 1954, when free discussion was possible, had expressed an entirely different dividing line, much later in history, from the timing written down by Mao in 1940. In 1957, following pressure and in what Perelomov deems to be an article of inferior scholarship, Tong came to a conclusion in keeping with Mao's views. In the fall of 1958 Perelomov had occasion to meet in Jinan with Tong. Reviewing his notes of that conversation, Perelomov finds that Tong had been evasive or silent on many questions. No scientific conversation had taken place. He adds, "Perhaps, this is explained by the presence of a representative of the administration."[40] (It is ironic that when I interviewed Perelomov in early 1978, our meeting was also in the presence of a third party who was to report on us and left me with a similar impression.) In the book Perelomov makes clear that the atmosphere described in the period 1973-1976 was detrimental to free intellectual dis-

---

[39] Ibid., pp. 221-26.
[40] Ibid., pp. 228, 234.

cussion and the search for an accurate understanding of China's history.

The closest thing to a summary position of recent Soviet thought about the Chinese intelligentsia is the chapter "Intelligentsia" in *Classes and Class Struggle in the PRC*, jointly written by Markova and G. V. Astaf'ev. The authors divide this social stratum in 1949 into four types: 1) the traditional gentry intelligentsia with a classical education; 2) the bourgeois intelligentsia educated in missionary schools or abroad; 3) the petty-bourgeois intelligentsia partially familiar with Western radical ideas, including some who had accepted Marxism-Leninism and spread its ideas among the working class in China; and 4) the revolutionary intelligentsia formed from progressive workers and peasants who occupied lower and middle ranks in the CCP, PLA, and administrative organs of liberated areas.[41] The leadership of the CCP included individuals from all of these backgrounds. To reeducate the diverse population of intellectuals required that they be treated in a comradely manner in which the masses respected them in return for their respect and trust. However Maoist ideology and policies identified the intelligentsia with the bourgeois class, increasingly confused rote learning of quotations from Mao with reeducation, and cultivated the distrust of the intelligentsia by the masses. The vast majority of the intelligentsia was able actively to participate in building socialism, but they were not used effectively. The most promising groups were especially persecuted and then in the Cultural Revolution humiliated, tortured, or even murdered. The role of nonspecialists in the arts and sciences was expanded at the expense of the professionals and creativity. In the mid-1970s the remaining intelligentsia could not participate fully in professional activities out of fear of committing some new mistake and from fatigue from all that they had gone through. The moral formation of the young generation of the intelligentsia had taken place in conditions of complete rejection

[41] *Klassy i klassovaia struktura v KNR*, p. 159.

of the basic human values and devoid of the achievements of both national and world culture. Despite all that they endured, some of the intelligentsia continued to care about the fate of the people and to adhere to their convictions. Persecution of dissidents and reeducation failed to stifle the protests of the intelligentsia. The same source qualifies these conclusions by arguing that the engineers and technicians were not persecuted on the same scale and that these personnel in certain military industries were not affected by the Cultural Revolution.[42]

The Post-Mao Era

The predominant Soviet viewpoint is that the situation of the Chinese intelligentsia has changed little despite the fact that many have been rehabilitated, their prestige has risen, and their cooperation in the "Four Modernizations" is required. The new leadership needed the intelligentsia in the struggle against the Gang of Four and as part of "democratization" to reassure its imperialist partners. But the position of this group remains difficult due to long-cultivated anti-intellectual attitudes and the continuation in local offices of those accustomed to using cudgels on literature and art. Attempts by intellectuals to stand up against violations of law are still often condemned or punished. Fear among the intelligentsia that the past will be repeated persists, as does distrust in the leadership. All this is exacerbated by severe material conditions. The 1981 crackdown on so-called "liberalization" was further evidence that the basis of Maoism persists and leads to renewed confrontation with a significant part of the intelligentsia.[43] Zhelokhovtsev adds to this characterization the point that the attempts in 1977-1978 to create in literature and culture the cult of personality of Hua Guofeng followed the same lines used previously in the deification of Mao, and that the Western press

42 Ibid., pp. 182, 186-87, 193-94.
43 Ibid., pp. 187-89.

erred in describing this as a conscious policy of de-Mao-ization.[44] In this view, criticism of the Maoist approach is mainly a concession to necessity and does not go nearly as far as the Chinese people want.

In the yearbooks issued by the Institute of the Far East, Markova analyzes the situation of the intelligentsia year by year, while as many as fifteen other entries examine selected areas of science, culture, and ideology. For 1978, Markova recognized some improvements, but also noted that many who were wrongly accused in the past had not yet been rehabilitated. She added that, "It is not accidental, even as they were proving that the intelligentsia belong to the proletariat class, the official ideologies stressed that one has to see also that among the intelligentsia as before there are people whose bourgeois ideology has not changed entirely." Such statements, she continued, demonstrate the tendency to use the concept of class struggle, as under Mao, to camouflage the struggle of political groups and the desire to keep open the possibility of a quick reversal to policies of repression.[45] For 1979 Markova recognized the continued rehabilitation of cadres, now extending back beyond those attacked in the Cultural Revolution to the group condemned in 1957. Throughout the year the Chinese press repeated that the intelligentsia should be trusted, and condemned as anti-Marxist earlier treatment of this group as if it were potentially hostile to socialism. Intellectuals were admitted into the party and were named to leadership posts in large numbers. But Markova made it clear that she regarded the intellectuals as still without much enthusiasm and fearful of retribution. She concluded that writers and artists could scarcely have welcomed Zhou Yang's resumption of leadership; he had previously participated in the persecutions before himself suffering in the Cultural Revolution.[46]

[44] Zhelokhovtsev, *Literaturnaia teoriia i politicheskaia bor'ba v KNR*, p. 192.

[45] *Kitaiskaia Narodnaia Respublika 1978*, pp. 271-75.

[46] *Kitaiskaia Narodnaia Respublika 1979*, pp. 259-64.

In each of these Soviet studies of the post-Mao policies toward intellectuals, there is grudging recognition of improvements, placed in the context of still serious problems and continuities with the Maoist era. Only in Deliusin's article, which was distributed in just one hundred copies as a rotoprint of the Institute of the International Workers' Movement, is the positive transformation of the intelligentsia highlighted. Not ignoring the devastating legacy of Maoism and the lingering attempt to preserve the cult of Mao, Deliusin observed at the end of 1977 that the situation was changing sharply. Professors and scientists had become heroes of the day. The Chinese press clearly stated the need for improving the work of the intelligentsia. Deliusin did not deny that fear had not disappeared, that many mouth the necessary words, but he stressed that a fresh wind was blowing and that a turning point had been reached in the fate of the intelligentsia.[47]

Conclusions

The essence of Western criticisms of communist policy toward intellectuals is that controls at all stages interfere with creativity and scientific advancement. The intelligentsia is recruited, in part, on the basis of political criteria; therefore the best people are often excluded from important and, especially, sensitive positions. Training is too ideological and isolated from international scholarship or is too narrowly specialized in an effort to keep the costs of education to a minimum. Once employed, specialists face further restrictions. Controls may limit access to foreign information and counterparts, create sensitive subjects that are not to be investigated, and restrict photocopying for fear of dissent and spontaneous associations for fear of factionalism. Western observers see intellectuals as the bearers of the cultural traditions of the past and as the best informed members of society concerning the real conditions in the

[47] Deliusin, "Sud'by intelligentsii v Kitae," pp. 20, 23.

outside world. They conclude that members of this group have a distinctive outlook on life that is least amenable to conversion by leaders who demand conformity.

From this viewpoint, there is a constant struggle, sometimes more open or intense and sometimes less, between officials and the intelligentsia. The officials need the intelligentsia and, over the long run, have no choice but to give them access to information not available to others. They also fear the intelligentsia and, for their own self-protection in a system built on censorship and a contrived view of history and world affairs, tightly restrict them. Criticisms draw attention to the character of restrictions and purges and the deleterious consequences for the performance of the economy, the advancement of science, the flowering of the arts, and the well-being of the people. Distrust of the intelligentsia exacts a heavy price in both efficiency and creativity. This is the viewpoint that the Soviets seek to refute; yet it is also their viewpoint about China. Soviet writers agree that socialism requires a reeducated and largely newly recruited intelligentsia. They also agree that this process occurs gradually and requires trust as well as guidance from the leadership. Regardless of their views on other matters, writers on China concur that Chinese policies toward the intelligentsia erred from the beginning and continued for thirty years to be ineffective or worse.

In some Soviet writings these criticisms of China are tempered by a caution that weights heavily the need to reeducate the old intelligentsia and to control the activities, publications, and artistic expressions of educated people. It appears that the danger from the right lurks ominously in the background. In other writings the intelligentsia appears instead as the defender of the workers in the struggle against abuses of government. The danger comes from China's leadership. Freedom of expression and the acquisition of knowledge by those who are most capable most quickly advances the country. Respect for educated people emerges as a foundation for a truly socialist society.

Differences of opinion about intellectuals are at the heart

of the controversies between hardliners and reformers in both post-Mao China and the post-Stalin Soviet Union. The hardliners, who in the USSR have retained the leading positions of power, demand continued surveillance and tight controls over intellectuals. They see the prime danger to socialism as coming from the right, and its initial manifestations appear in the views and artistic works of intellectuals. The reformers cannot counter with a full-fledged critique of aged and ignorant leaders who act almost arbitrarily without adequate knowledge or concern for expert advice. Nevertheless, their criticisms of Chinese policies toward learning and expertise expose many of the fundamental problems in the Soviet Union. With regard to the place of traditional thought and the old intelligentsia trained before the revolution, certain Soviets consider these to be resources of value to the new order. Distrust by leaders too eager to sweep away the remnants of the past leads to damaging consequences—for the intellectuals as a whole, for the masses of people who could be favorably influenced by them, and especially for the officials whose policies will be guided by ignorance and whose power will not be checked by persons who are best prepared to articulate the causes of mistakes. Chinese leaders used force rather than persuasion, demanded ritual obedience rather than seeking reasoned debate. They lost the benefits that could be achieved by a free exchange of views and a free, creative atmosphere. In this criticism the reformers part company from the hardliners who condemn such freedom, for example the "Hundred Flowers" movement of 1956-1957, as a breeding ground for a rightist assault on socialism.

The Soviet consensus about intellectuals appears to be more fragile than that about peasants and workers. The issue in this case centers clearly on control versus creativity. The orthodox view is that controls must not be greatly relaxed because the intelligentsia represents a threat from the right. The intellectuals constitute the true enemy of socialism. Through various transmutations and vaguely articulated assumptions, the orthodox group identifies the intelligentsia with the petty-bourgeoisie or with some cloudy concept of the right. In contrast, the reformers find no basis at all for a threat from the right. The danger that lurks in a socialist state comes from ignorant officials who are intolerant of knowledgeable criticism. The reformers are calling for a revival of the social sciences with independence to investigate actual social conditions and freedom to present critical findings. The two camps are fundamentally opposed on the question of intellectuals, including the role of scholars in socialist society. These differences are consistent with the differing styles of scholarship advocated and practiced by each group. As discussed in Chapter 1, it is the reformers who are identified with genuine principles of scholarship, e.g. in Deliusin's praise of diversity, Kiuzadjan's emphasis on learning from Western specialists, and Gel'bras's attention to overcoming shortcomings in previous Soviet writings.

However fragile the consensus may be, there does exist a common critical perspective on the treatment of intellectuals in China and, by extension, in socialist societies. This perspective has much in common with Western criticisms of the Soviet Union as well as China. It rejects a tense atmosphere of political pressure, involving secret denunciations. It opposes continuous interference in regular classwork oriented toward professional training and in the selection of students and employment of specialists with proven ability. The Soviet consensus also recognizes the need to draw heavily on the contemporary culture of bourgeois societies. Above all, Soviets approve of professionalism. Intellectuals should be treated with respect and rewarded materially. They must be given some scope for originality without fear of making mistakes. Steps should be taken to keep them satisfied and motivated to work well in their fields. Criticisms of Chinese shortcomings in these areas closely resemble Western criticisms of socialism in both countries.

The consensus breaks down on what may be the central issue in the Soviet reform perspective: intellectual freedom.

Officials and their representatives stand in the way of experts. In the final analysis, the officials determine what can be studied and what conclusions can be drawn from these studies. Separating social scientists from the truth produces inefficient, and sometimes tragic, consequences. In China, the differences between the communist party and the intelligentsia were depicted as red versus expert. A similar, though less intense, clash exists in the Soviet Union; it is obscured by the oblique arguments necessary for public expression. Soviet studies of China provide us with the rare opportunity to detect two differing concerns about the problems of intellectuals under socialism.

· 5 ·

OFFICIALS

Contrasts are ubiquitous in the Soviet treatment of the positive development of their own country and the negative development of China, but one contrast stands out as vividly as proletariat and capitalist. That is the distinction between the dedicated, virtuous officials who have brought progress to the Soviet Union and the incompetent, venal officials who have abused power and caused great hardships in China. The glorified treatment of communist party officials, military officers, and other leaders in Soviet society leaves no room for sociological analysis. Isolated cases of corruption are publicized (in Andropov's anticorruption program of 1983-1984 accusations became frequent), but no systematic explanations are tolerated. Only in the study of China is there scope for discussion of the position of officials in a socialist or quasisocialist society. For this reason, of all the topics in the sociology of China none has greater potential to extend or modify the Soviet worldview. In the Chinese context, Soviets can at last assess the relations of officials who call themselves communists to the other social classes and groups of their society.

Only in the late 1970s did detailed studies begin to appear on the various categories that constitute Chinese officialdom. Most have been written by Soviets who appear to enjoy secure protection in the orthodox camp. Yet, without producing monographs on this subject, leading reformers such as Burlatsky, Deliusin, and Gel'bras have also managed to record their views about officials. They extend the criticisms offered by other writers on China into an analysis of two deep-seated problems of leadership failure: 1) the accumulation of power in the hands of incompetent officials; and 2) the social psychology of nondemocratic and, for a long period, brutalized rule.

There is still no book-length study in Russia of the officials of China. This group is not referred to as an elite or a new class. Because of the extremely sensitive nature of the analysis of officials in a communist-led society, there is an air of incompleteness—of unreality—in the Soviet discussion that goes beyond the unstated parallels to the Soviet Union in other chapters. In particular, the orthodox group, with its convoluted application of ideological labels, falls far short of the ideals of empirical sociology. The effort by the orthodox camp to force into the discussion the tiny national bourgeoisie and to give a rightist cast to the entire category of officials may twist the reality of China more sharply than for any other topic examined in this book.

The indirect, historical approach of reform scholars in their treatment of officials concentrates on the continuities with traditional society. This approach has two advantages: it shifts part of the blame for shortcomings in China to the uncontroversial target of premodern society and it justifies serious scholarship by pointing to the need for intensive research into Chinese history. Historical research paved the way for the direct analysis of PRC management and officials that began only in the post-Mao era. It has also, albeit through mirror images, opened our view to what Soviets think about the role of officials in a communist-led system.

THE LEGACY OF THE PAST

Confucian China attached a great deal of importance to officials, establishing clear models for their recruitment, their personal character, and their formal relations with the people. Even when the political system degenerated under Manchu rule and the difficult conditions of the nineteenth century, the Confucian teachings remained at the forefront of exam-oriented education and national debate until the first decade of this century.

Soviet authors recognize that Confucianism retained a hold on the Chinese people long after the examination system was abolished in 1905 and the dynastic system ended in 1911. Some writers express appreciation for the extraordinary civilization that existed in China. A recent collection of articles under the title *Confucianism in China* refers to the "rich culture" and "great thinkers from Confucius to Sun Yat-sen."[1] Deliusin's introduction to the volume argues that "The Chinese problem cannot be understood if one studies only those processes that take place before our eyes; it can be correctly and objectively comprehended only when the researcher, analyzing the contemporary period, knows well the features of the historical development of China, the traditional methods of political and military struggle, the main trends of the sociopolitical thought of ancient centuries."[2] Deliusin goes on to talk of the continuing and steadfast influence of ancient political philosophers on the psychology, thought, and norms of behavior of the Chinese. The articles in the book examine aspects of Confucianism in successive periods, ending with a review of the struggle against Confucianism during the second decade of this century. More on the place of tradition in this period of change can be found in a 1971 collection of articles on the May Fourth Movement and in a 1979 collection on political thought concerned with social development.[3]

Elsewhere Deliusin writes that Confucius repeatedly reappears in the political life of China. He refers to the influences of traditional political and socioeconomic ideas and traditional institutions of state and law on the formation of Maoism and on contemporary life.[4] He notes such continuities as: 1) the broad role of the state in economic life; 2) the view that agriculture is the base of the economy and the most important factor in stability, and that the urban population is parasitic; 3) the role of state authority as the protector of the highest moral values and the designator of the norms that should guide each Chinese in

[1] *Konfutsianstvo v Kitae: problemy, teorii i praktiki*, p. 3.
[2] Ibid.
[3] *Dvizhenie "4 maia" 1919 goda v Kitae*; and *Kitai: poiski putei sotsial'nogo razvitiia.*
[4] *Kitai: traditsii i sovremennost'*, pp. 4-15.

daily life; and 4) the existence of traditional methods of educating the bureaucratic administrative apparatus, which to a significant extent correspond to contemporary means of preparing cadres based on learning and memorizing dogma. Deliusin observes that "Each person who is acquainted with the contemporary life of China, is struck by the opposite concepts of *ganbu* [cadre] and *laobaixing* [people], which force one to recall the customary division of society for old China into *guan* [official] and *min* [people]."[5] Deliusin carries further than any other Soviet the argument that the position of the contemporary official follows the traditions of Confucian officials.

Meliksetov expands on the assessment of the ruling class characteristic of Chinese despotism prior to the advent of communist rule. He sees it as a "collective exploiter," as a class-state, with social status a function of proximity to power, and a large part of the income of the ruling gentry coming from carrying out bureaucratic and public functions.[6] Pointing to the observation of Deliusin that the three-level people's communes cannot be correctly interpreted without consideration of traditional Chinese conceptions, Meliksetov supports Marx's hypothesis that the absence of private property in the European sense is the key to understanding Asian history. In other words, the Chinese people even in the twentieth century continued to lack private rights as they were exploited by a new despotism or local militarism that stood in the way of society's progressive development. Deformed class relations, especially the slow growth of the bourgeoisie and of organizations to defend class interests, enabled the Kuomintang to turn more and more into a "substitute class." The state acted as "the most important integrative factor of Chinese society."[7] Meliksetov has not extended this analysis to the PRC, but it would seem likely that he finds the same traditions operating and would agree

[5] Ibid., pp. 5-7.

[6] A. V. Meliksetov, *Sotsial'no-ekonomicheskaia politika Gomin'dana 1927-1949 gg.*, p. 8.

[7] Ibid., pp. 34, 37.

with Deliusin's view about the role of the state and its officials.

Gel'bras makes a unique contribution to Soviet studies of China by tracing the concept of ganbu back before the 1949 victory. He notes that the first attempt in the Marxist literature on China to conceive the essence of this social category and its role in the PRC was in 1968 by the Hungarian P. Polonyi. Clearly Gel'bras considers the problem of officials in a socialist society an important one.

Many negative influences of Chinese history are revealed in Gel'bras's analysis of the birth of the ganbu stratum. At the end of the 1920s the revolutionary struggle in rural regions was influenced by strong remnants of patriarchal-kin relations. The fact that the struggle centered in out-of-the-way rural regions made it very difficult for workers and intellectuals to join in. The revolutionary movement came under the powerful influence of the social psychology of the poorest peasants and lumpen proletariat elements with their centuries-old traditions of secret societies. Groups formed in the CCP and the PLA that exerted an enormous influence on events not only in the 1920s-1930s but also in the 1960s-1970s. Mao concentrated on using the contradictions among leadership groups in the interest of his own faction rather than to liquidate the groups inside the party. In the 1950s and 1960s nothing was printed in the open press on these groups although this subject resounded at closed party meetings. Gel'bras uses terms such as "patriarchal" and "localist" to refer to these groups, suggestive of the Confucian precedents for these types of behavior.[8]

CLASS STRUGGLE AGAINST THE BOURGEOISIE

According to the Soviet viewpoint, victory in 1949 did not end the struggle for power by the bourgeoisie. Portions of this class continued to threaten the consolidation of so-

---

[8] Gel'bras, *Sotsial'no-politicheskaia struktura KNR 50-60-e gody*, pp. 160-63.

cialism. These were the enemies against whom officials entrusted with the reins of party and state had to do battle. While agreeing in principle on the necessity of a struggle between capitalism and socialism in China of the 1950s, Soviets disagree on the nature of the threat posed and the wisdom of the policies that the Chinese adopted. A review of their changing and divergent views of the national bourgeoisie is important to understand their overall assessments of the social class system in China.

The Soviet view of China in the late 1950s is recorded in a history of contemporary China published in 1959.[9] The four authors of the part that treats the period 1949-1957 are V. I. Glunin, B. P. Gurevich, G. D. Sukharchuk, and A. V. Meliksetov, all among the more able Soviet specialists on China. Shortly thereafter the Institute of Chinese Studies was closed, and these four went their separate ways. Three of the group remained active in the 1970s and 1980s as leading specialists on Republican China, and Gurevich turned even further back to Chinese Central Asian relations in the nineteenth century. Along with others at this ill-fated institute, they had apparently been judged guilty of excessively positive evaluations of the PRC, but they managed to reorient their academic careers in the following years of virtual silence about the contemporary society by switching to other periods of Chinese history. Their published views in the late 1950s clearly reflect unqualified approval of the policies in China that would later be seen as controversial.

In 1959, these authors depict a classic battle between the Chinese people, represented by the party and the government, and the bourgeoisie. On the one side were the officials seeking to restore the economy and to achieve a democratic transformation. On the other side, the reactionary forces waged a ferocious class struggle against these aims. The threat was real and serious, and it justified the repressive and violent countermeasures by the state. Accord-

---

[9] *Ocherki istorii Kitaia v noveishee vremia.*

ing to this view, actions intended to suppress the counter-revolutionaries, such as the death sentences handed down by the people's tribunals that helped the peasants in their struggle with the landlords, were in the interest of the people. Rather than receding, however, the threat became more serious. By the end of 1951 the conflict, or as the Soviets write the contradiction, between the bourgeoisie and the proletariat (broadly defined) had intensified. The fault is placed at the hands of the former, who tried to turn the country onto the capitalist path of development and to evade government restrictions. The bourgeoisie waged a massive struggle, committing illegal acts and forming secret associations. They created a serious danger for the socialist revolution, but the party saw the danger in time and responded appropriately with campaigns in 1951 and 1952 against the right and with tight controls on bourgeois elements.[10] Serving as a form of class struggle between the proletariat and the bourgeoisie, these campaigns opened the road to a peaceful transition to socialism. Soviets in 1959 justified the early campaigns and the tough measures against the Chinese bourgeoisie.

During the first five-year plan, the struggle against the bourgeoisie remained intense. From 1953 to 1955 it mainly took the form of structural change in the economy aimed at containing and reducing the influence of this class. But to the extent that the ideological and political struggle by the bourgeoisie against the party intensified and even succeeded in exerting a negative influence on some elements inside the party, there were distortions of the correct line. This struggle launched by the right justified vigorous actions to deal with the enemies of socialism. This 1959 history of China applauds all of the campaigns and restrictive measures taken against the "right," including the 1954-1955 purges against the antiparty bloc of Gao Gang and Rao Shushi, who were accused of an unprincipled attempt to seize power. The book refers approvingly to the election pro-

[10] Ibid., pp. 506-12.

cedures followed in the PRC, including the preference given to the working class and the strengthened unity of the popular-democratic front including the national bourgeoisie. It praises the 1954 Constitution of the PRC for not only fixing the rights of citizens but guaranteeing their realization. In this book, there is only support for the attacks against bourgeois ideology and the identification of the old intelligentsia with the social base of the national bourgeoisie and the kulaks in the campaigns of 1954-1955. As justification, the authors contend that counterrevolutionary elements appeared in disguised forms everywhere, especially in the first half of 1955, and their hostile actions increased, including murders and other crimes. The campaign against them in the second half of 1955 is praised as a necessary step for the preservation of the life and property of the people and for the success of socialist construction. These 1959 appraisals refer to collectivization as a great success, bringing about the victory of the socialist revolution in the countryside. They also approve of the 1956 call for the long-term coexistence and mutual control of the CCP and the democratic parties and groups, considering this united front appropriate for reeducating the bourgeoisie in conditions where the center of gravity of the class struggle had moved to the sphere of ideology.[11]

Recognizing that the majority of the Chinese intelligentsia still adhered to bourgeois views, including a portion that was antagonistic to Marxism, the authors consider the task of the "Hundred Flowers" period to have been the reeducation of the intelligentsia and at the same time the elimination of dogmatism in science, literature, and art. Yet, they add that the contradiction between the working class and the bourgeoisie was serious; indeed it was antagonistic, as China's leaders insisted. This necessitated a course of open battle, which, if delayed for a time, would be pursued after the CCP was confident of socialism's victory. In this period, counterrevolutionary elements gained leading posts

[11] Ibid., pp. 537, 540-41, 543, 568, 581-82.

in certain newspapers and democratic parties. They became active in 1956 and, taking advantage of Mao's call for free critical discussion, attacked the socialist revolution and tried to restore capitalism. Under these circumstances, the authors agree with Mao that only an open, uncompromising battle could resolve the contradictions with the right, that is the bourgeoisie. The campaign against rightists in 1957-1958 was important in reeducating the intelligentsia and raising the socialist consciousness and the position of the working class.[12] Soviet views of the national bourgeoisie may appear contradictory for they give unqualified support to the twists and turns of Chinese policies in the first decade of the PRC. Although the Soviet authors may have appeared reform-oriented in the Soviet context of the late 1950s, e.g. for their approval of the elimination of dogmatism in science and the arts, they also accepted a premise which by now has become associated with a hardline approach, that a serious and expanding assault against socialism was being carried on by the bourgeoisie in China, which justified harsh repressive measures.

In 1967 one of the first publications of the newly formed Institute of the Far East was a brochure with a greatly revised appraisal of events in China.[13] In addition to criticizing hasty collectivization in 1955, the forced tempo of industrial development in 1956, and the premature formation of craft and commercial cooperatives in 1956, the authors found fault with elements of militarization and military-bureaucratic methods in policies of the period 1949-1957. From 1949-1954 military control was exercised. For a long time, the working class and its mass organizations were not represented in the military control organs designated from above. Special regions in some parts of China continued to be ruled by non-elected authorities. In other words, China's officials did not represent its leading class.

The authors note also that the most representative lead-

[12] Ibid., pp. 502, 594-97.
[13] B. Zanegin, A. Mironov, and Ia. Mikhailov, *K sobitiiam v Kitae.*

ers often became targets of oppression. The targets of campaigns in 1955-1956 were mainly those who adhered to earlier party decisions about gradual transformation. As a means to accomplish socioeconomic transformation, primitive measures and force were widely applied by those who remained in power. Ideological campaigns were accompanied by terror, leading to mass suicide. Repression occurred regularly in the course of party purges. In campaigns against rightists, administrative organs, not the courts that should have had jurisdiction, handed down sentences, even death sentences. All of these errors are tied in the Soviet analysis to Mao's views of the functions of power in a socialist state and of the dictatorship of the proletariat as, above all, force and repression. Relying on the cult of personality, Mao strengthened his position by undermining party and state democracy, and after 1962 by restructuring party and state organs on the basis of organizational principles of the army. Officials worked in organizations tightly controlled from above and were obedient tools of their leaders.[14] The problem of a threat from the right backed by the bourgeoisie has disappeared in this analysis, as China's leaders themselves and the officials who obey them appear as the chief threats to socialism.

But the negative influence of rightist elements in Chinese society continued to be asserted by some Soviets. If the events of the 1950s to 1970s are depicted as a petty-bourgeois counterrevolution (as they are, for instance, by Lazarev),[15] then the place of the bourgeoisie cannot be overlooked. Lazarev explains that the liquidation of the big exploiters created favorable conditions for the small-scale owners. Even after cooperatives (collective farms) were set up, this social type continued to exist. Because the cooperatives had a primitive technology and the leaders of China permitted recent petty-bourgeois elements to escape from under the influence and leadership of the proletariat, this

[14] Ibid., pp. 37-39, 43-44.
[15] Lazarev, *Klassovaia bor'ba v KNR*, p. 12.

class could become active. Moreover, Lazarev asserts, the class had a serious partner, the national bourgeoisie, which retained substantial material resources. After the national bourgeoisie lost control as private owners, they remained in high managerial posts and also received incomes not dependent on their work. Lazarev argues that the leadership of the CCP mistakenly regarded the contradictions between this class and the proletariat as nonantagonistic (differences that can be resolved without dangerous conflict) and thus allowed it to continue acting on behalf of its class interests.

According to this view, in the early 1960s Mao made a sharp turnaround in his orientation—now to the extreme right. Although part of the bourgeois class had been repressed for its attempted counterattack in 1957, another part was accepted among the people. Rather than preparing the party to attack the counterrevolutionary class, Mao launched an attack against the elements supporting socialism. Power was transferred from the working class to a "conglomerate of petty-bourgeois elements." Among the causes of the Cultural Revolution, Lazarev counts Mao's advances to the national bourgeoisie and his mixing up of exploiting and non-exploiting classes in one concept, "the people." "The initiators of the 'cultural revolution' were many times more favorably inclined to the national bourgeoisie than to the working class, the peasantry and the intelligentsia." Recognizing that (in the first stages of this violent campaign) there were ultimatums against the bourgeoisie, too, and certain of them were raided and lost personal belongings, Lazarev nonetheless concludes that their capital was untouched and they were soon reassured, as were the overseas Chinese. Moreover, neither the leading political figures from their ranks nor former officials under the Kuomintang suffered. The bourgeois-democratic parties were spared. While the working class lost its leading position in society, the bourgeoisie remained secure. After Mao's death, says Lazarev, while other classes, including the intelligentsia, did not benefit from a genuine relaxation of controls, the bourgeoisie gained markedly. Bank deposits and other property were returned to them along with wages that had been withheld. Restrictions were rescinded that had for a time limited the entry of their children into the CCP and Komsomol, the army, higher education, and work. The leadership clearly sought to motivate the national bourgeoisie, and overseas Chinese, to invest their resources in "modernization." Lazarev concludes that "Policies of Peking leaders concerning the remnants of the exploiting classes objectively support the fact that in China the counterrevolutionary process continues and deepens."[16]

The 1979 yearbook on China distinguishes between the ignored interests of the half-million former capitalists and the favorable policies toward the extremely small stratum of huge capitalists. The latter had contacts with the West that the Chinese leadership intended to use in realizing its programs for economic development. In the final analysis, this section of the yearbook concludes, the new policies could split even more the basic classes of society, who are opposed to the capitalists, from their leaders—the cadres.[17] Favoritism for the national bourgeoisie was one cause of this widening gulf.

Two recent books devote an entire chapter to China's national bourgeoisie. V. I. Vanin of the Institute of the Far East is the author of the chapter in *Classes and Class Structure in the PRC*. He criticizes Maoist ideology for its thesis on the exceptional nature of the Chinese national bourgeoisie, which asserts that because of its patriotism and support for socialism it is the most remarkable bourgeoisie in the world. The Chinese failed to recognize, during the course of the transition to socialism, the turning point when the contradiction between the working class and the bourgeoisie inevitably became the major contradiction. They failed to expropriate the property of the bourgeoisie and to isolate it.

[16] Ibid., pp. 21-26, 153-54, 163, 170-71, 261-62.
[17] *Kitaiskaia Narodnaia Respublika 1979*, p. 80.

Vanin explains these failures, taking into account the nature of the revolutionary movement, the low level of capitalist development, the isolation of this group from foreign capital, and the fact that in the course of the long revolutionary movement, counterrevolutionary bourgeois elements were in the main crushed.[18]

Despite policies from 1950-1957 that greatly reduced this small stratum's influence, according to Vanin, it remained considerable for several reasons. First, capitalists continued to receive an exploiter's income; parasitic elements existed in the fixed percentage return on the capital they had turned over. Second, the majority continued to work in enterprises and to receive excessive incomes. Third, special forms of representation were preserved, especially the "democratic" parties, which acquired a strong antisocialist tendency after large numbers of bourgeois elements joined in 1956. Fourth, this stratum bore bourgeois nationalist ideology and had certain opportunities for spreading its influence. In Vanin's opinion, it was necessary to devote attention to "the final liquidation of the national bourgeoisie."[19] Although the bourgeoisie received guarantees in the form of the "five constants," including protection of their political position and income from capital, they continued to battle to obtain illegal income and to oppose socialism. Mao even approved of control over activities of the communist party by the bourgeois parties, rejecting the monopoly of the CCP in the leadership of society. This course of coexistence and mutual control opened the way for the bourgeoisie to intensify its struggle against socialism. Later in 1957 the battle against the right wing of the bourgeoisie and against rightists in official posts had great significance for building socialism, but, Vanin concludes, the campaign was misdirected and the national bourgeoisie regrouped and reemerged as an important force.[20]

[18] *Klassy i klassovaia struktura v KNR*, pp. 201-202, 205-206.
[19] Ibid., pp. 228-33.
[20] Ibid., pp. 238-42.

According to Vanin, Mao's conception of class struggle and the role of the bourgeoisie under socialism justified not physically liquidating them. Moreover, Mao believed that a new bourgeoisie continually is formed. His "vulgar sociological" designations of class were based on employment, ideological factors, or scale of income, not on place in production and relation to the means of production. In practice, the Chinese leadership did not direct class struggle against the national bourgeoisie. In the mid-1960s, it even encouraged the "democratic" parties to become more active. Rightist elements were granted amnesties. And the Cultural Revolution was not directed against the national bourgeoisie. Indeed, opportunities increased for strengthening bourgeois influence. Dissatisfaction throughout China with the privileged position of the national bourgeoisie led to confiscations by the Red Guards, but the official press did not demand the liquidation of their special rights, and leaders came to their defense and awarded them more than the value of the property they had owned. "The artificial preservation of the national bourgeoisie as a special stratum, placed in a privileged position, not only 'conserved' bourgeois ideology, but also created favorable conditions for its spread."[21] In a petty-bourgeois environment, Vanin goes on, the influence of the bourgeoisie could reach far. In this case, their influence was extended through nationalist tendencies. The Cultural Revolution opened the way for an increase in private ownership activities, including the black market and underground enterprises. The former capitalists did not have much economic force, but somehow Vanin sees them as contributing to the environment conducive to capitalism. More recently in an effort to attract qualified personnel to responsible positions, the Chinese leadership has relied on persons from the national bourgeoisie, which Vanin argues, could lead to the increased influence of this stratum.[22] Recognizing various

[21] Ibid., pp. 245-54.
[22] Ibid., p. 257.

motives that underlie the 1979 measures favoring this group, Vanin nevertheless sees the outcome as a further threat to socialism.

Gel'bras has also devoted a chapter to the Chinese bourgeoisie in his 1980 book. He agrees with Vanin on the importance of this group and of the overseas Chinese associated with it. At the same time, he avoids many of the oversimplifications and assumptions that enable Vanin to link this group to counterrevolution. Gel'bras makes clear that the development of the national bourgeoisie into a class was suppressed and that Mao and his associates never were defenders of its class interests. However, he adds, the effect of Chinese policies was to set apart persons from this background in an estate. They formed a special group among the officials and the scientific and technical intelligentsia, enjoying the advantages and privileges of the ganbu and not experiencing all the horror felt by the intelligentsia.[23] The domestic policies of China's leaders, at least since the 1960s, have not contradicted the interests of this estate. The leaders are dependent on this group, behind which stand millions of overseas Chinese, international connections, and even the possibility of reunification with Taiwan.

Gel'bras contrasts two periods in the history of the relationship between the national bourgeoisie and the Chinese leadership. During much of the 1950s, the younger generation of this group were not welcomed in the schools, were forced to renounce their parents or to spy on members of their families, and encountered difficulties in forced job placements after graduation. The class tended to oppose the socialist transformation and friendly relations with the USSR. By the 1970s, the second period, higher government authority had realized its dependence on the national bourgeoisie, its specialists and technocrats. These persons acted as advocates for centralized bureaucratic and technocratic tendencies in the society. The bourgeoisie recognized that the only way to defend their estate privileges

---

[23] Gel'bras, *Sotsial'no-politicheskaia struktura KNR 50-60-e gody*, p. 159.

and to improve conditions in which they could function was through the existence of a strong central authority. Gel'bras concludes, "The preservation of an estate of the national bourgeoisie can become or already has become one of the factors of the social isolation and aloofness of the managerial, scientific and technocratic apparatus."[24]

THE GANBU

Two recent books, which I have already referred to as representing the orthodox and reform views, respectively, and which are each divided into chapters on separate social classes, give different weight to China's cadres (*ganbu*). In the 1981 book produced at the Institute of the Far East under Sladkovsky's general direction, there are separate chapters on: the working class, the peasantry, the intelligentsia, the national bourgeoisie, and the army. In Gel'bras's 1980 book, the chapters focus on: the working class, the peasantry, the intelligentsia, the national bourgeoisie, and the ganbu. Except for the final category, the volumes agree on the principal divisions in the society. The only other extended treatment of ganbu by the Soviets is in the 1981 book of which Gel'bras is the primary author, where Kul'pin prepared the section called "ganbu and peasants."[25]

What rationale is given for separate analysis of this group? Gel'bras begins his chapter with the statement that, "In contemporary Chinese there has arisen the daily turn of phrase '*ganbu he qunzhong*' (ganbu and masses), naturally reflecting the separation of the first from the other classes and strata of the population. For a long time already in China not a single person could be found who could not from the first glance unmistakably single out the ganbu in any crowd or group of people by manner of bearing, clothing, footwear, and other signs that would be elusive for the uninitiated person." Gel'bras notes that the Chinese defi-

[24] Ibid., pp. 156-58.
[25] *Rabochii klass v sotsial'no-politicheskoi sisteme KNR.*

nition distinguishes the ganbu as leaders from employees, office workers, or soldiers. Furthermore, the ganbu are divided into locals and outsiders, old and new—categories that to this day have not lost significance. Different viewpoints among groups of cadres have remained substantial, according to Gel'bras, from long before the revolution. Such terms as "spheres of influence" and "regionalism" apply to the activities of these groups, which, Gel'bras argues, can be differentiated according to their social type, position, and ideological viewpoint. He distinguishes five viewpoints in all. One viewpoint favored a strong state and strict discipline to achieve its hierarchical-statist tendencies. Cadres of this persuasion gravitated toward bureaucratism, patriarchal despotism, and support for an all-powerful central state apparatus. Another perspective was the patriarchal-militarist tendency, reflecting the lumpen proletariat masses, who scorned educated people. This often became a destructive force and could be observed in cadres prepared to support anyone who would look out for their personal positions in the army, the party, or elsewhere. A third group reflected the petty-bourgeois-kulak tendency. It was encouraged by the call, associated with the concept of new democracy, for the long-term coexistence of socialist and capitalist elements. Fourth, the anarchist-egalitarian tendency was characteristic of those who supported "full equality." Finally the revolutionary-democratic tendency included what Gel'bras considers Marxist-Leninist forces, which sometimes faced a united front of representatives of all other tendencies. In this complex and divisive environment, the personal characteristics of the cadre were shaped. Increasingly widespread were "mutual suspicion, the practice of denunciations, treachery, time-serving, careerism, conformism, haughty manners and individualism, duplicity and secrecy."[26]

Gel'bras goes on to distinguish seven main social types

[26] Gel'bras, *Sotsial'no-politicheskaia struktura KNR 50-60-e gody*, pp. 160, 166-67, 173.

182

of ganbu—going beyond the two types, mandarin and specialist, proposed by Polonyi. First is the "lumpen-bureaucrat" (*liumpen-biurokrat*), not lumpen by social origin or position but by political manner. This category consists of deceitful persons, engaged in embezzlement of public property and distortion. "They need to keep everybody in fear in order to overcome their own fear of everyone. They are scornful of work, honor, knowledge. Their entire world—it is a world of things and delights and, simultaneously, careers.... For them, nothing is sacred, including human life."[27] Second Gel'bras singles out the "fanatic-good soldier" (*fanatik-boevik*). Often this is a relative, a person of the same locale or a colleague of a higher ganbu, tied to him by long years of service. Typically illiterate or little educated individuals of this type become blind adherents of a cause which is embraced by their group, prepared to go to any lengths, even murder. Whereas the lumpen-bureaucrats consider nothing sacred and could easily stab a comrade in the back, the fanatics are thick-headed followers who are devoted to their group's mission.

Third on Gel'bras's list is the "enlightened gentry" (*prosveshchennyi shen'shi*). Persons in this category are educated and sincere. Depending on circumstances in China, they have been called "bourgeois," "revolutionary intelligentsia," or "revolutionary elements having bad class background." Gel'bras finds these people easily deceived, ready to sacrifice everything for the liberation of the people, but, in fact, giving their life and honor over to adventurers and lovers of power. Mao played masterfully on their good intentions. When they realize their actual role in some dirty deed, some in this group become demoralized and think about giving up their leadership duties. Fourth is the "specialist" (*spetsialist*), who is professionally educated and often knows foreign languages and has traveled outside China. This technocrat is ready to take on any political guise in the interest of production and of increasing the greatness

[27] Ibid., pp. 199-201.

of the nation. Like the "enlightened gentry," these "specialists" have been accused of bourgeois views, but, unlike them, they are more purposeful in the interests they serve and are not easily led astray by good intentions.

Gel'bras's fifth type of ganbu is the "unfortunate proprietor" (*goremyka-khoziain*), who works as a political and economic organizer of production. Not always educated nor even literate, cadres of this type are knowledgeable about concrete matters and express the interests of a specific sector or region. They strive to improve the economy of their brigade, commune, or region, obliged constantly to wheel and deal for these interests. Tenacious and purposeful, they are frequently punished, only later to be restored to their posts. Their actions are often taken at the expense of neighboring units and the state; therefore they paralyze state regulation of the economy and contribute to anarchy in production and the market.

A sixth type is the "independent pastor" (*udel'nyi pastyr'*), who staunchly defends the traditional ways of his village. Most widespread among production team and brigade leaders in backward areas, persons in this category lack education and outside political experience. They owe their positions to their organizing abilities, and they express the interests of lineages and kin, on whose behalf they engage in any kind of intrigue, deceit, or illegal act. In comparison to the "unfortunate proprietors," the "independent pastors" are less able to deal effectively with outsiders and have a narrower field of vision, reflecting the meager commercialization of the local economy.

Finally, Gel'bras identifies a type of "politician" (*politik*). This is an educated person, convinced of his ideals. Members of this category form the nucleus of various leadership groups. The most extreme designations are applied to them, such as "proletarian revolutionary," "class enemy," or counterrevolutionary. In comparison to other groups, here one finds the most clearly expressed class positions and class consciousness. A "politician" sees issues on a broad scale, sometimes reflecting the interests of regions or of large-scale contemporary industry.

These diverse types of ganbu described by Gel'bras, to some extent representing different generations, could not do a satisfactory job of managing China. Many of them were uneducated and incompetent. The need for managers had never been so great as it was after 1949, but the problems were so severe, Gel'bras concludes, that "Such a society could not be managed in the full sense of this word." These problems were complicated by the separation of units "owing to the underdevelopment of production, infrastructure, and the national market" and by the enormous scale and speed of changes.[28]

Kul'pin describes the relationship between ganbu and peasants as having "at times a very tense character. In response to policies that extracted not only the surplus but even part of the necessary product, uprisings occurred in the villages. After cooperation [collectivization] the essence of the state policy of extraction of the surplus and part of the necessary product did not change." What had applied to separate households, now applied to the peasant collectives; the state squeezed more out of the village than it could afford to give up. According to Kul'pin, in the 1960s and 1970s the leaders of the rural units were all appointed from above rather than being elected. Thus they became functionaries of a single state apparatus. All of them became simple executors of orders from above. When maximal amounts of local harvests were subject to obligatory sales at low prices, the lower-level ganbu, who were peasants themselves and were united by informal ties to other villagers, were tempted to defend local interests. Moreover they had to be concerned with increasing output. Nevertheless, despite isolated instances of defense of peasants and criticism of state policies, Kul'pin considers the interests of the ganbu to have been clearly on the side of the state. Career interests took precedence; the ganbu were

[28] Ibid., p. 201.

ready to drive the peasants to full destitution. The demands placed on the local cadres, such as expanding lands planted in grain to the detriment of the ecology, did not develop their competence. "The economic conditions created by the state demanded from officials neither knowledge, professional mastery nor enthusiasm, but the capacity for putting into practice in an uncompromising way the directions of higher organs."[29] The interests of the peasants were sacrificed to the demands of the state. When the peasants were driven to despair and, even in the face of political and economic sanctions, grew openly defiant, the ganbu sought the aid of the militia or even the army. The ganbu enforced unpopular measures, including militarized methods to organize labor, in order to produce more intensive work.

Other characteristics of the ganbu are delineated by Gel'bras. They are mainly men; women as a rule are entrusted with posts exclusively at a low level. They are chiefly Han Chinese; already underrepresented, the non-Han cadres suffered a serious blow in the Cultural Revolution. Originally the primary source of ganbu were demobilized soldiers of the PLA. In addition many of the high echelon officials were from families of landlords. Pointing to the dearth of data on social origins, Gel'bras nonetheless concludes that a significant part of the ganbu of all generations consisted of nonproletariat and nonpeasant strata of the population by birth.[30] As ganbu they enjoyed a privileged position, especially following the reorganization of 1956. None of the policies adopted by China's leaders could resolve the divisions within the ganbu on their proper role in society—on organizational and educational policies affecting them and their relations to the masses. The process of democratization failed. Bureaucratization expanded but not elections that would have enabled the people to be represented.

[29] *Rabochii klass v sotsial'no-politicheskoi sisteme KNR*, pp. 114, 115-16, 118.

[30] Gel'bras, *Sotsial'no-politicheskaia struktura KNR 50-60-e gody*, pp. 177-79.

According to Gel'bras, power gravitated to the ganbu. "In the first half of the 1960s the activities of the entire system of meetings of peoples' representatives were gradually curtailed, and absolute power was concentrated in the hands of the ganbu, freed from the necessity of giving an accounting before the people." A huge, all-powerful bureaucracy emerged. The state authority and its organs intervened directly in all facets of daily life, relying on coercion as the only possibility for maximum concentration of the surplus product of the entire society and maximum forced savings. The state interfered in births, in the use of the family budget, in the assignment of all labor power. "A gigantic organization formed, covering like a net the entire body of Chinese society, penetrating all pores of its life." The cadres acquired features of an exclusive estate, e.g. with their own information through periodicals unavailable to the general public. It became necessary under these circumstances for China's leaders to introduce special mechanisms to make cadres form ties with the masses such as required participation in physical labor and sending cadres to live and work in lower-level units, often in the countryside. Gel'bras argues that there was distrust, mutual denunciation, and surveillance over the ganbu. The caste-like character of the ganbu and their power over subordinates did not prevent their decay. Out of control, the cadres subordinated their work to their career ambitions, clawing for posts and sinking into corruption. Gel'bras writes that the tyranny of the ganbu took on a frightening scale.[31] State authority, as exercised by the cadres, became an independent force over society.

In 1976 Ia. M. Berger had argued against the view that the ganbu is a separate stratum.[32] He insisted that the majority of the lower cadres in the village were on the side of the peasants and that it was very problematic to consider

[31] Ibid., pp. 189, 191-93.
[32] Ia. M. Berger, "Gosudarstvo i derevnia v sovremennom Kitae: tezisy," *Obshchestvo i gosudarstvo v Kitae* 7:3 (1976), pp. 477-78.

the ganbu a stratum. Gel'bras finds Berger correct in concluding that there is an absence of unity in the ranks of the ganbu and acknowledges that to regard the ganbu as an "artificial caste" in no way means perceiving them as some kind of social monolith.[33] But he differs from Berger in the importance he attaches to this group. Both in his overall characterization of this group and his detailed classification of it, Gel'bras has demonstrated that its significance is far greater than its numbers (20-25 million in the 1960s) would indicate. He presents a powerful argument for the analysis of officials as a separate force in Chinese society.

THE ARMY

Soviet authors describe and explain the militarization of Chinese society. Lacking strong support from any social class, Mao Zedong relied on the People's Liberation Army as his primary base of power. This backing made possible such measures as the excessive extraction of rural production from the peasants, forced labor for persons of all classes, and recurrent campaigns against the intelligentsia. The state amassed enormous power to regulate and direct the lives of individuals on the basis of its ownership of the means of production, control over the work force, and receipt of a significant share of the product of labor.[34] Taxes in kind and assigned labor similar to corvée predominated as the state's methods to control the economy. As a result, relations based on personal dependency prevailed, unprotected by elementary rights of citizenship. Closed microsocieties became the local organizational foundations for this arrangement because small-scale production could not be highly centralized or run directly by the state. Because it repeatedly tampered with or even eliminated market mechanisms and social relations vital to a rural economy,

[33] Gel'bras, *Sotsial'no-politicheskaia struktura KNR 50-60-e gody*, p. 197.
[34] Ibid., pp. 66-67.

the state needed a reliable and active security force and army to keep discontents in check.

Soviet sources agree that the Chinese army has played and continues to play an enormous role in Chinese society, a circumstance the Soviets regard as an "abnormal situation." It results from Mao's conception "of the role of force in the development of society and the possibilities of military organization," including his view of intense class struggle under socialism which, along with foreign conditions, justifies the omnipresence of the army. The book *Classes and Class Structure in the PRC* criticizes Mao for giving the PLA too great a role in the political and economic life of the regions under communist control prior to 1949. This role was not called for by military conditions, but by Mao's view that army discipline plays a decisive part in the sociopolitical rebuilding of society. After 1949 Mao considered the army to be the main source of cadres for the creation of a state apparatus, and the PLA continued to supply cadres in large numbers in later years. He gave excessive power to military-control organs that had jurisdiction over local party organizations and authorities. The PLA helped disseminate propaganda among the population. It had a large role in running the border regions. The army was very active in collectivization and the campaign against rightists in 1957. From the end of the 1950s Mao devoted great energy to establishing his personal control over the army; the cult of personality reached large dimensions there in the years of the Great Leap Forward. Of course, it was the Cultural Revolution and the revolutionary committees that followed that brought the army most deeply into local affairs. Relying on it, Mao built up what Soviets refer to as a "military-bureaucratic dictatorship."[35]

A book by B. N. Gorbachev details the sociopolitical role of the Chinese army from 1958 to 1969. It notes that the army began to play an exceptional role in the years of the so-called "Cultural Revolution," when it became "the main

---

[35] *Klassy i klassovaia struktura v KNR*, pp. 273, 274-84.

weapon for crushing party, state, and social organizations, and took under its control the economy, all social life in the country and occupied the central place in the political mechanism of the PRC."[36] Later efforts were made to return the army to its barracks, but its power was by this time too great. The dictatorship could not function without armed force, although a wide-ranging purge of army ranks occurred in 1971. Despite the purge, the faction later called the "Gang of Four" and its supporters could not gain sufficient support from the army to remain in power after Mao's death.

Gorbachev stresses the regionalism within the PLA. Because their armies were engaged in a wide range of functions, local commanders concentrated significant power in their own hands. This often enabled these military officers to follow a course independent of the center. Reviewing attempts to increase direct central control and to transfer officers, Gorbachev is concerned largely with the army's role in central politics. However, he does touch on the quality of the officers and their organization. His conclusion is that, "The traditional belief of Chinese in family, clan, blood relations, home village and province is fully prevalent also among the military."[37] A system of personal devotion exists in the army. Officers look on their trusted subordinates as followers and act as their patrons and protectors. Continuous rivalry is the natural outcome from the operation of these traditional fiefdoms within the military organization.

More detail on the army's role in political struggle and on the meaning of the labels "military-bureaucratic regime" or "dictatorship" appears in a book by G. N. Mos'ko that describes a decade of transition as China's leaders turned increasingly to the military. Mos'ko concludes that by the end of the 1960s "armed forces occupied a commanding

[36] B. N. Gorbachev, *Sotsial'no-politicheskaia rol' kitaiskoi armii (1958-1969)*, pp. 4-5.

[37] Ibid., pp. 124-29, 196.

position in all spheres of life: economic, political, ideological."[38]

The chapter on the army in the 1982 book *Classes and Class Structure in the PRC* asserts that military expenses were high relative to the state budget, noting that, although China is one of the leading nations in military expenditures, it ranks 125th among 150 U.N. members in per capita income. The book adds, "The Chinese leadership artificially divides the economy into two sectors to a significant extent set apart: the military and civilian." The first sector has developed a fully contemporary industrial base with the best material resources and is supplied with significantly better qualified cadres, while the second must to a large extent satisfy its own needs, using modest local resources with primarily primitive technology and manual labor. The book also makes the point that, "Because of continually increasing military expenses there is a sharp limitation on state appropriations for health care, education, sociocultural arrangements, housing, and public construction. The financing of the army and the functioning of the military sector of the economy is realized all the more at the expense of the living needs of the Chinese people."[39]

Soviet sources do not overlook the social composition and privileges of the Chinese army. One view is that the Maoists have sought to rely on the most backward strata—the poor and lower middle peasants. Poorly educated and rural soldiers are more easily used to realize Mao's aims. But from the end of the 1960s the percentage of workers in the army increased as the needs of a modern army became more complex. The role of the intelligentsia has also been growing. Referring to these developments as "progressive processes of change in the social structure of the army," Soviets believe the results will be negative for the Maoist regime in the long term, leading "to a gradual erosion of the al-

[38] G. N. Mos'ko, *Armiia Kitaia: orudie avantiuristicheskoi politiki Maoistov*, p. 68.

[39] *Klassy i klassovaia struktura v KNR*, pp. 291-92.

liance of the military with the party-administrative leadership."[40]

In his 1973 book, Gel'bras appears to take a stronger stand than other Soviet observers on the privileges of the army and the ganbu and their separation from the people. He writes that military service provides a mass of privileges and entails a special position. "Not one social stratum of the population in the country has such material and moral support, gains such social benefits, as the army." Only army officers are guaranteed a specified number of deputies in all elected organs of power. One officer often can occupy many posts simultaneously, being at once secretary of a local party organization, chairman of a people's committee, and director of a factory. "These people made use of closed information differentiated by service rank, received special official rewards, special payments and privileges. All that is needed they received in specially assigned foodstuffs and manufactured goods: they are served in closed clubs." Gel'bras refers to these military cadres as a specific stratum, and even a caste protected from the control of the rank-and-file party members and workers. Mao relied heavily on the army and used it as the major source for cadres in state, party, economic, and mass organizations, but he also took advantage of deep popular dissatisfaction with the cadres "to organize the struggle against them under the slogan of battle with 'the lords, sitting on the neck of the people.' "[41] To free himself of military opposition, in the aftermath of the Cultural Revolution Mao also began the campaign to restore the party.

One source contrasts a genuine Marxist-Leninist approach to bourgeois and petty-bourgeois sociological and political thought, which either greatly exaggerates the role of the army, as do Maoists, or sees any participation of it in political and socioeconomic activity as a social pathol-

[40] Ibid., pp. 306-12, 315.
[41] Gel'bras, *Kitai: krizis prodolzhaetsia*, pp. 27-28.

ogy.[42] Marxism-Leninism does not deny that in special historical situations the army is able to play an independent and even decisive role in the social life of the country, but that role was to last only for a short period. The progressive role of the army in our times, the source continues, is for all practical purposes limited to the struggle for national independence and the liquidation of precapitalist forms of social relations. Clearly this is not an endorsement of the use of the army in China in recent years.

THE CHINESE COMMUNIST PARTY

It is easier for Soviets to criticize the theoretical basis of Maoism than to analyze the structure of the CCP. Many books have appeared on Mao's thought and on the history of leadership disputes in the Chinese communist movement.[43] Only one book has been published on party membership, a 1980 volume by I. F. Fedorov and V. G. Zubakov entitled, *Membership in the CCP: How the Party of the "Thought of Mao Zedong" Was Built.*[44] Issued in 100,000 copies, this book does not draw on a substantial scholarly base. Without addressing many general questions about how the organization and role of the communist party in society could lead to widespread shortcomings, Fedorov and Zubakov identify many mistakes in the development of the party in

[42] *Klassy i klassovaia struktura v KNR*, p. 272.

[43] In order of appearance these books are: M. Altaiskii and V. Georgiev, *Antimarksistskaia sushchnost' filosofskikh vzgliadov Mao Tszeduna*; O. Vladimirov and V. Ryazantsev, *Stranitsy politicheskoi biografii Mao Tszeduna*; L. P. Deliusin, *Agrarno-krest'ianskii vopros v politike KPK (1921-1928)*; A. M. Rumiantsev, *Istokii evoliutsiia "idei Mao Tszeduna"; Kritika teoreticheskikh osnov Maoizma*; P. P. Vladimirov, *Osobyi raion Kitaia, 1942-1945*; Van Min, *Polveka KPK i predatel'stvo Mao Tszeduna; Ideino-politicheskaia sushchnost' Maoizma*; A. S. Titov, *Iz istorii bor'by i raskola v rukovodstve KPK 1935-1936 gg.*; L. P. Deliusin, *Spor o sotsializme v Kitae*; A. M. Grigor'ev, *Revoliutsionnoe dvizhenie v Kitae v 1927-1931 gg.*; V. M. Gubaidulin, *Revoliutsionnaia vlast' v osvobozhdennykh raionakh Kitaia (1937-1945 gg.)*.

[44] I. F. Fedorov and V. G. Zubakov, *Chlenstvo v KPK: kak stroilas' partiia "Idei Mao Tszeduna."*

the PRC. Before reviewing their analysis, we should examine how other authors describe the origins of these errors prior to 1949.

Two books by Deliusin on the CCP in the 1920s point to problems that would remain in later decades. He notes the absence of a scientific understanding of socioeconomic conditions, the tendency to overlook the complex character of class relations, and the lack of action by the intelligentsia and the party in gradually transforming the thinking of the peasant masses and creating democratic organs of authority in the village. Deliusin depicts the impatience of radical elements of the petty bourgeoisie who formed the first nucleus of the CCP. They were in such a hurry for the proletariat to seize power that they counted on establishing a dictatorship of the proletariat without the active participation of the working class itself. Deliusin describes the arrogance of party leaders, who slighted two essential forces in the building of a truly socialist society—the informed understanding of nationally specific conditions by intellectuals who could carefully analyze social structure, and the democratic participation of the masses through organizations that genuinely promoted active involvement. From the beginning the Chinese Communist Party did not attach sufficient importance to these "healthy" and fundamental forces in the building of socialism.[45]

A. M. Grigor'ev finds that 1927-1931 was the decisive period in the history of the CCP. In this period the top echelon of the leadership changed, as did the basic social composition of the party. The CCP became largely a party of peasants. Groups of cadres formed, which would continue to vie in intraparty struggles for the next half-century.[46] Apart from these observations, Grigor'ev says little about the structure and membership of the party, nor do

[45] L. P. Deliusin, *Agrarno-krest'ianskii vopros v politike KPK*, pp. 5, 444, and *Spor o sotsializme v Kitae*, p. 138.
[46] A. M. Grigor'ev, *Revoliutsionnoe dvizhenie v Kitae 1927-1931 gg.*, p. 4.

the other Soviet authors who write about the power struggles and policies in the history of the CCP.

Fedorov and Zubakov begin to fill the void in analyses of party structure in their explanations of how the leaders of the CCP departed from the principles of party building attributed (along with many other Soviet assertions about the proper socialist policies) to V. I. Lenin. They argue that, especially in conditions of mass illiteracy and nationalist remnants of petty-bourgeois and feudal ideology, strict centralism and discipline in the party are needed. Under these circumstances, great care must be taken in building the party. "The experience of the CPSU, for example, shows that it never tried to force an increase in its ranks at the expense of quality, that at each step of its development it selected the best representatives of the working class, who devoted themselves to serving the revolution, the business of building socialism and communism." The Chinese communists faced the key question of party formation on a nation-wide scale beginning in May 1949 with 3.3 million members, 61 percent of whom were illiterate and more than 13 percent scarcely literate. Only 3 percent were workers; most were poor and middle peasants, petty-bourgeois intellectuals, or children of well-to-do landlords and bourgeoisie opposed to the Kuomintang. Among party cadres less than one-half percent were workers. The authors argue that this composition was avoidable and, in any case, it should have been quickly transformed once the PRC was established. It resulted from Mao's division of society into classes based on property rather than on relationship to the means of production.[47] An erroneous understanding of social classes led to serious mistakes in recruitment.

By 1956 the CCP had 10,730,000 members. Many young members, according to Fedorov and Zubakov, lacked a general education and were weakly prepared theoretically and politically. Although the percentage of workers was rising

[47] I. F. Fedorov and V. G. Zubakov, *Chlenstvo v KPK: kak stroilas' partiia "Idei Mao Tszeduna,"* pp. 4, 9, 11-12.

and the new recruits were revolutionary enthusiasts, there was insufficient attention to the class affiliations, moral qualities, and ideological convictions of the new members. Large numbers entered hastily in the course of competitions among units for the greatest enrollments. Despite these criticisms of the CCP, the authors conclude that the main questions of party building were correctly resolved in this period. Many correct conclusions were drawn at the Eighth Party Congress in 1956 on the need to reform the party, to combat conceit and intolerance of criticism, to clean out the ballast of those who had wormed themselves in for fame and position. Fedorov and Zubakov also write approvingly of the call to drive counterrevolutionaries from the CCP, although they note with concern that the congress did not condemn the Maoist campaign methods of 1942-1945 or call for caution in repeating the experience of a mass purge.[48]

This Soviet examination of the CCP insists that over several decades, apart from an interlude in the 1950s when there was some improvement, the wrong people were recruited into the party and that the healthy forces were driven out. Above all, Mao and his supporters enrolled activists from political campaigns, especially inexperienced youth. The main criterion for admission was personal devotion to Mao, an approach that became especially widespread in the mass recruitment of new members from 1969. To speed up the process, it was decided no longer to require a waiting period as a candidate member prior to full party membership. This hasty recruitment was one factor that contributed to lower standards. The door was opened wide for petty-bourgeois elements. Indeed, Fedorov and Zubakov argue that among the leaders in the Central Committee of the CCP there was a large group from the middle and upper nonworking strata of society and few from workers' and peasants' families. As a result, party members were easily subjected to the influence of bourgeois ideology. In

48 Ibid., pp. 14, 18-21, 23-24.

the period of party restoration of 1969-1973, recruits were mainly peasants, employees, soldiers, Red Guards, activists of the Cultural Revolution, or young workers below the age of 25. At the insistence of Mao's wife, Jiang Jing, women entered in larger numbers than before, but this was because she counted on her authority among them. Few members of national minorities were admitted and few intellectuals. Party members were not interested in studying or reading. They sought to live in luxury at the expense of the state, separated from the masses, fighting with each other for higher posts. They were motivated by personal interests and caught up in factional intrigues.[49]

Fedorov and Zubakov give a good deal of attention to unnecessary repressive measures within the CCP. They make clear that purges are justified in Marxist-Leninist parties and insist that the purges of the 1920s and 1930s in the CPSU, with the victory of socialism, were necessary. Yet, they argue that the purges in China were different. Peng Dehuai had underlined the perniciousness of the cult of personality and the serious problem of democracy in the lower party organizations. Following the repression of Peng in 1959, mass persecution descended upon the lower party cells. Mao tolerated not even the slightest opposition, especially by those who spoke out against the cult of personality or the repeated violation of party norms. In 1963-1965 the creative intelligentsia in the party was purged. During the Cultural Revolution Red Guards dealt sadistically with party leaders and members; more than three-quarters of the Central Committee, almost two-thirds of its Politburo, and almost all members of the Secretariat were repressed. A significant portion of the cadres in the CCP were driven out by the Maoists; only the party organizations in the army continued to function. In 1969 a new party began to form under the former name of the Communist Party of China. Blind obedience to the party replaced the principle of democratic centralism. The rights of party members were sharply curtailed. Even the right to elect delegates to congresses was lost; delegates were designated from above. Maoists "politically and physically destroyed, creating an atmosphere of tension and distrust in the party."[50] Democracy and intellectual creativity in the CCP were eliminated.

The Soviets also describe the role of mass murders in the history of the CCP. Mao's rise to power was made possible when as many as 400,000 communists perished between 1927 and 1935, especially members of the working class including the flower of the party. Not all were lost to revolutionary struggle; some died from blows struck within the party at Mao's hand. During the Cultural Revolution 5 million communists suffered death or incapacitation. The Soviets cite as evidence an article in *Renmin Ribao* of September 4, 1979, that in Inner Mongolia in the Cultural Revolution only as a result of three fabricated matters "up to 100,000 cadres of Mongol and Chinese nationalities suffered, there were maimed and killed tens of thousands of people." Other statistics are presented on large-scale murder and many cruel forms of discipline against party members, especially of the independent thinkers. Fedorov and Zubakov present a grim picture of terror and oppression of cadres and within party circles, of a party manipulated from above and not involved in decision making from below.[51]

While not focusing directly on the communist party, L. M. Gudoshnikov writes about the political system in the PRC and proposes a number of generalizations. He calls it: 1) a regime of personal authority, which is at the heart of the military-bureaucratic dictatorship; and 2) a country in which there is a strong military presence within the party and administrative apparatus. Noting the reestablishment of party committees beginning in 1969-1970, Gudoshnikov claims that they "did not weaken the military influence in

[50] Ibid., pp. 27, 30, 32-33, 37, 63.
[51] Ibid., pp. 49, 65.

the political mechanism of the country, but rather strengthened it." The army maintained the leading role. Gudoshnikov finds also: 3) a merging of the apparatus of the party
and administrative organs; 4) the absence of popular representation and the refusal to form organs of power and
other leading organs by means of elections; 5) a merging
into single institutions the organs of the court, the procu-
racy, and public security; and 6) the absence of active, mass
public organizations. Reviewing the evidence on concentration camps, Gudoshnikov claims that forced labor was
widespread and that, in Guangdong province alone, there
were a million prisoners in various forms of concentration
camps on the eve of the Cultural Revolution.[52]

THE POST-MAO ERA

Running through Soviet writings is the theme that China
has been poorly managed. The people in charge, whatever
their organizational identification, have lacked competence
and respect for democratic procedures. To what extent,
then, according to these sources, did the management of
the society improve in the years immediately following Mao
Zedong's death?

A book by V. N. Remyga answers that question for the
industrial sector. It concludes that management remains
inadequate even though the Beijing leadership is trying to
avoid serious problems by reducing the use of administrative means in favor of material incentives and "economic"
means. In the early 1980s the system still relies on the
forced development of industry under central control largely
at the expense of the local sector. The military sector claims
so many resources that it leads to losses elsewhere and
"blocks the development of productive forces. . . . The system of management of industry . . . acquires an antinational
antisocialist direction." Firms still lack independent control,

[52] L. M. Gudoshnikov, *Politicheskii mekhanizm Kitaiskoi Narodnoi Respubliki*, pp. 189-92, 165.

e.g. over hiring and firing their labor force, although recent steps move in that direction. Perhaps because of the similarities of the planning process in the USSR and the PRC, Remyga's detailed analysis of the intricacies of the process and its ineffective elements appears well-informed. Evidence is presented about new procedures to elect lower cadres in the PRC, although the author criticizes the process as narrowly formal. In other words, the elections do not constitute real representation. The author mentions that among other reforms in 1979 courses on managing enterprises were set up. Nevertheless Remyga's main conclusion reaffirms that the system continues to be oriented to "maximally concentrating material and financial resources in the hands of the state for further intensification of the military-economic potential of the country."[53]

The conclusions in Soviet writings on recent changes in the CCP are no more optimistic. Fedorov and Zubakov insist that, after Mao's death, policies concerning the party remained Maoist, both the spirit of Maoism and the measures for staffing the party. The methods of the purge of the Gang of Four were, as before, Maoist rather than a democratic or a careful approach. The party membership has not really changed much despite proposals to the contrary and despite regulations reintroducing a stage of candidacy to the party, demanding tightened discipline, and insisting on collective leadership. Purges and repression have continued and widened. Party members are guilty of seeking personal gain and of ignoring the masses. Many act out of personal animosities; they are seeking revenge. The party remains about 70 percent peasants and only 7 percent workers.[54] Few among the cadres have much education or specialization. In the CCP there is widespread dissatisfaction and anarchism. This Soviet view gives no hint that a different kind of party may be emerging.

[53] V. N. Remyga, *Sistema upravleniia promyshlennost'iu KNR (1949-1980)*, pp. 123, 147-48.

[54] Fedorov and Zubakov, *Chlenstvo v KPK: kak stroilas' partiia "Idei Mao Tszeduna,"* pp. 68-89, 98.

The Soviet yearbooks on China for 1978 and 1979 also take a glum view of changes in the CCP. G. A. Stepanova stresses the persistence of Maoism within the party despite certain correctives. She describes for 1978 the purges and the campaign for rehabilitation, both of which involved large numbers of people. She notes the unfortunate persistence of joint leadership posts in the party and the provincial administrative apparatus. Divisions in the leadership reached down among party members. Stepanova argues, "For many cadre workers the CCP is characterized by fright, fear of committing a blunder, indecisiveness." The result is passivity and a lack of initiative. Acknowledging changes at the Third Plenum in late 1978, she nonetheless concludes, "these measures cannot bring a recovery of health to party life."[55] A year later Stepanova found that the principle of collective leadership was being ignored in major decisions and that, amid intraparty strife and sharp turnabouts in approach at the top, many cadres were in a state of disorientation and passivity and preferred to temporize.[56] The problems were so serious that questions of party organization and discipline remained on the pages of the press throughout the year. Although for the first time since the Cultural Revolution party and administrative function began to be separated, party and military commissar posts continued to be combined.

At the Twenty-sixth Congress of the CPSU in 1981, Leonid I. Brezhnev acknowledged that change was occurring in the internal policies of China. He added that time would tell what the true meaning of these changes would be, and to what extent the current leadership was succeeding in overcoming the Maoist legacy.[57] This limited recognition of movement away from Maoism was soon followed by

---

[55] *Kitaiskaia Narodnaia Respublika 1978*, pp. 44, 47.

[56] *Kitaiskaia Narodnaia Respublika 1979*, p. 45.

[57] "Iz doklada general'nogo sekretaria TsK KPSS tovarishcha L. I. Brezhneva 'Otchet tsentral'nogo komiteta KPSS XXVI s'ezdu Kommunisticheskoi Partii Sovetskogo Soiuza i ocherednye zadachi partii v oblasti vnutrennei i vneshnei politiki,' " *Opasnyi kurs* 11, p. 3.

improved bilateral relations, as leaders of China and the Soviet Union proceeded toward the negotiations that were announced in September 1982. In this environment, a widening split could be noticed between a dominant group of Sinologists who continued to insist that Maoism without Mao persisted in the People's Republic and a number of small groups who in one way or another disagreed.[58]

Even the dominant group, centered in the Institute of the Far East and reflected in its journal, *Problemy Dal'nego Vostoka*, began to show greater recognition of the considerable change taking place in China. An article in that journal in spring 1982 acknowledged that over the previous five to six years not a few changes had occurred: constitutional organs of power and management were restored, mass organizations had become formally active, the democratic parties had again come alive; a system of direct elections had been introduced in state organs at the county level, for the first time in the history of the PRC legal codes had been adopted, and Maoist repressions had been condemned. But, the article continues, China had turned sharply to the right, falling back from positions already occupied by socialism. This could be seen not only in economic measures and foreign policy but also in the political structure. The authors argue that attempts have failed to lead the party out of its serious ideological and organizational crisis and that "democratization" has mostly the character of a façade. Cadres sabotage the decisions of the center. They abuse power, are corrupt, and serve divisive local, factional, and group interests.[59]

An article in the previous issue of the same journal (translated by the Soviets as *Far Eastern Affairs*) had put the case for continuity more strongly, insisting, "It is already clear that the Chinese leaders, generally retaining the positions of Maoism, are clinging in every way to the Maoist prin-

[58] Rozman, "Moscow's China-watchers in the Post-Mao Era."

[59] V. Ia. Matiaev and V. P. Fetov, "Kitai: nekotorye aspekty vnutrennego razvitiia," pp. 39, 40-41, 45.

ciples on the concrete questions of party construction and ideological and political work." The article also criticizes China's new leaders for rehabilitating from November 1978 bourgeois elements who had been labeled rightists for their plans in the 1950s to make a right-wing turn in China's development. It calls this "an act of loyalty toward the Chinese bourgeoisie on the part of the Deng Xiaoping grouping" committed, in all likelihood, "in order to win the favor of the overseas partner in the military-political alliance then taking shape."[60] According to this view, neither the purges nor the rehabilitation of recent years were directed at restoring justice. Rather they were meant to stabilize and unite China while subordinating the apparatus to the leadership's ends of turning China into a mighty military power.

Elsewhere in Soviet writings the difficulties of forging a competent and dedicated corps of leaders in China are attributed largely to the legacy of Maoism rather than to the mistakes of Deng Xiaoping and his supporters. Holdovers from the Maoist era remain in positions of power, enabling them to stand in the way of genuine reform. E. S. Kul'pin repeats the remarks of a provincial first secretary that many cadres received without enthusiasm measures introduced by the new leadership. Cadres responded to policy changes by waging a struggle for power in the village and against reduction in their privileges. She concludes that, as the authorities began to carry out measures to limit the power of the cadres in 1978-1979, the latter did not want to become mere officials executing the will of the state and struggled to maintain their exploitation of the peasants and unlimited power.[61] This approach holds that the primary problem is how a new leadership intent on reform can rein in abuses by millions of officials and cadres. The legacy of the cult of personality and political terror cannot be easily eradicated.

[60] K. Yegorov, "The Policy of Rehabilitation of Cadres and Certain Aspects of the Political Struggle in China," *Far Eastern Affairs* 1982:1, pp. 87, 96.

[61] *Rabochii klass v sotsial'no-politicheskoi sisteme KNR*, pp. 120, 126.

Appearing in April 1982, in the popular journal, *Novyi Mir*, an article by Fedor Burlatsky presented the strongest case yet in the Soviet Union for the difficulty of overcoming an entrenched legacy of repression in China. Entitled, "The Interregnum, or a Chronicle of the Times of Deng Xiaoping," this article describes the "transition of the country to legality and order, the end of the customs of preceding epochs, when hundreds of thousands of people without trial and investigation were subjected to slaughter, persecution, physical destruction." Burlatsky finds that China is still far from realizing the elementary norms of justice, that to turn back a quarter-century to a system which once existed is "extremely complicated by the deep deformation of the entire political and public life, of customs and human relations, of the social psychology in conditions of the regime of the personal authority of Mao Zedong." He refers to the "widest dissemination through society of immorality, inhumanity, falsehood, and dishonor, in other words, the breakdown of the socio-psychological foundations, on which the entire public edifice is held up."[62]

Burlatsky directly examines the situation of the 39 million members of the CCP. He observes that two-fifths of them are cadres or army officers and most of the others have public responsibilities in unions, cooperatives, etc. Thus "the party practically coincides with the governing stratum—the ganbu. Precisely in the hands of this stratum is found power and political influence in the entire country." It is the party and state apparatus that Burlatsky finds most affected by moral spoilage. Drawing on a document of the Fifth Plenum of the Central Committee of the CCP in February 1980, he lists the vices found among party members who have become officials: 1) they turn into lords who only take care of their own gain; 2) they conduct affairs without investigating questions; 3) they engage in petty tyranny, humiliating people; 4) they are duplicitous; 5) they per-

---

[62] Fedor Burlatsky, "Mezhdutsarstvie, ili khronika vremen Den Siaopina," *Novyi Mir* 1982:4, pp. 206, 215.

secute and take vengeance on critics; 6) they engage in factionalism, interfering with the conduct of the party's political line; 7) they do not oppose people and actions inciting counterrevolutionary activity; 8) they fawn on and connive with political enemies; 9) when they commit errors, they cover them up rather than acknowledging them; 10) without principle, they swim with the tide; 11) they divulge secrets; 12) they chase after privileges; 13) they breed familism, arbitrarily responding to party decisions. The most serious of these failings Burlatsky finds to be lies and falsehoods that are the norm of political life and have penetrated into all pores of Chinese society. He adds that the ganbu in many ways remind one of the mandarins and bureaucrats of old China. As to the future, he considers the party and state apparatus oriented to their self-preservation, not toward a return to socialist principles. Reforms will inevitably continue to encounter the opposition of the vast stratum of ganbu. The vices of the system are no longer tied to the activities of particular individuals occupying the leadership; the system is at fault because socialist principles have been deformed. While recognizing that many recent reforms can somewhat improve the economy, Burlatsky insists that different reforms are required to restore culture, civilization, humanity, and morality.[63] Clearly the competence of the cadres is essential to overcoming decades of deterioration in these fundamental respects.

CONCLUSIONS

While the previous three chapters have treated the victims of Maoism, this chapter examines groups whose position is more ambiguous. Because of the intense suspicions of top leaders and internecine struggles among factions, those who have been the primary beneficiaries of the social order created in the PRC have also numbered among its most

[63] Ibid., p. 216-17, 218, 220, 227.

brutalized victims. Turnover in many leadership posts has been great, but the successors have not been distinguished by either competence or dedication to principle. In the 1980s the existing officials in party, army, and administrative posts are largely a legacy of past mistakes in recruitment, training, and organizational methods. They cannot do an adequate job of leading the country out of the morass in which it has long been mired.

This general Soviet consensus breaks down when questions of how officials should operate are phrased in specific terms. Essentially two points of view can be detected. On the one side are those who stress the dangers of a swing to the right. These writers are fearful of an expanded role for the national bourgeoisie and call for greater centralization and discipline in the party. On the other side are those who argue that, in effect, the process of de-Maoization is being delayed and may be derailed by the deeply rooted legacy of nondemocratic procedures. The ruling stratum is reluctant to give up its prerogatives. Experts are not being given an adequate voice in running the country. It takes little imagination to identify the obvious parallels between these two viewpoints on China and the differences visible on the internal matter of de-Stalinization and continued reform of the Soviet system.

The alternative Soviet perceptions of what is wrong in China are reminiscent of what Soviets refer to as the "fantasies of bourgeois Sovietologists," for example Robert Sharlet, concerning the existence of two opposing and contending groups in the USSR.[64] One group is the "school of state's rights," consisting of dogmatists in favor of state interference in all matters. The other group is the "school of constitutional rights," who support freedom of the individual and limitations on state power over citizens. The official critics of Sovietology deny the existence of these groups, but in Soviet writings on China there is evidence

[64] A. I. Luk'ianov, G. I. Denisov, E. L. Kuz'min, and N. N. Razumovich, *Sovetskaia konstitutsiia i mify sovetologov*, p. 14.

of divergent views about socialism that roughly correspond to these perspectives.

While accusing bourgeois observers of being unwilling to recognize that socialism moves on a rising line, Soviets are guilty of belittling the gains in China since 1976. Soviets accuse Sovietologists of imagining that the population of the USSR is passive about constitutional changes depicted by Westerners as no more than a new appearance of Soviet totalitarianism but asserted to be significant advances. Yet at the same time Soviets view the Chinese as passive and undeceived by constitutional cosmetics of a persistent repressive order. And while some Soviet spokesmen challenge Westerners who contend that the 1977 Soviet Constitution does not guarantee individual rights or protect the individual from the state, others criticize the Chinese reforms in the post-Mao era for not substantially correcting the horrendous record on human rights of the PRC.[65] Even if one relies on Soviet reports of Western criticisms of their political system and the officials who serve it, there is no difficulty in finding many parallels to Soviet commentaries on China.

Western criticisms of both the Soviet Union and China point to at least three basic elements in relations between the elite in charge and the masses they govern: 1) the threat of arbitrary punishment; 2) the possibility of an abrupt change of living conditions for large groups or even the majority of the population; and 3) the search for protection and sponsorship. The first of these refers to the ability of officials to penalize or even arrest those individuals, or entire categories of people, whom they oppose. Because so many of the opportunities and benefits of socialist society such as housing, schooling, and work are made available through state agencies, officials have wide-ranging possibilities for punishing those who cross them. The second criticism focuses on the power of high officials to change basic policies including the conditions of work or leisure.

[65] Ibid., pp. 19, 35, 120-22.

Because the terms of access to material resources are largely a matter of central regulation, the rules that govern their use or distribution may change suddenly, which can alter the life circumstances of vast numbers of people. Finally, critics of conditions characterized by uncertainty and fear point to the response of many individuals, in search of protection or gain, who try to form and to take advantage of personal connections. We found in this chapter that these Western critiques are largely shared by Soviets writing about Chinese officials.

Two seemingly contradictory impressions of the organizational status of officials can be gleaned from these critical views of a communist-led society. On the one hand, the officials are bureaucrats working within large-scale, centralized organizations. With few exceptions, they have no voice in the main decisions of their organizations. On the other hand, many of the officials, although not necessarily those at low levels, have ample opportunity to find leeway for favoritism in their own areas of responsibility. Thus they may turn into petty despots in their relations with ordinary citizens, able to exploit them individually and as a class. Impersonal bureaucracy and petty tyranny march hand in hand. This is what Burlatsky and others appear to be saying.

How is the Soviet worldview modified by the debate about officials in China? First, there is the persistent theme that the socialist revolution and the transition to socialism do not signify a full break with tradition, even in the relations between the leadership and the people. The social psychology of the past lives on even within the communist party and must be analyzed by historically informed social scientists. Second, the debate over China exposes the lingering impact of terror and repression. The people do not quickly or easily recover from such measures, and the officials themselves do not simply revert to honest and vigorous methods. Third, by differentiating diverse types of officials, the debate points to the value of sociological analysis of this category as a separate entity in socialist societies.

Fourth, the analysis suggests implicit reforms to reduce the dangers from the state. Kul'pin draws attention to officials who do not defend the people but merely seek to advance their own careers in state service. She implies that ways must be found to represent the interests of the masses, to defend them against the mistakes and abuses of their leaders. The literature on officials in China also takes note of the qualifications of those entrusted with power. Better selection procedures are one means to reduce the likelihood of abuse of power. The orthodox and reform camps give different emphasis to many of these themes. Their consensus may be narrowly limited to a repudiation of grave excesses in China—and, by extension, the worst abuses of Stalinism. On the question of officials the consensus breaks down; there are sharp—perhaps even fundamental—differences of opinion among Soviet writers.

· 6 ·

NATIONAL MINORITIES

From the mid-1960s, when the Sino-Soviet conflict became a dispute over territory and over the consequences of historical imperialism, the situation of minorities along the mutual border came to the forefront. A separate sector was set up at the newly established Institute of the Far East to focus on the minorities in China. The purpose of exposing the mistreatment of the major ethnic minorities in China remained unclear. Were the accusations that the minorities have suffered materially and been subjected to political repression intended to help China's leaders return to the path of socialism? Were they intended to justify military assistance to peoples who were encouraged to break away from the territorial grouping of the People's Republic of China? The intentional ambiguity left Soviet options open while placing some pressure on Chinese leaders that included the possibility of Soviet military involvement.

With the stakes so high and foreign policy so clearly at issue, there was little room among the Soviets for discordant notes on the theme of national minorities. Reform voices remained silent, perhaps in recognition that within Soviet domestic policy discussions the issue was too sensitive to place on the reform agenda. There is some diversity in the Soviet position, but it consists only of an even more extreme statement of harsh criticisms that appear to justify rebellion against Chinese authorities. There is no indication that what is being proposed represents a proposal for change in the Soviet Union toward greater equality of nationalities.

Despite the restricted range of this discussion on the position of minorities, the overall critical stance does repeat, in many respects, criticisms directed from the West against Soviet as well as Chinese policies. It is also a clearer repudiation than anything found in Soviet writings about their own Stalinist period of what may go wrong in a socialist setting. Even in this discussion in which the reform camp takes no part, we find echoes of what the Soviets refer to as anticommunism.

THE LEGACY OF THE PAST

In the introduction to his book *The History of China and the Present*, S. L. Tikhvinsky states, "Among the multiple socioeconomic factors that have made possible the emergence of the antisocialist course of the Peking leadership, not a small role was played by the tradition of old China. The materials in this collection of articles show what an enormous weight of reactionary traditions and chauvinist superstitions was obtained in the legacy of the Chinese People's Republic from the multicentury rule of exploiting classes of slave and feudal China."[1] Tikhvinsky, the only historian of China awarded the high rank of academician in recent decades, chooses as the first selections in this book some of his articles on China's historical international relations and then turns near the end of the book to the topic of "Great Han hegemonism." He addresses such questions as what were the main principles on which Chinese ruling circles built up relations with neighboring peoples and what were the continuities in China's aggressive policies.

Tikhvinsky paints a highly simplified and one-sided picture of Chinese aggression over 2,000 years. He links to the perception of China as the center of the world, the demand for superiority in all international relations and the search for conquests to subject all outsiders. The vocabulary he uses is indicative of the general tone of condemnation. He writes of the Qing empire's "aggressive and great power aspirations," and lumps together Chenghis Khan and Kangxi as "murderous conquerors."[2]

In a more recent introduction, written for the book *China*

[1] S. L. Tikhvinsky, *Istoriia Kitaia i sovremennost'*, p. 9.
[2] Ibid., pp. 28, 31.

and Neighbors: in Modern and Contemporary Times, Tikhvinsky
further develops his viewpoint on the continuities visible
in Chinese history. "Chinese nationalism, which manifested
itself especially perniciously in relations of China with its
neighbors, has a long history; xenophobia and Sinocen-
trism to an equal extent were present in feudal, bourgeois,
petty-bourgeois ideology and utopian peasant socialism in
China. With the aid of Confucian ideology feudal rulers
attempted to enlarge greatly the feeling in the Chinese
people of belonging to a special ethnic community 'selected
by Heaven,' that led to the appearance of false ideas about
the exclusive nature of the Chinese people, its history, culture, place in the world, to conformism in relation to their
own conservative traditions, to open xenophobia. The great
power traditions of ancient and medieval Chinese diplo-
macy left a deep imprint on the subsequent history of relations of China with its neighbors." Moving ahead to the
twentieth century, Tikhvinsky finds that Sinocentrist, great
power ideas were used by Chinese bourgeois revolutionary-
democrats in their attitudes toward neighboring peoples.[3]
In recent decades these traditions are the source of foreign
policies aimed at the Soviet Union and domestic policies
directed at national minorities. In Tikhvinsky's view, which
has not been publicly criticized or even indirectly contradicted by Soviet authors, the Han Chinese pose a danger
to other peoples because of their deeply inculcated worldview. This view is not inconsistent with the statement of
T. R. Rakhimov that Chinese rule over other nationalities
assumes "the most barbarous, savage, inhuman forms."[4]

Historical factors figure into three lines of Soviet criticism
of Chinese dealings with minority peoples. First, writers
point out that many of these peoples are very different
from the Chinese. Rakhimov, a specialist on these minorities, writes, "The non-Chinese peoples inhabiting South
and Southwest China constitute roughly 70 percent of the

[3] *Kitai i sosedi,* pp. 5, 7.
[4] T. R. Rakhimov, *Sud'by nekhanskikh narodov v KNR,* pp. 24-25.

total number of the numerically small peoples of China. With the exception of the Tungkang, they are closely linked with the peoples of Southeast Asia by origin, language and economic and cultural traditions." He adds, "The Chuang, Uighurs, Mongols, Tibetans, and many other peoples differ fundamentally from the Chinese culturally and linguistically." Second, Soviets portray the minority peoples as "having unceasingly fought their oppressors for national freedom and independence." When they were under Chinese control, it was because of conquest through military expansion. From the Chinese, they could expect no more than physical annihilation, forced assimilation, or being driven from the best lands into the deserts or mountains. Rakhimov asserts, "Many hundreds of thousands of Mongols, Tibetans, Uighurs, and other peoples were ruthlessly annihilated in the course of these wars of conquest." The case for Chinese rule over Tibet is also weakened because the administration of that territory even after it was incorporated in 1792 remained "entirely in the hands of the Tibetan government."[5] Third, the nature of historical rule is depicted as exploitative, cruel, and aimed at destroying what was nationally distinctive. The way the Han Chinese conducted themselves is presented in very harsh terms.[6] On the basis of these three factors, there appears to be little justification for Chinese rule over (or federation with) many, if not all, of the minority peoples.

Rakhimov singles out the struggle of the Uighurs in Sinjiang in 1944-1949 as the last major attempt prior to the formation of the PRC to achieve liberation from China's brutal tyranny. He points out that as three districts in Sinjiang were cleared of the Kuomintang, a people's democratic government was set up. The Chinese name of Sinjiang was dropped, and in its place the East Turkestan

---

[5] T. R. Rakhimov, "Great-Hanist Chauvinism Instead of the Leninist Teaching on the National Question," *Leninism and Modern China's Problems*, pp. 99-101.

[6] A. A. Moskalev, *Politika KNR v natsional'no-iazykovom voprose*, pp. 10-11.

Republic was proclaimed.[7] Clearly he regards this effort to create an independent state as justified.

Did Maoism affect Chinese communist relations with ethnic minorities before 1949? The answer Rakhimov gives on the basis of statements at party congresses is no. "In the period from 1921 to 1949 the Communist Party of China acted in accordance with the proletarian stand and principles on the national question and fought to translate these principles into reality. This conformed to the Leninist teaching on the right of nations to self-determination."[8] The non-Han peoples could look forward to setting up national states within a federal republic and even to the right to succession as a means of ensuring a voluntary union. In the programs worked out by the CCP they were guaranteed liberation from tyranny. Elsewhere Rakhimov concludes that Mao's views posed a threat to this position. Already in 1938 Mao's rewording of the rights of nationalities indicates to Rakhimov that he was actually against their right to self-determination although the former position was not openly or directly overturned.[9]

It is worth noting that Soviet accusations against the Chinese and their leaders were echoed in the vitriolic statements from Beijing to the late 1970s about Soviet policies toward minority nationalities. Writings on China seek to refute these charges, accusing the Chinese of conveying ideas from the Western anti-Soviet literature. The notion that the PRC maintained traditional Chinese expansionist aims resembles Beijing's view that the relations between Russia and neighboring peoples were characterized by aggression and conquest. Soviets charge that Maoist authors distort the voluntary entry of Georgia, Armenia, and the peoples of Central Asia and Siberia into the structure of Russia. At the same time as they accuse the Chinese of finding nothing but an unending string of unjust conquests

[7] Rakhimov, "Great-Hanist Chauvinism Instead of the Leninist Teaching on the National Question," p. 100.

[8] Ibid., p. 103.

[9] Rakhimov, *Sud'by nekhanskikh narodov v KNR*, pp. 50-51.

in Russian history, Soviet critics of the PRC present an equally oversimplified view of the continuities in China's aggressive nationalism.

ETHNIC POLICIES: POLITICAL DIMENSIONS

From the beginning of the PRC there were signs of Great Han chauvinism. Rakhimov gives a number of examples visible during the early years. First he accuses China's leaders of deliberately and greatly understating the numerical strength of their minorities, whom he refers to as the "non-Chinese people."[10] He explains that prior to 1949 this population was considered to be about 10 percent of the total in China, but the 1953-1954 census gives a figure of only 6 percent. In the case of the Mongols, the discrepancy is even greater; instead of 5-6 million as the Chinese had formerly written, the official number did not exceed 1.5 million. Rakhimov fails to note how unreliable the precensus estimates of minority numbers have been considered in Chinese studies. He simply asserts that the 1953 understatements were deliberate and part of a policy aimed at forcible assimilation.

Second, Rakhimov identifies a policy of dividing minority areas in order to reduce the autonomy of their populations. Most Tibetans in China live outside the Tibetan Autonomous Region, which itself was set up in 1965, as many as fourteen years after the Chinese had pledged to guarantee Tibetan autonomy. The Zhuang living on opposite sides of a river in Guizhou province have been unjustifiably separated into two nationalities. And in 1954, on the pretext of giving "fraternal assistance" to the Mongolians and uniting all areas with Mongolians into one unit, the Inner Mongolian Autonomous Region was expanded to make the Mongols a minority of no more than 10 percent of the population in their own region. Many nationalities such as

[10] Rakhimov, "Great-Hanist Chauvinism Instead of the Leninist Teaching on the National Question," p. 98.

the Manchurians with well over a million people did not receive autonomy even at the county level.[11] Rakhimov also attaches importance to the use of names. Arguing that the Uighurs, the largest national group in Sinjiang, wanted to rename that area Uighuristan rather than keeping a name associated with Chinese imperial conquests, he asserts that the Chinese disregarded their discontent. Legitimate expressions of national will and independence were rejected. The Chinese assessed these "as a manifestation of bourgeois nationalism, as a separatist movement."[12]

Third, once in power, the Chinese backtracked concerning promises of self-determination. When a speech Mao delivered in 1945 was reissued in his collected works in 1952, Mao deleted phrases in which this right was declared. In the 1954 constitution this right was taken away. Despite other positive provisions, there were no firm guarantees of the rights and freedoms of the non-Han peoples; rights that were simply declared were not observed in practice and the will of these peoples was ignored. In Sinjiang the continued employment of former Kuomintang officials who had committed crimes occurred over the protest of local peoples, and thousands of participants in the national-liberation struggle of 1944-1949 were punished on the basis of false accusations.[13] The Han Chinese predominated in local administrative organs in minority areas and in the course of campaigns behaved coarsely and tyrannically. Many of these mistakes, and others too, were cited at the Eighth Congress in 1956, but that barely began to function as a basis for improvement when in 1957-1958 more serious manifestations of Great Han nationalism became evident.

From the mid-1950s the presumption behind minority policies shifted to the view that the non-Han peoples have no ethnic territories and therefore there is no justification

---

[11] *Kitaiskaia Narodnaia Respublika 1973*, p. 243.

[12] Rakhimov, "Great-Hanist Chauvinism Instead of the Leninist Teaching on the National Question," pp. 105-107.

[13] Rakhimov, *Sud'by nekhanskikh narodov v KNR*, pp. 51-60.

for the right of self-determination.[14] Supported by distorted perceptions of Chinese history, this view holds that from long ago China was a single multinational state. All peoples should be considered Chinese, even, as Tikhvinsky put it, if for a short period during the past 2,000 and more years Chinese troops crossed their territory during the course of some war of conquest.[15] The struggle against "local nationalism" that began in 1957 was a violation of China's constitutional principles. Boundary adjustments, mass resettlements of Han Chinese, and the posting of large army units increased the presence of Chinese in administrative units with a substantial minority presence.[16] In the Great Leap Forward, the Maoists declared that the nationality question was resolved. This paved the way for open discrimination against the non-Han nationalities. Articles openly called for the assimilation of the non-Han peoples.[17]

The Soviet evaluation of the next two decades of Chinese policies fits the familiar picture of two low points in the Great Leap Forward and the Cultural Revolution and two partial corrections in the early 1960s and 1970s. At their nadir, policies sunk to a low of enormous callousness. Rakhimov describes the tragedy of the Great Leap in various ways: discrimination that deprived the nationalities of "elementary human rights"; "Chinese colonialism—this is a system of not only political oppression, but also cultural"; "the extremely heavy burden of compulsory deliveries of grain to the state [which] condemned the non-Han population of the PRC to an existence of semi-starvation"; "a mass purge among the national cadres and their persecution"; and "a program of forced assimilation of the non-Han peoples." Commensurate with the greater and longer lasting suffering of the Cultural Revolution, Rakhimov uses

[14] Ibid., p. 67.
[15] S. L. Tikhvinsky, "Bor'ba s apologetikoi velikokhan'skogo gegemonizma: vazhnaia zadacha istoricheskoi naukoi," *Ak'tual'nye problemy bor'by s maoistskimi fal'sifikatsiiami v oblasti istorii*, p. 96.
[16] Rakhimov, *Sud'by nekhanskikh narodov v KNR*, pp. 69-72.
[17] *Kitaiskaia Narodnaia Respublika 1973*, p. 244.

even stronger language: "The widest strata of the local population were subjected to terror and mass repressions." He sees this as a time when power at all levels was transferred to Chinese soldiers, thus liquidating all national autonomy. The army continued to control all areas of life even after there was some camouflage of the continued forceful Sinification in the 1970s.[18] Having repressed the vast majority of national cadres, China's leadership found that the Han Chinese cadres working in these areas could not function adequately without knowledge of local languages; some of the old cadres were rehabilitated and young activists of the local minorities were recruited, but this was less the restoration of self-government than the establishment of a network of obedient messengers.[19]

In short, after a brief interlude in 1949-1957 of a generally correct course despite repeated mistakes, the next two decades brought policies based largely on force and terror. The minorities were ruled by the Han Chinese, often through the army. Their cadres were readily cast aside and victimized. Their territories were divided to suit the purposes of Han control. In response the minority nationalities rose at times in rebellion or, out of fear of severe and bloody retaliation, found more indirect ways of expressing their discontent. This is the gloomy vision of China's nationality policies found in Soviet sources.

ETHNIC POLICIES: CULTURAL DIMENSIONS

A. A. Moskalev specializes on PRC policies concerning the languages of national minorities. In the absence of Soviet specialists on other areas of local life such as religion and family, Moskalev's writing stands out as the principal investigation of changes in the ways of life of entire nationalities. According to him, a great deal depended on the rapid resolution of language problems—on raising the cul-

---

[18] Rakhimov, *Sud'by nekhanskikh narodov v KNR*, pp. 73-80, 85, 105.
[19] *Kitaiskaia Narodnaia Respublika 1973*, pp. 245-46.

tural level of the non-Han peoples and enlisting them in economic development.[20] This was a key to success in building harmonious relations and in achieving a cultural transformation vital to socialism.

Instead of harmonious relations, however, China's leaders sought control and dominance. They resorted to many methods that affected language use. Moskalev discusses mass migrations, including forced resettlement of minority peoples, as a strategy of assimilation.

During the first years of the PRC, legal provisions contained much that favored the free development of nationality languages and the granting of equality to them. Nevertheless, Moskalev indicates, the statutes lacked firm guarantees of rights and freedoms; the statements had a predominantly declarative character without adequate assurance that they would be enforced. Furthermore there were few specialists and little information on which to base policies. In addition, there were leaders and workers in this area who did not respect the decisions that had been taken and made it difficult to implement them. The problems, thus, were legal, scholarly, and political and were exacerbated by inadequate personnel policies. In 1954, on nationalistic grounds, Mao rejected the specialists' suggestions to use Latin or Cyrillic for establishing a phonetic alphabet for languages that lacked a written script, an act Moskalev points to as one factor that delayed progress in this area. At the same time, he concludes, the Soviet experience and Soviet advisers, especially T. R. Rakhimov, were extending great help to the Chinese.[21]

Whereas the slow pace of advance in the language situation was the primary characteristic of the years 1949-1956 and was correctly recognized in 1956 as requiring serious attention, the following period saw the generally positive

[20] A. A. Moskalev, *Politika KNR v natsional'no-iazykovom voprose*, and "O politike v natsional'no-iazykovom voprose," *Problemy Dal'nego Vostoka* 1978:3, pp. 135-42.

[21] Moskalev, *Politika KNR v natsional'no-iazykovom voprose*, pp. 48-49, 53-57, 79.

tendencies of these early years replaced by more negative trends. There was a transition in Beijing's language policies to blatantly coercive methods. Texts failed even to cite the principle of volunteerism as the basis for nationality relations and decisions were made at meetings to which representatives of non-Han nationalities were not even invited. Language policies were now dictated with little else in mind apart from the aim of accelerating Sinification. For instance, in the spring of 1958 at the second conference on nationality languages the Maoists insisted that the only way to supplement the vocabulary of these languages was with Chinese words and terms. During and after the antirightist campaign of 1957-1958, they attacked the defenders of the "purity" of nationality languages as "rightist elements" and "local nationalists." In the process, contacts of any sort with peoples outside the PRC, even the ties between Mongols in Inner Mongolia and those in the Mongolian People's Republic, were attacked. The Chinese closed their national minorities off to the outside world as part of their strategy of Sinification.[22]

The Great Leap Forward brought new justifications for not creating written languages for small nationalities and for replacing the languages of some others with Chinese script. Moskalev argues that nationalities were forced to give up their written languages and were left without any written form. This process of liquidating scripts continued in the Cultural Revolution, with destructive consequences for education and culture in general. There was even an attempt to force all peoples to adopt the language and script of Beijing, using the justification that all China was approaching communism. Although correctives to the extreme policies of the Great Leap Forward were introduced in the early 1960s, Moskalev states, the approach based on coercive methods, distrust of scholarship, and the spreading of the Chinese language continued.[23]

[22] Ibid., pp. 98-99, 104-105.
[23] Ibid., pp. 109, 126-27.

Moskalev contrasts the real cultural revolution in the USSR, which in a short time during the late 1920s and early 1930s resolved the complex problem of creating scripts for many peoples, with the so-called Cultural Revolution in China, which made illegal the scripts of non-Han peoples and sharply reduced the spheres in which their languages functioned.[24] Maoists insisted that there no longer was a nationality question and that to argue that the separate interests of non-Han nationalities must be recognized was a rightist deviation. In this light, the use of separate languages was construed as harmful to unity. The Institutes of Nationalities and schools to prepare minority cadres and teachers were closed. In these years Maoists even systematically destroyed books and manuscripts in national languages. Great works perished in fires or were turned into pulp as a result of what Moskalev calls these barbarian policies.

Attributing improvements in the situation of minority languages to tactical factors in the early 1970s, especially to an awareness of the need for cadres of local nationality, Moskalev considers the general approach to the problem in China as in essence unchanged.[25] By the mid-1970s there was some tolerance for a narrow circle of languages, but Chinese was forcibly imposed as the language of instruction in schools. The 1975 Constitution of the PRC maintained the discriminatory character of language policies.

Other areas of minority culture were subjected to similar onslaughts, according to Soviet sources. "In the 1970s Maoists continued to adhere to the course of actual liquidation of the national culture of non-Han peoples." The Maoists destroyed vast numbers of monuments and art. They "forced marriages between local inhabitants and Chinese (resettlers and soldiers)."[26] In Tibet the Red Guards broke into homes

---

[24] Ibid., pp. 128-29.
[25] Ibid., pp. 134-40.
[26] Rakhimov, *Sud'by nekhanskikh narodov v KNR*, p. 100, and "Great-Hanist Chauvinism Instead of the Leninist Teaching on the National Question," p. 109.

and forced the local population to give up their national clothes, religious objects, etc., and to cut their hair short. In Sinjiang, they required native peoples to eat pork and cremate their dead.[27] Although the destruction of religious buildings and the repression of religion are mentioned in passing, Soviet sources give little detail in these areas. They apparently avoid topics where Soviet policies might appear similarly culpable, and concentrate on the area of language, in which some parallels are likely to be overlooked in the face of the far more extreme measures adopted in China.

ETHNIC POLICIES: ECONOMIC DIMENSIONS

In the first years of the PRC, land reform and the socialist transformation of agriculture and commerce occurred more slowly in many areas inhabited by national minorities. Some Soviet sources merely acknowledge this divergence or suggest that it was a realistic response to different conditions in each region. However, L. M. Gudoshnikov of the Institute of the Far East offers another interpretation. He notes that land reform left almost untouched the property of religious institutions apart from their land and that in livestock regions occupied by national minorities care was taken not to damage relations with feudal elites. As a result of this inaction the social effects of the revolution were unequal for the Han Chinese and the majority of "non-Chinese" people, which, according to Gudoshnikov, led to a perception that the nationality question remained unresolved.[28] He appears to regard this moderation as a mistake, perhaps suggesting that he is little concerned with the voluntary participation of these peoples.

Gudoshnikov mentions other factors as having had negative economic consequences in later years, such as: 1) the transfer of many of the best lands to "Chinese" migrants;

[27] L. M. Gudoshnikov, "Velikoderzhavnyi shovinizm rukovodstva KNR v voprosakh natsional'no-gosudarstvennogo stroitel'stva," *Opasnyi kurs* 5, pp. 243-44.

[28] Ibid., pp. 234-35.

2) the establishment of communes with virtually one aim: to extract the maximum product in order to supply Chinese soldiers stationed in the area as well as to supply the cities settled mainly by Chinese; and 3) the repression within each minority of the national intelligentsia, almost all of whom passed through reeducation labor camps in the late 1950s and early 1960s.[29] In the 1960s and 1970s the economies of the nationality regions are depicted as backward extremes of China, receiving little assistance for economic growth apart from that necessary to strengthen the areas as military bases. They were denied even the minimal assistance they had been granted in the first years of the PRC. The economies of these areas served as a source of supplies for the Chinese soldiers based there.[30] They were obliged to grow mainly grain even if the result seriously damaged their rural economies. Under these conditions the non-Han peoples often sabotaged enterprises and communes; trains and motor transport were accompanied by armed escorts.[31]

The 1976 yearbook of the PRC presents information on the state of the economy and its leadership around the time of Mao's death. The authors of this section, Rakhimov and V. A. Bogoslovskii, expose Chinese press reports that cadres of local nationalities number more than 65 percent of the total in the Sinjiang-Uighur Autonomous Region and 61 percent in Tibet. The authors regard these figures as distortions because local cadres are primarily in charge of low-level units; at higher levels the representation of non-Han peoples falls sharply, and in the military command stationed there, they are practically absent.[32] The economy continued to receive little financial aid from the state, but considerable money was spent on building highways, many of which had military significance. Agriculture could not meet the needs of the local population, the soldiers, and the arriving migrants. In this yearbook and other Soviet

[29] Ibid., p. 240.
[30] *Kitaiskaia Narodnaia Respublika 1973*, p. 248.
[31] *Kitaiskaia Narodnaia Respublika 1974*, p. 48.
[32] *Kitaiskaia Narodnaia Respublika 1976*, p. 74.

sources there is unmitigated criticism of the economic failures of the PRC in regions identified with non-Han populations.

THE CASE OF TIBET

A book on Tibet by V. A. Bogoslovskii appeared in 1978. It was published under the general editorship of Sladkovsky and its responsible editor—each Soviet monograph has in addition to the author a person who takes responsibility—was Rakhimov. Along with Rakhimov and Moskalev, Bogoslovskii works at the Institute of the Far East studying ethnic minorities in the PRC. Centered on one minority, his views reiterate the principal Soviet criticisms of China's policies.

Bogoslovskii points out the historical distinctiveness of the Tibetan people. They had long-standing, stable political institutions and a long history of an independent state. Tibet differed greatly from China in religion and socioeconomic development, and Chinese civilization had exerted no real influence on Tibet. Bogoslovskii finds it unusual that there was so little evidence of class antagonism both before 1949 and through the 1950s. He relates this to the stagnation and isolation of Tibetan society, the sharply and clearly differentiated position of classes, and various aspects of the role of Buddhism.[33] Criticizing Chinese writings on the history of Sino-Tibetan relations, Bogoslovskii finds the Tibetans hostile to Chinese administration and unwilling to cede any of their independence. Not until the invasion of the PLA did Tibetans agree to negotiate with Beijing in 1951 and to sign a document giving up their autonomy.

Once established in Tibet, the Chinese consistently sought to increase their control and the means—especially transportation and troops—to project it. During 1951-1959, the Chinese generally maintained a united front policy of ac-

[33] Bogoslovskii, *Tibetskii raion KNR*, pp. 15, 13-14.

cepting a continued role for the Tibetan upper classes. Some early steps were taken under Chinese military authority to develop industry, agriculture, education, and health care, but China's main concern was to change Tibet's administrative system. Unsuccessful in repeated efforts to integrate Tibet through new administrative organs, the PRC leadership also failed to win over the Tibetan masses. When Chinese authorities in the mid and late 1950s made some attempts to isolate the Tibetan upper classes without abandoning the united front altogether, the Chinese failed to comprehend the actual state of social relations, the persistent influence of religion, and the fact that "their actions appeared in the eyes of the Tibetans as encroachments by atheistic-outsiders on ancient national traditions and sanctified religions."[34] Erring in their policies to split Tibet into opposing social classes, the Chinese inadvertently promoted an interclass consolidation which prompted anti-Chinese attitudes to spread deeply among the lower classes. Following the March 1959 uprising that was brutally suppressed, the military control of the PLA became secure throughout Tibet. This made it possible for the Beijing leadership to impose the changes in society it desired without waiting longer for Tibetan consent.

From 1959 to 1965 the old theocratic system of administration in Tibet was ended. Large numbers of former personal servants and monks were returned to their native villages, which created a problem because these people were unprepared to farm, especially to open up new lands in the harsh environment of Tibet. The increase in the size of the army in Tibet due to the 1959 uprising and to border conflicts with India placed added burdens on agricultural output. Before the land reform had been completed, collectivization was already being carried out in 1960. This hasty course failed, and the methods by which it was conducted, especially the seizure of land only recently promised to the peasants, provoked intense dissatisfaction. Des-

[34] Ibid., p. 73.

perate agricultural conditions required modifications in policy, which came in 1961, but the food situation remained serious. The system was geared to the extraction of the maximum resources to meet the needs of the Chinese army stationed in Tibet and to secure Beijing's control. "The reforms were carried out from above, by Chinese authorities, in conditions of mass repression and destruction of the traditional institutions of Tibetan society." Bogoslovskii even argues that no matter how justifiable the abrupt methods of 1959 against the monasteries, which had supported the uprising, the repression touched almost every family and seriously aggravated the situation in Tibet. Recognizing the progressive nature of confiscating church land and ending the political role of religious institutions, he nevertheless sees the reform of administration and the agrarian reform as having been directed above all at liquidating all forces (even potential ones) who could give voice to nationalist demands; i.e. mass repression had gone too far, and reform was accomplished by coercive means.[35] In short, the reforms were imposed and their timing was bad; they made enemies even of those Tibetan people who had not previously been so antagonistic to the Chinese.

Bogoslovskii's book continues the story of the Chinese oppression of Tibet up to 1976. He does not overlook the measures taken from 1959 to 1965 to develop industry and trade and especially education. But he finds the new system of education "deformed" by Chinese nationalist policies, which did not allow the history and literature of the Tibetan people to be taught. At this time the forced Sinification of the Tibetan language also began.[36] These manifestations of Great Han tendencies caused additional dissatisfaction among the Tibetans.

The Cultural Revolution in Tibet liquidated the remaining elements of the autonomy of the native population. Native cadres were repressed. Constitutional organs of power were disbanded. All power both factually and formally was

[35] Ibid., pp. 100-102, 106, 107-15.
[36] Ibid., pp. 130-31.

in the hands of the army, the establishment of revolutionary committees having formalized military authority. Few Tibetans were even included. The Cultural Revolution also brought communes to Tibet, with a barracks form of organization of labor and daily life. The position of the Tibetans declined further as soldiers came into the villages at harvest time to confiscate most of the output, leaving many of the peasants to eat roots and to die of hunger. The Chinese demanded considerable forced labor to meet the needs of intensive military construction. Groups of Red Guards descended on Tibet and ran rampant through the homes and communities of the native population. Bogoslovskii concludes that Tibetans were deprived of elementary human rights. Punishment could come for not wanting to join a commune or for working poorly in it and for a woman who wore national dress or who observed religious practices. The Tibetan language was forbidden in state institutions and in a new type of primary school. Militarization and regimentation extended into the daily life of people, with restrictions on whom one could marry. The Tibetans responded to the policies of the Chinese with active resistance, sabotage, and emigration as well as passive resistance. The Chinese sought assimilation, but could not achieve it with these blatantly oppressive measures. Modifications that occurred in some of the harsher policies in the early 1970s are seen mainly as a strategic appeal beyond the borders of China, especially to Tibetan emigrants.[37] Nonetheless, Bogoslovskii recognizes that by the mid-1970s the working class had grown considerably, primary school education was widespread, and other major changes in the social structure of Tibet were taking place.

THE POST-MAO ERA

Year after year the yearbooks of the PRC repeat that no basic changes have occurred in nationality policies. Acknowledging that in 1977 China gave significant attention

[37] Ibid., pp. 146, 153, 178-79.

to these problems, Moskalev nevertheless concludes the section in that year's volume with the assertion that changes in policy after Mao's death and the removal of the "Gang of Four" were on the whole only of a "tactical character."[38] He remarks, too, that the economic difficulties of the nationality regions worsened due to drought, that speculation was rampant, and that the further militarization of the economy placed an added burden on the shoulders of the workers of these nationalities. They were forced to build military objects, especially roads.

A year later it was Bogoslovskii's turn to discuss the nationality question. He suggests that the correct perspective for viewing Hua Guofeng's proposals in February 1978 ostensibly to ameliorate the situation of the non-Han peoples is Hua's call for further strengthening the unity of all nationalities, by which Hua meant unquestioning obedience to the orders of the CCP leadership. The leadership needed the help of non-Han peoples in meeting its military needs. With these goals in mind, Hua called for guaranteeing equality and autonomy, actively training cadres of the nationalities, developing their languages and scripts, and respecting their customs. Bogoslovskii observes that the leadership formally "returns" to the principles present in laws and positions declared prior to the Cultural Revolution, but he places the word "returns" in quotation marks. He cites official statistics on gains in production, but counters them with information on agriculture in these regions that suggests mostly failures.[39] Despite the rehabilitation of many cadres purged earlier, he argues, repressive measures continued. The resettlement of Chinese in minority regions continued in 1978, but these were mainly specialists.

Moskalev's 1979 assessment continues to stress the mass dissatisfaction of the non-Han peoples with the policies of Beijing. Agriculture and herding remained poor, all aspects of public life were militarized, and conditions for the

[38] *Kitaiskaia Narodnaia Respublika 1977*, p. 53.
[39] *Kitaiskaia Narodnaia Respublika 1978*, pp. 77-78.

normal development of languages and culture were still absent. What modifications of policy that had taken place during the year were tactical, loosening up in certain spheres while maintaining a cruel regime of military control in the nationality regions. He notes that in 1979 much attention was given to evaluating the state of the nationalities problem in Tibet. Conferences were held and problems were acknowledged. Some positive steps were taken and positive pronouncements were made during the year, but Moskalev finds negative developments also: 1) the professed conclusion that on the whole the PRC had for over 30 years followed correct policies on nationality questions; and 2) the increased role of the army. Where reforms occurred, as in the restoration of words in Uighur and Kazakh languages that had been removed in favor of Chinese-based terms, they are depicted as necessary due to the extreme unpopularity of the previous policies, or, as in the case of appointing more non-Han cadres, as a tactic aimed at giving the appearance of attention to local interests while preserving the dominant position for the Han cadres.[40] Again the conclusion is that no basic change has taken place. In his 1981 book on the policies concerning the languages of the nationalities, Moskalev goes into more detail on plans and promises, but he again concludes that the freedom of use by non-Han peoples of their own languages and scripts continues to remain essentially nominal.[41]

In addition to Bogoslovskii's book on Tibet, another monograph on China's minority populations is Moskalev's 1979 book on two autonomous regions, the Guangxi-Zhuang and the Ningxia-Hui regions. The author examines the general characteristics of each region and the stages of transformation, including the period of the Cultural Revolution and the 1970s. The section headings on the latter period leave no doubt about Moskalev's conclusions: "The rise of militarization," "The low level of industry and ag-

---

[40] *Kitaiskaia Narodnaia Respublika 1979*, pp. 71, 75-76.
[41] Moskalev, *Politika KNR v natsional'no-iazykovom voprose*, p. 171.

riculture," "The discriminatory course of the Maoists in relation to the national literature and arts," "The decline in the area of education and health care," etc. In the final sections on each region, the reforms of 1977-1978 are depicted in pessimistic tones. Among the findings are that China's leaders continue to shunt non-Han cadres into secondary posts, all areas of life in the autonomous regions are militarized, the local peoples are still required to rely on their own resources, and the national distinctiveness of the peoples is scarcely taken into account. "Autonomy as before bears a purely nominal character. . . . The promise 'to respect' the customs and habits of the non-Han nationalities, 'to take into account' their peculiarities and life needs, the specifics of national regions, etc., bear therefore a propagandistic, declarative character."[42] Thus in a study focused on two regions, Moskalev makes many of the same negative assessments of PRC policies that are found in his other writings from the post-Mao years.

AN EXTREME POSITION

In 1979, Victor Louis, a Soviet journalist and suspected KGB spokesman, was able to get his book *The Coming Decline of the Chinese Empire* published in New York. In it, according to Harrison E. Salisbury, who wrote a dissenting introduction, Louis seeks "to lay a foundation, however dubious it may be, on which the Soviet Union could justify launching an attack on the People's Republic, a preemptive strike to keep China from seizing Soviet territory and, at the same time, to carry out 'a liberating mission' in favor of oppressed minority peoples within China." The first part of the book is divided into separate chapters on Manchuria, the Mongols, Tibet, and Sinjiang. Although it was not published in the Soviet Union, the book provides a Soviet view of national minorities in the PRC. In an extreme form,

---

[42] A. A. Moskalev, *Guansi-Chzhuanskii i Ninsia-Khueiskii avtonomnye raiony KNR*, pp. 128-31, 99.

Louis presents views found in other Soviet writings on China.[43]

One aim of Louis's book is to show that there are persuasive historical reasons for the independence of the minority areas on the border of the PRC. In addition to Tibet and Inner Mongolia, Louis includes Manchuria in the list of areas that deserve to be independent. He writes, "The roots of Manchurian independence were far too strong to be destroyed through punitive military action alone"; and "The three-million-strong Manchurian people are still very much alive. But though far less numerous peoples elsewhere enjoy autonomy, independence, and even United Nations membership, the people of Manchuria have been robbed of all these cherished attributes of nationhood. But for how long?"[44]

Louis's second aim is to argue that the minority peoples themselves are intensely eager for separation from China. Louis discusses the wave of resurgent nationalism in Inner Mongolia and the "indestructible desire" to reunify with the Mongolian People's Republic, referring to the opponents of the PRC leadership as "liberation forces."[45] Persecuted by the Chinese authorities, the minority nationalities are, in Louis's opinion, eager to secede.

Louis's third aim is to point out the tragedy that Chinese rule has brought to the lands of ethnic minorities. In his chapter on Tibet, he writes, "An entire nation has been placed at the mercy of a foreign colonial machine that has deliberately set out to destroy or assimilate it. . . . The Dalai Lama was not exaggerating when he declared that the Tibetan race was threatened with total extinction, or that if the present situation in Tibet continues its people face the menace of complete annihilation." Louis cites large figures for those killed in purges aimed at local nationalities, e.g. he refers to a 1969 Austrian report that 300,000 local res-

---

[43] Victor Louis, *The Coming Decline of the Chinese Empire*, p. xvii.
[44] Ibid., pp. 20, 21.
[45] Ibid., pp. 38-40, 44.

idents had been massacred in Eastern Turkestan (Sinjiang). Louis also links the post-Mao policies to those that preceded. The new policies are portrayed as "a safety valve" and an effort by current leaders to dissociate themselves from "all deeds that provoked dissatisfaction and hatred," while "giving nothing away that has been done to achieve assimilation and national unity."[46]

In the course of his comments, Louis criticizes PRC methods to achieve complete assimilation. He discusses migration policies aimed at flooding regions with Chinese immigrants, language policies aimed at bringing about unification, and "humiliations and mockery of the religious feelings of Moslems."[47] Such policies provide one basis for Louis's conclusion that the minority peoples want to secede and are engaged in a legitimate struggle for their self-determination.

Conclusions

On the problem of China's national minorities there is a high degree of consensus among Soviet writers. While it is Victor Louis's distinct contribution to build on this consensus an undisguised justification for Soviet intervention to help dislodge the minority regions from China's control, his basic criticisms of Chinese relations with the non-Han nationalities are consistent with the views expressed elsewhere. In all matters, the Soviets rebuke the Chinese authorities for policies of national discrimination and Great Han chauvinism. They find evidence for intense discrimination in at least seven areas: 1) the imposition of a colonial administration; 2) personnel policies in which native populations are seriously underrepresented in high-level and influential positions; 3) persecution of members of nationalities who object to measures of control and discrimination or who openly persist in their adherence to traditional be-

---

[46] Ibid., pp. 58-59, 86.
[47] Ibid., pp. 94-100.

liefs concerning their peoples; 4) suppression of the scripts and languages of the national minorities and their replacement by the Chinese language; 5) destruction of local customs, monuments, and religions; 6) a deliberate migration policy in support of vast numbers of Han settlers and the forced resettlement of some native populations; 7) economic exploitation, including heavy taxes, forced labor, low investment in the civilian sector, and severely depressed standards of living.

Criticisms of human rights violations appear repeatedly in Soviet writings on the national minorities of the PRC. They repeat charges that these people are denied freedom of speech, have their religious beliefs infringed on, and are persecuted and imprisoned for disagreeing with Sinification policies. Analyzing the provisions of the 1978 Constitution of the PRC, the pronouncements of Chinese leaders in favor of minority rights at the end of the 1970s and the beginning of the 1980s, and the procedures of elected bodies in the autonomous regions, Soviets find only camouflage, deceit, and demagoguery. As Rakhimov asserts, "Statutes of the constitution on self-government of the non-Han peoples, on their freedom and equality are the usual farce of the Chinese leadership."[48] The Chinese authorities are doing a better job of masking their real intentions, but the aim of their policies remains as before the forced assimilation of peoples who deeply oppose the policies imposed on them.

More than in other Soviet writings on groups and classes in the PRC, comparisons with Soviet conditions appear fairly often in discussions of national minorities. Invariably the history of the Soviet Union stands as a model for the correct approach to fraternal relations. The basic explanation for the difference between the two countries, Rakhimov declares, is that "in the Soviet Union national autonomy is based on recognition of the rights of peoples to self-determination, while in China the non-Han peoples are deprived

[48] Rakhimov, *Sud'by nekhanskikh narodov v KNR*, pp. 111, 143.

of this right."[49] There is no indication that these writings on China are in any way intended to reassess Soviet history or to encourage reforms in contemporary Soviet conditions.

The literature on the ethnic minorities of the People's Republic presents a monolithic view of what has gone wrong in a state originally on the path to socialism. The lack of diversity may be due to the fact that this topic has been virtually monopolized by the Institute of the Far East and by high ranking figures such as Tikhvinsky. Just as foreign relations in general and Sino-Soviet relations in particular are sensitive topics, in which dissenting views are scarce or even absent altogether, minority relations in the PRC may be a subject on which the official line is unambiguous and the dangers of straying into criticisms of the Soviet Union are obvious.

[49] Ibid., p. 146.

· 7 ·

CONCLUSIONS

The central issues that figure in the international debate over the costs and benefits of socialism are easily identified. Does the violence launched by communist leaders in the course of rural reorganizations, recurrent campaigns, and political purges represent a ruthless violation of basic human rights, or is it a justifiable means of reeducation and punishment? Do the methods used to increase and reallocate labor participation signify state coercion, or are they a new and more equitable form of individual and collective incentives? Is the massive reorganization of peasants, workers, intellectuals, and ethnic minorities a device for tightened control from above, or is it a means for heightened participation from below? Does a communist-led society intimidate experts or does it make possible the fullest advance and application of scientific knowledge? Despite some brief or indirect criticisms—which had become infrequent by the 1970s—of Stalinist excesses, published materials in the Soviet Union clearly accept the second alternative in response to each of these questions. Soviet spokesmen vigorously reject the criticisms implied in the first set of alternatives as being distortions attributable to "anticommunism."

Where can one find Soviet academics, officials, and journalists discussing these fundamental themes of socialism in detail? Certainly not in the official histories of the Soviet Union nor even in the narrowly focused criticisms in the press and academic literature of problems in Soviet society. Direct evidence on contrasting views about Soviet history is scarce. The refutations of "anticommunist" criticisms raise many central issues, but the responses are so defensive and one-sided that it is hopeless to look for a genuine discussion there. The vast Soviet literature on China has long been

235

neglected, perhaps in part because outsiders expected to find this material as superficial and predictable as Soviet writings on "anticommunism." Enough examples exist of widely circulated, heavy-handed, political treatises on China to reinforce this expectation and to discourage readers from probing deeply into this field. Otherwise informative books may also have simplistic and one-sided sections, for example on Soviet assistance to the PRC in the 1950s.[1]

It is probable that few Western specialists in either Chinese studies or Soviet studies have been aware that a substantial volume of materials exists with detailed information on the social classes of the PRC. It will, I think, come as a surprise to many that numerous Soviet authors know Chinese, draw on primary sources, are acquainted with Western secondary sources, and seek to add something new to the existing state of knowledge, not only in the Soviet Union but in the international community of specialists on China. They produce serious scholarship that should be familiar to conscientious researchers on China writing on similar subjects. It deserves to be of wider interest too, because these Soviet studies of China—published during the 1970s and early 1980s—open up new vistas into five distinct areas of scholarship.

First, the literature on Chinese social classes shows how the Soviet worldview was appreciably extended during the Brezhnev era. The prevalent view of this era as being a time of a generally stagnant worldview has some merit, but it needs to be qualified especially by the reinterpretations of socialism found in the literature on China. Second, when juxtaposed with Soviet refutations of "anticommunism," these writings offer a new perspective on the ideological struggle in which the Soviets are engaged. They reveal the great extent to which the principal, external criticisms of the failings of a communist-led system are shared within the Soviet Union in official and academic circles. Third,

[1] A. P. Davydov, *Profsoiuzy Kitaia: istoriia i sovremennost' (1949-1980 gody)*, pp. 18-32; and *Promyshlennost' KNR*, pp. 14-24.

the differences found in Soviet studies of China present a rare look at how different groups of academic specialists and officials diverge in their outlook on socialism, with relevance to their views not only on highly sensitive problems of Soviet history but also, by implication, on the present and future of Soviet society. They are suggestive of what a reform agenda for the Soviet Union might look like. Fourth, this literature has merit precisely for what it sets out to do. It contributes to Chinese studies, especially to the sociological understanding of China. Finally, it is important for understanding Sino-Soviet relations. Analysis of Soviet perceptions of internal conditions in China is one way to advance the study of the Sino-Soviet relationship—an important area within the field of international relations. The following sections of this chapter summarize what can be learned about these five themes from the Soviet literature on China.

EXTENDING THE SOVIET WORLDVIEW

It is not without reason that independent observers find the Soviet perspective on historical development, the contemporary world order, and the nature of their own society to be sterile, uncreative, and dogmatic. This is inevitable to the extent that a body of literature written between the 1840s and 1920s is cited uncritically as the basis for current interpretations. Creativity is stifled by orthodox views dictated from above concerning all major policy initiatives in Soviet history and most major foreign policy developments in modern times. Writing about Russian history, Soviet society, and world relations, Soviet specialists in the decades after Stalin's death have managed to introduce a degree of creativity, but the limitations have been tight on matters of any significance to the overall worldview. Nor is the recent literature on China likely substantially to alter this overall view unless its implications are made more explicit for Soviet history and international communism. Nonetheless, it opens a wedge that extends the worldview and, more importantly, shows how this outlook on social change could be extended much further.

The legacy of traditional societies in the transition to socialism is one concern of the Soviet perspective. Writings on China point to mistakes that should be avoided, the major one being the failure to understand the specific conditions and traditions of the country in question. In studies of China this mistake resulted in part from the automatic transfer of such Russian categories as kulak to conditions in which they did not conform well to reality. More generally, in the course of their criticisms of CCP policies in Chinese history, Soviets call for achieving a clear scientific understanding of existing social relations.[2] Mistakes result from ignorance and incorrect assumptions by leaders who ignore or silence expert advice. Especially dangerous are assumptions that exaggerate the level of class antagonisms and revolutionary consciousness. For various historical reasons, poor peasants may be relatively passive and unlikely to oppose their more well-to-do neighbors. The proletariat may remain weak and without strong leadership, and the intelligentsia may be seriously limited by ethnocentrism and other conditions. These prerevolutionary features should be well understood by the communist party as it sets out to reorganize social relations. Arrogance and the suppression of dissent by officials who lack respect for intellectuals are the root cause of dogmatism, and dogmatism leads to mistakes.

It is understandable that a principal contribution of specialists to their country's worldview (in an era of rapid professionalization as separate area studies and social science disciplines have expanded) is that expert advice matters. They argue that policy must be based on knowledge. Along with others, the China specialists have helped amend the Soviet worldview to acknowledge that a danger to socialism

---

[2] Gel'bras, *Sotsial'no-politicheskaia struktura KNR 50-60-e gody*, pp. 30-31; Deliusin, *Agrarno-krest'ianskii vopros v politike KPK*, p. 5.

arises from leaders who launch policies that are not based on the wisdom gained from experts.

The need for gradual and voluntary change is a second theme in Soviet studies of China. The success or failure of policies such as collectivization depends on the voluntary participation of the people concerned.[3] Consistent with this judgment is the belief that people must feel that they are involved and have a say in decision making. If they feel helpless before higher authorities and if change is forced upon them, the people will be apathetic or worse in facing the goals of socialism. Collectivization and communization occurred against the will of Chinese peasants; unions ignored the interests of Chinese workers; campaigns were targeted against intellectuals in general; national minorities suffered as a group with no opportunity for self-government. In each case, the state failed to give people a say in their own future.

Although the concept of democratic procedures has been reinterpreted to limit many individual rights, its repeated invocation by Soviets in the concrete circumstances of Chinese history does give it specific content in support of basic human rights. The line of criticism that objects to coercive methods in China broadens the Soviet worldview to favor mass participation and genuine representation. It opposes direct controls by the army or police. Rejecting an atmosphere of terror, this view advocates tolerance of criticism and recognition of individual rights.[4] It calls for patience and persuasion in the administration of society.

Third, the Soviet worldview has been elaborated on as part of the favorable attitude toward personal and group monetary incentives expressed in studies of China. Soviets accept the notion of human nature that sees people as eager to improve their living standards and as responsive to material incentives. Peasants need adequate prices for what

---

[3] *Klassy i klassovaia struktura v KNR*, p. 103.

[4] *Rabochii klass v sotsial'no-politicheskoi sisteme KNR*, p. 123; and L. S. Kiuzadjan, *Ideologicheskie kampanii v KNR 1949-1966*, pp. 26-31.

they produce. Peasants and workers need income differentials sufficient to induce greater output. The entire population requires improved consumer goods and services to satisfy their material needs. Soviets fault China for over-investing in its military and in heavy industry and for denying people private plots and markets.[5]

A corollary of this stress on rewards is the rejection of intimidation or force to get people to work harder. A government must be concerned about the morale of people. Writers seem to stress this theme especially with regard to the intelligentsia, whose creative output depends on more than material rewards.[6] The conditions of work as well as the rewards for its completion are basic determinants of the quantity and, especially, the quality of output.

Preference for an orderly, predictable environment is a fourth theme that recurs through Soviet studies of China. The Soviets favor regularized procedures, not arbitrary ones. They advocate the rule of law and the operation of formal procedures, not personalized and dependent relationships. In writings by Lazarev, Burlatsky, and others, increasing attention centers on the social psychology of daily life.[7] The implications of this approach are particularly clear concerning the role of officials. They must operate as bureaucrats under strict guidelines and following precise legal procedures.

In China regular procedures were ignored at all levels. At the top, the cult of personality denied collective leadership. The major organizations including the communist party were restructured along military lines rather than operating according to normal administrative procedures. In their interactions with ordinary citizens, officials were

[5] *Sel'skoe khoziaistvo KNR 1949-1974*, pp. 346-47, and O. Borisov, "Nekotorye aspekty politiki Kitaia," *Kommunist* 1981:6, p. 113.

[6] *Sud'by kul'tury KNR (1949-1974)*, p. 96; and S. D. Markova, *Maoizm i intelligentsiia*, pp. 26-27.

[7] G. F. Saltykov, *Sotsial'no-psikhologicheskie faktory v politicheskoi zhizni rabochego klassa KNR 70-kh godov*; and Fedor Burlatsky, "Mezhdutsarstvie, ili khronika vremen Den Siaopina."

not held accountable. They abused their power and often became corrupt. The implication of this line of criticism for the Soviet worldview is that precise controls, laws, and procedures are necessary to create a proper environment for honest and efficient social relations.

Of course, specialists on China are not alone in advocating these principles of scientific understanding of society, democratic procedures, material incentives, and impersonal forms of authority. During the eighteen years of Leonid Brezhnev's leadership, these were generally popular themes. They were firmly incorporated into the Soviet worldview and were reenforced by code words such as the scientific technological revolution for advancement of knowledge and socialist legality for democratic procedures. Nevertheless, a wide gap has continued to exist between these idealized concepts and the realities of Soviet society. The gap results largely from two circumstances that were especially obvious during Stalin's rule and remain very much evident today. First, high-sounding principles are qualified by other principles that make their realization impossible. What is given with one hand is taken by the other. Above all, the demands for increased controls and an expanded role of the communist party limit scientific inquiry, democratic rights, and checks and balances in the use of power. Second, the gap between ideal and actuality is widened by the lack of specificity about conditions in communist-led societies that influence the fate of these principles. Little has been written about what went wrong in the Stalinist era. Even today as Brezhnev's successors drive to improve material incentives and reduce abuses of authority, there is little candor in treatments of the history and causes of these deviations.

In this context, studies of China show how principles central to the proper functioning of a socialist system can be violated. They present historical details and a broad social context for assessing what goes wrong under the communist party's leadership. Publications on China and Maoism from the mid-1960s have been a surrogate for internal studies of Soviet history and Stalinism, e.g. on the cult of personality and collectivization. As such, they have enriched the evolving Soviet worldview.

The existence of an official worldview has not placed an ideological straightjacket on Chinese studies in the Soviet Union. A primary reason for this is that China does not fit the standard dichotomy of radiant socialism versus unjust capitalism or even the recently added Third-World categories for multi-formations that blend feudalism, capitalism, and sometimes socialism. The challenge of China required a new approach that could not avoid the theme of shortcomings en route to socialism. A second reason is that the general, Soviet worldview is no longer in most fields intended to silence scholarly inquiry. Informed and careful scholars are considered essential in this new age of the scientific technological revolution; a place has been carved out of the fields of history and the social sciences for new, empirical disciplines such as sociology, and there is talk of new orientations such as historical sociology.

There remains a single, officially approved worldview in the Soviet Union. Academic researchers must adapt to it and refrain from attacking it directly. Even the most narrow-minded defenders of the orthodox position and the most fervent reformers who work within the system must accept, as the ground rules for their analysis, the basic rubric of this worldview. It should also be recognized that both orthodox and reform specialists on China have contributed to a common set of adjustments of the Soviet official viewpoint concerning the need for professional knowledge in managing a socialist society, the preference for gradual and voluntary changes based on persuasion, the primary reliance on material incentives to motivate performance, and the impersonal exercise of authority on the basis of legal procedures. They must work within a common worldview, and they have together guided change in a particular direction. Although later in this chapter and throughout the preceding chapters I emphasize the differences that separate the orthodox and reform camps, it

242

would be misleading not to identify similarities. Nowhere are these similarities more striking than in the practice of repeating Western criticisms directed against the Soviet Union and China in their own criticisms of China.

REFUTING ANTICOMMUNISM

The official Soviet position in the Brezhnev era, later forcefully restated under Andropov and Chernenko, is that the ideological struggle is intensifying.[8] On the one side is the proletarian position represented by the Soviet Union. It is based on a scientific understanding, and it defends truth. On the other side is the bourgeois position and, the Soviet Union's second principal challenger, the Maoist position, which may be described as petty-bourgeois or Han chauvinist. These positions are built on falsifications. One of the primary duties of China specialists is to expose these falsifications, to fight against anticommunism.

Soviet institutes and publishing organs must justify their publications on China as serving this ideological struggle. They do this in several ways. One method is to expose shortcomings in "bourgeois" writings on China. Soviets accuse these writings of being directed against their own society, either by praising the Chinese for trying to overcome problems evident in Soviet life or by insisting that the failures of China are shared by the Soviet Union and the socialist world in general.[9] They also accuse Westerners of distorting the history of Sino-Soviet relations.[10] In some cases, especially in the book, *Contemporary China in Foreign*

[8] A. I. Luk'ianov, et al., *Sovetskaia konstitutsiia i mify sovetologov*, p. 3; and "Fight Reagan 'Crusade,' Soviet Aide Says," *The New York Times*, June 15, 1983, p. A3.

[9] O. B. Borisov, "Polozhenie v KNR i nekotorye zadachi sovetskogo kitaevedeniia," pp. 11-12; *Sovremennyi Kitai v zarubezhnykh issledovaniiakh*, pp. 7, 31; and A. N. Zhelokhovtsev, *Literaturnaia teoriia i politicheskaia bor'ba v KNR*, p. 188.

[10] Raisa Mirovitskaya and Yuri Semyonov, *The Soviet Union and China: A Brief History of Relations*, p. 5.

Research,[11] Soviets have pointed to serious shortcomings in Western writings that idealized Maoism and the Cultural Revolution at a time when Soviet criticisms were more on target.

More important than these direct refutations of different views of China are the indirect methods of demonstrating why "anticommunists" are wrong. The massive Soviet expansion of Chinese studies has been approved, in part, to meet this need. It has been essential to dissociate China from the Soviet Union. This is not an easy task to accomplish, however, because genuine comparative methods would have exposed too many shortcomings of Soviet history. As a result, Soviets have adopted a variety of approaches to convey differences without going deeply into comparisons. The first is to present an idealized view of Soviet policies (more a statement of principles than a study of history) drawn largely from the writings of Lenin and secondarily from those of the Brezhnev leadership. In general, nothing is said about Stalinism. Rarely do writers on China even mention the problems of contemporary Soviet society even though many of them are widely discussed (if even in a limited, non-comparative context) in the Soviet press. The second approach is to confine comparisons to a few general points. This selectivity maximizes the perception of differences. Third, Soviet spokesmen take the offensive in accusing their international counterparts of behaving according to the rules they themselves are required to follow. It is foreign specialists, especially Americans, who are deeply committed to the ideological struggle and who must reject objectivity and truth.[12] Soviet authors do not candidly acknowledge their substantial debt to Western studies of the PRC. Hints of convergence are anathema in this area as in others.

In their eagerness to dissociate their society from China, however, Soviets embrace many of the principal criticisms

[11] *Sovremennyi Kitai v zarubezhnykh issledovaniiakh.*

[12] I. I. Klimin, *Agrarnaia politika KPSS (1917-1937 gg.): deistvitel'nost' i burzhuaznye vymysly*; and M. A. Shalin, *Antikommunizm i ideologicheskaia bor'ba na sovremennom etape.*

that they identify with "anticommunism," but restrict their application to China. At home, this may encourage people to appreciate how much better off they are today than the Chinese. Because of the obvious similarities with the Stalinist era, this implied comparison gives people a vivid reminder of how much worse things could be and how far they have come. Abroad, Soviets can argue that they stand firmly opposed to the violations of basic rights and the serious inefficiencies of which they have been accused. The vigor and extent of criticisms against Chinese policies have since the 1960s separated the contemporary Soviet Union from its Maoist adversary.

Along with the large literature exposing bourgeois falsifications of Soviet socialism, the even larger literature exposing Chinese deviations from socialism is intended as a refutation of "anticommunism." Whatever the merits of these writings as persuasion, however, they fail as scholarship with respect to refuting their alleged enemies. Because the Soviets print only brief excerpts from the writings they consider to be "anticommunist" and because they do not make systematic and substantial comparisons between the USSR and the PRC, they cannot demonstrate that these two countries have not in fact each committed the mistakes and abuses of which Western observers have accused them.

We may surmise that there are two sharply divergent Soviet positions on the ideological struggle with the West in Chinese studies. The view handed down from above and espoused by leading administrators such as Rakhmanin, Tikhvinsky, and Sladkovsky is that "anticommunism" is the general characteristic of Western scholarship and that a high priority should be given to doing battle with it.[13] Spokesmen at the Institute of the Far East accept this position, showing hostility to foreign specialists on China and emphasizing the superiority of Soviet studies. In contrast, at the Institute of Oriental Studies in Deliusin's Department

[13] M. Sladkovsky, "In Opposition to Great-Han Chauvinism," *Far Eastern Affairs* 1981:4, p. 21; and O. B. Borisov, *Vnutrenniaia i vneshniaia politika Kitaia v 70-e gody*, p. 3.

of China, the atmosphere is more purely scholarly. Scholars may express a debt to their Western counterparts and an eagerness to learn more about recent research in the West. For many writers on China, it is unlikely that the ideological struggle is a genuine concern. Their writings indicate an openness to the best scholarship, whatever its origins, in order to improve their own research.[14]

For most criticisms, the following pair of equations holds: Western criticisms of the Soviet Union = both orthodox and reform Soviet criticisms of China = changes in the Soviet worldview since the Stalinist era. In the next section I propose another pair of equations that pertains to a limited but strategic set of criticisms: selected Western criticisms of the Soviet Union = reform Soviet criticisms of China that are not shared by the orthodox writers = a reform agenda for change in the Soviet Union. Before proceeding to a discussion of the differences in Soviet views, it is important to examine the first equation between Western criticisms of the Soviet Union and the widest range of Soviet criticisms of China.

What does it mean to conclude that Soviets echo what they call "anticommunism?" It does not mean a rejection of the society in which they live. Those Western criticisms that reject the very essence of socialist societies—the vitality of Marxism-Leninism as a guide to social change, the leading role of the communist party, centralized planning, state and collective ownership of the means of production—are not repeated in Soviet publications on China. There is, of course, no way of telling to what extent, in the absence of censorship, they would be present. Circumstances permit no more than criticism from within the system. Discussions of China are held strictly accountable to the same basic standards on these central ideological topics.

The repetition of criticisms long directed against the Soviet Union in the context of writings on China also should not be necessarily construed as an obvious subterfuge for internal criticisms of Soviet history and life. Almost no com-

---

[14] *Kitai: obshchestvo i gosudarstvo*, p. 3.

parisons are permitted that openly acknowledge the similarity of mistakes in the two countries. In many cases, the Soviet Union is specifically exempted by a Soviet author from the criticisms against China. On the surface, the conclusions often assert that the PRC failed while the USSR succeeded. Considerable effort is made to restrict the implications of the criticisms to China. The orthodox camp makes the greater effort, but it is unlikely that even they are unaware of the abundant similarities between the two countries and of the Soviet reader's consciousness of those similarities. The dearth of comparisons is an admission that the alternatives are more damaging than silence.

Since Khrushchev's de-Stalinization speech in 1956, there has been a desperate need in the Soviet Union for an open discussion of differences of opinion about Soviet society—past, present, and future. That mood has not disappeared simply because it has been severely stifled. It is inconceivable that Soviets writing about many of the most sensitive issues of their own country's experience should not be attuned to the parallels and differences. Following this reasoning, we should conclude that those who echo "anticommunist" criticisms are conscious of the relevance of these issues to the Soviet Union and, depending on their viewpoint, seek within the limits of their flexibility to dull or sharpen the reader's appreciation of similarities. The differences in criticisms of China between the orthodox and reform thinkers suggest that, while both sides are "echoing," they have different objectives in influencing Soviet public opinion. The orthodox group wants its readers to emphasize differences between the two settings, as in the situation of ethnic minorities, and to conclude either that China is a special case from which little can be learned for domestic application or that China is another case of a threat to socialism from the right, reinforcing traditional Soviet concerns about enemies on the right at home and abroad. The reform group appears to want readers to draw different lessons—to arrive at a real appreciation for the legacy of Stalinism via an understanding of Maoism and to influence the prospects for change in Soviet policies.

The alternatives to repeating criticisms associated with anticommunism were simply not viable. For most of the period 1960-1966, the Soviets refrained from discussing the nature of Chinese society, but this silence could not easily be maintained in the face of increasingly hostile relations and the absence of an adequate explanation for the Chinese heresy in the existing Soviet worldview. Another response was to deny that China had anything in common with socialism. The focus on traditional society had some promise from this point of view, but there was no way to ignore the fact that China was in many ways following in the Soviet Union's footsteps at least up to 1957. Another approach that gained popularity in the late 1960s was to blame Mao and perhaps a small number of his associates, but an ideology grounded in relations among social classes could not easily accommodate this personalized interpretation. There was no easy escape from a discussion of how socialism could go wrong; increasingly through the 1970s Soviet specialists on China plunged deeper into this topic. Soviet officials decided to expand specialized research on China and to form a corps of experts who could explain events there. They also sought to arouse public opinion against China at home and abroad. The obvious outcome of these decisions was to repeat the criticisms of China already widespread in the West. For their own convenience, they generally neglected to mention the origins of these criticisms and the fact that the same criticisms are applied to their own country. The Soviets performed this trick in large part by artificially separating two types of publications concerned with a common set of problems of socialism, calling one type anticommunist and the other Marxist-Leninist scholarship on China.

PRESENTING DIVERGENT SOVIET VIEWS

As I have mentioned in Chapter 1, a basic difference exists between the Soviet orthodox group and the reformers in their methods of scholarship. The leading orthodox figures set the course in broad strokes. Their generalized writings offer firm conclusions, with little ambiguity or scholarly depth. They often publish with Politizdat, the political publishing arm; their journal articles are likely to be reprinted in *Opasnyi kurs*, the almost annual collection of hostile commentaries on the PRC.[15] Under these leaders in the field toil hundreds of journeymen who specialize narrowly on one aspect of modern or contemporary China. While their work usually reveals detailed familiarity with the Chinese press and with some of the secondary literature, it is bounded within strict confines and by conclusions fully in compliance with the dictates of their superiors. In the reformers' camp are small groups of specialists working away from the bastion of the orthodox viewpoint, the Institute of the Far East. (There are also several individual scholars at this institute, whose valuable monographs suggest a broader perspective or a deeper interest in traditional China than is customary among their colleagues.)[16] The annual conference volumes, *Society and State in China*, put out under Deliusin's leadership best reflect the inquisitive spirit, diversity, and search for high scholarly standards of the reformers.[17] In recent years these volumes have not treated post-1949 China, but I have located enough studies by representatives of this category to identify their views on a wide range of issues that appear in Chapters 2 through 5, although not on the subject of minority nationalities treated in Chapter 6.

Certainly one of the main differences between these two groups in the method of treatment of Chinese social classes is their approach to comparisons. The orthodox group has, to a great extent, maintained the style of the Stalinist and Khrushchev eras of readily transferring to China categories and assumptions drawn from Russian and Soviet history. In contrast, Meliksetov and Gel'bras have led the way in

---

[15] *Opasnyi kurs*, vols. 4-11 (1973-1981).

[16] L. S. Perelomov, *Konfutsiantsvo i legizm v politicheskoi istorii Kitaia*; and A. S. Mugruzin, *Agrarnye otnosheniia v Kitae v 20-40-kh godakh XX v.*

[17] *Obshchestvo i gosudarstvo v Kitae*, conferences 4-13 (1973-82).

criticizing the state of Soviet research on China through the 1960s and in warning against the continued transfer of Soviet terms such as "landlord" and "rich peasant," burdened by the assumptions associated with them.[18] The reformers have argued forcefully for the need to understand China on its own terms, to take into account its distinctiveness, e.g., the diverse strata of its working class.[19] Their approach does not reject comparisons and generalizations, but places trust primarily in historical literacy. The orthodox group places more weight on deductive methods, associated with quotations from Lenin and implicit comparisons with an idealized Soviet Union.

The two viewpoints clash in their treatment of the legacy of traditional China. Not only does the traditional society enter more fully into the arguments of the reformers (although the gap in this respect has narrowed in recent years) but the implications for the transition to socialism are different. To the reformers, China's heritage of despotism and lack of attention to individual rights complicates the path to socialism.[20] Existing democratic traditions and institutions, which have been developed by the bourgeoisie, help a society evolve under communist leadership toward socialism. In their absence, the rights of individuals may not be respected in the new society.

Both schools of thought in the Soviet Union recognize China's backwardness in economic development and social relations. But they appear to draw different conclusions from it. The reformers emphasize that a gradual approach to reforms must be taken, readying the people or awaiting their support for new policies. They criticize revolutionaries and communists in China before 1949 for exaggerating the development of the society; they also criticize

---

[18] A. V. Meliksetov, *Sotsial'no-ekonomicheskaia politika Gomin'dana 1927-1949 gg.*, pp. 22-25; and V. G. Gel'bras, *Sotsial'no-politicheskaia struktura KNR 50-60-e gody*, pp. 30-31.

[19] A. V. Meliksetov, "Nekotorye osobennosti formirovaniia rabochego klassa Kitaia k nachalu noveishego vremeni," p. 8.

[20] *Kitai: traditsii i sovremennost'*, pp. 5-7.

subsequent Soviet writers for misunderstanding the readiness of Chinese society in 1911, 1927, and again after 1949 for a new stage of development.[21] The orthodox school appears to use backwardness as a justification for greater central control. Carrying Lenin's extension of Marx one step further, they see communist party leadership as compensating for not fully mature social relations. After the revolution, too, strong party leadership and a powerful state lead the small working class on the path to socialism. Adherents of this viewpoint also recognize that the backwardness of the traditional society slows the transition, but they are more optimistic that leaders can take charge and are more sanguine about the consequences of centralization.

A consequence of backwardness and distinctiveness in premodern social structure was the state of class conflict in China at the time of the communist victory. The reformers offer detailed evidence about weak class antagonisms.[22] They cite this as justification for not moving quickly or in an extreme manner against the upper classes and for confining the most negative class labels to a small minority. A scientific and specific understanding of class divisions and other social relationships in the countryside and in the urban work force can prevent excessive violence and unpopular policies. The orthodox group expresses more concern for rooting out bourgeois influences and seems to take their existence for granted without much examination of existing social relations.

Correspondingly the two sides disagree on some of the principal problems facing the Chinese in the transition to socialism. The orthodox group warns of the threat from capitalism, justifying tough measures to try to reduce capitalist influences.[23] The reform group draws different con-

---

[21] L. P. Deliusin, *Agrarno-krest'ianskii vopros v politike KPK*, pp. 5, 442-43; and V. G. Gel'bras, *Sotsial'no-politicheskaia struktura KNR 50-60-e gody*, pp. 46-48.

[22] Gel'bras, *Sotsial'no-politicheskaia struktura KNR 50-60-e gody*, pp. 22-49.

[23] V. I. Lazarev, *Klassovaia bor'ba v KNR*, pp. 19-21.

clusions from China's history of the early and mid-1950s. Evaluating land reform, the reformers stress that it went too far in weakening the middle peasants and in eliminating the rich peasants. They warn, too, that the destruction of traditional associations and dependency relations created a vacuum that contributed to excessive centralization.[24] Relying on the poor, the Chinese authorities were influenced to select excessively egalitarian and nondemocratic policies. Furthermore, one Soviet reform view suggests that brutality in the course of land reform and other early campaigns bred later violence.[25] The reform perspective highlights the dangers of excessive conflict and violence and advocates moderation based on careful understanding of actual conditions.

On no issue is the reformers' case for moderation clearer than in the opinions expressed about the intelligentsia. The reformers argue that Chinese intellectuals were largely on the side of the revolution.[26] They were ready to help build socialism, and their contributions could have made an enormous difference. In order to serve the cause of socialism, however, intellectuals must be trusted and respected for their creativity. They must be drawn into the decision-making process as experts, as specialists who conduct careful investigations and present the results based on their independent research. Their complaints must be heard. Human rights violations that muzzle the intelligentsia have far-reaching negative consequences. In contrast, the orthodox forces warn of the continued bourgeois influence of this group. To combat this threat they demand more thorough reeducation of intellectuals after the revolution and are wary about recruiting officials from this stratum.[27] In their view, the old intelligentsia carries traditions that must be

[24] L. S. Perelomov, *Konfutsiantsvo i legizm v politicheskoi istorii Kitaia*, p. 226.

[25] Fedor Burlatsky, *Mao Tse-tung: An Ideological and Psychological Portrait*, p. 102.

[26] Gel'bras, *Sotsial'no-politicheskaia struktura KNR 50-60-e gody*, p. 135.

[27] *Sud'by kul'tury KNR (1949-1974)*, pp. 89-90.

rooted out. The orthodox group places more reliance on the political authorities and on the adequacy of their understanding of society. The gap between the two perspectives centers on the difference between control and freedom, between demands for obedience and reeducation and requests for the free exchange of views and independent criticism.

Of all the differences of opinion, none is more central to the dispute over China than the debate about officials discussed in Chapter 5. For the orthodox side, the solutions to China's problems are increased centralization and discipline. Through the buildup of a communist party with tighter discipline, the problems of officials could be addressed. Outside influences, especially that of the national bourgeoisie, must also be eliminated.[28] The reformers advocate more fundamental changes, although they tend to do so obliquely. They call for eradicating the deeply entrenched habits of nondemocratic procedures and abuses of privilege.[29] The ruling stratum must relinquish its prerogatives, otherwise de-Maoization will not proceed very far. Reformers appear to favor a new breed of officials who are educated, specialists by training, and rely on expert information. They clearly advocate different methods of governance—ones less subject to abuse and favoritism.

The differences between the orthodox group and reformers concerning the role of knowledge and expertise extend to other social classes and strata. The reform orientation advocates meritocracy in all spheres of life. It proposes giving increased responsibility to the older, qualified, experienced workers. It approves of a shift of rural leadership to the peasants who demonstrate their ability to understand agricultural problems and increase production.[30] In the dichotomy between red and expert, to the extent

[28] I. F. Fedorov and V. G. Zubakov, *Chlenstvo v KPK: kak stroilas' partiia "Idei Mao Tszeduna,"* pp. 8-9, 145.

[29] *Rabochii klass v sotsial'no-politicheskoi sisteme KNR*, p. 126.

[30] A. P. Davydov, *Profsoiuzy KNR 1953-1958*, pp. 89-116; *Rabochii klass v sotsial'no-politicheskoi sisteme KNR*, pp. 114-18.

CONCLUSIONS

that issues can be broached openly, reformers side with the experts. On the basic need to extend reliance on expertise, Soviet specialists are in agreement, but on the need for a sharp shift in the balance in favor of the experts over the reds who lack expertise there appears to be a split in Soviet reactions.

There are also divisions concerning participation. The reformers harshly criticize state coercion. They oppose unions controlled from the top and urge greater worker participation and defense of worker interests.[31] They advocate increased worker participation in management too. In order to counteract widespread apathy, they urge that controls be relaxed in favor of genuine grass-roots involvement by large numbers of people and particularly by groups of people employed together.[32] These groups must be able to express their real interests and defend them through organizations capable of representing them. The controls demanded by the orthodox perspective clash with these proposals for much greater representation much as they come into conflict with the expanded role of knowledge the reformers support. Reformers see compatible solutions to both problems as knowledgeable people rise through the intelligentsia and the ranks of workers to assume positions of responsibility, including official positions at all levels. They value genuine elective procedures. The orthodox writers begin with a wider definition of the bourgeoisie and use this to justify far more restrictions on representation as well as knowledge.

The two sides do not agree on the priority of the well-being of the people. For the reformers this is the key indicator of the system's success. The state must not exploit the people, but instead should encourage them to produce more through material incentives such as improved consumer goods. Reform writers appear to support the post-

[31] A. V. Kholodkovskaia, "Kampaniia 'uporiadocheniia i stroitel'stva profsoiuzov' i ee vliianie na rabochii klass (1973-1975 gg.)," p. 17.

[32] A. V. Kholodkovskaia, *Rabochii klass Kitaia v period "uregulirovaniia" (1961-1965)*, pp. 85-89.

254

Mao principle that peasants who enrich themselves through hard work should be praised and to consider the responsibility system a proper response to the people's desire for an expanded private sector and rewards commensurate with their increased labor. ⁵The orthodox group places more restrictions on material rewards. Alert to threats to central planning and to the maintenance of local control over the economy by party officials, this group fears that the expanded private sector or rewards strictly based on production would turn the country to the right.[33]

Finally the orthodox and reform assessments of China disagree in the importance they attach to impersonal procedures and the rule of law. The former view sees bourgeois and petty-bourgeois forces as ready to escape and to influence society as soon as tight controls are relaxed. While precise laws are useful in creating predictable conditions for maintaining order, there should be flexibility to maintain central control. In contrast, according to the view of reformers, laws must protect citizens from the repressive state and the army. It is the officials who use the guise of eliminating bourgeois elements to terrorize society and abuse legal procedures.[34] Individuals must be protected against excessive force and given the means to self-preservation through knowledge of the past, bonds with their family, and cultivation of a rich spiritual world. The two viewpoints clash in the balance they recommend between, on the one hand, individual freedom and group control and, on the other, individual rights and responsibilities to the state.

These differences between orthodoxy and reform come to a head in attitudes toward the post-Mao era. The one group sees hope in the improved position of the intelligentsia and of material incentives, but it finds fundamental change impossible without a transfer of power from the officials or at least much expanded representation of the

[33] O. B. Borisov, "Polozhenie v KNR i nekotorye zadachi sovetskogo kitaevedeniia," pp. 11-21.

[34] Fedor Burlatsky, "Mezhdutsarstvie, ili khronika vremen Den Siaopina," pp. 206-27.

people and fundamentally reformed legal guarantees and procedures. The other group sees danger from bourgeois forms of reward and downplays any possibility of casting aside Maoism unless national leaders redirect their foreign policy and turn inside China to groups within the CCP who want to tighten centralization and control. Neither group is optimistic about China in the short term. The reformers more warmly welcomed reforms in the late 1970s, but apparently decided that the legacy of Maoism among officials could not be overcome. Still they find opportunities to comment favorably on some steps that indicate what must be done. The orthodox group seems resigned to repeat the pessimistic conclusion that China has Maoism without Mao, while biding its time until a shift in national leaders might create an opening for improved Sino-Soviet relations.[35] Without principle, they actually adhere to a kind of foreign relations determinism: the nature of a society is judged by the extent of its allegiance to the Soviet Union. Only the reformers appear to accept the principle that the basic determinant of conditions in a society is its structure of social class relations.

The central difference in the viewpoints of Soviet specialists on China, and perhaps of other Soviets, concerns the nature of the threat to socialism. Is the threat likely to come from the right, by way of internal and external bourgeois influence? If so, controls must be tightened, democratic and legal procedures must be limited, and the well-being of the people must be given low priority in order to channel resources into the state's coffers and curtail the revitalization of the so-called bourgeoisie or intellectuals similarly inclined. Is the threat from the state, through officials intolerant of criticism and abuse of their power? If so, controls must be relaxed and the people must be granted more protection and representation. The implications of each assessment generally lead to opposite recommendations for domestic policies in the Soviet Union as

[35] Gilbert Rozman, "Moscow's China-Watchers in the Post-Mao Era," pp. 236-41.

well as to conflicting interpretations of what went wrong in the People's Republic of China.

The equation of Western criticisms of the Soviet Union, Soviet reform-oriented criticisms of China, and a Soviet reform agenda for internal change rests first of all on views of the state (or the party) and its officials. Despotic traditions, ruthlessness against class enemies, over-reliance on coercive controls, and reliance on those deemed most loyal—these are tendencies with dangerous consequences for the people. All three perspectives criticize these tendencies and call for safeguards against the state. They regard the officials as intoxicated by power and a threat to the well-being of society. They consider the intellectuals to be the leading advocates of human rights and improvements in the society. The Soviet reformers label these safeguards socialism. They articulate a path of peaceful change from within to improve socialism and to erase deviations from it. In the case of China, they see each social class as struggling toward goals consistent with socialism and the post-Mao leadership as carrying out reforms in the same direction. It remains unclear how they expect change to come about in their own country except through fuller and more accurate information. They write as advocates of change, but it is difficult to know how optimistic their true beliefs are. Judging strictly by what is written, the Western critics of the Soviet Union are invariably less optimistic about the prospects for reform in a communist-led society.

What are the goals of the reformers? The clear-cut goals are to encourage change in China, to provide accurate information on that country, and to influence Soviet public opinion on China. If it became clear that they were also openly pursuing reform in the Soviet Union, the consequences would likely be grave. The only internal Soviet struggle they hint at in their writings is that against poor scholarship. The standards advocated by the reform group are consistent with scholarly ideals in the West. In this respect, they qualify as superior observers of China in comparison to the orthodox group, which relies on more dogmatic, intolerant, and deductive methods. We cannot prove that the reformers are purposeful advocates of reform in the Soviet Union. We may, however, extract from their writings about China the following six-step reform appraisal and agenda.

A REFORM VIEW OF SOCIALIST SOCIETY

A. Route to Socialism
   1. Socialism should emerge gradually, with extra safeguards to protect individual rights in a society with a heritage of despotism or a weak bourgeoisie that had not succeeded in building democratic institutions. This challenges earlier views of the dictatorship of the proletariat.
   2. Socialism should build on a very broad coalition. Few people need be labeled class enemies, and contradictory influences can decline gradually through persuasion. Resort to violence on a large scale has negative consequences. This challenges earlier notions of class struggle.
   3. Collectivization should not be carried out without widespread popular backing in the countryside and a clear understanding of favorable economic consequences for the rural population. This is in direct opposition to collectivization as it has occurred.
B. Relations within Socialism
   4. Experts must be encouraged to speak freely and to carry on independent research. Officials must be prevented from interfering with these rights. This standpoint opposes most forms of censorship and the controls by the communist party over freedom of expression.
   5. Industrious workers, peasants, and intellectuals should be encouraged to produce more and to excel. They should form a meritorious elite on the basis of their qualifications, experience, and superior performance. This position challenges appointments based on political criteria and existing disincentives to strenuous personal efforts.

6. Resources should be concentrated on improving the
   well-being of the people. This objective clashes with
   the priority given to the military and heavy industry.

How serious is this reform critique of the socialist system?
It does not call for an overthrow of the system but concentrates on change from within. In these respects it is not
radical. It is, however, a far-reaching critique in that it
suggests that the wrong people are in power, they have the
wrong priorities, they repress those who could do the most
for the society, and their basic procedures are dangerous
to the happiness and well-being of the people. Only reforms
in support of expertise, participation, and incentives can
set the system on a favorable course.

The reformers label the outcome of this agenda "socialism." To be sure, in some respects, such as forms of ownership, it would resemble contemporary socialism. But in
many other respects—perhaps most respects—this reorganized society would resemble Western democracies. The
agenda is presented piecemeal and indirectly, so there is
no opportunity to look for weak links or even contradictions
among the separate parts. It is of necessity presented in
total isolation from assessments of capitalist societies; the
possibility of convergence or increasing similarities in the
long run is not discussed. Most likely the ideal is to avoid
the shortcomings of contemporary capitalist societies.
Nonetheless, if one takes into account the common criticisms of what happened in China, and by implication the
Soviet Union, and the reform agenda's likely impact on
Soviet society, it is difficult to avoid the conclusion that a
substantial convergence with capitalist societies is antici-
pated. This concept, which is anathema to Soviet leaders,
is the logical outcome of a reform agenda.

Advancing Scholarship on China

The vast Soviet literature on contemporary China does more
than help us to understand how the Soviet worldview is
changing and how Soviets hold conflicting visions of what

socialism should be. It also does what it directly sets out to accomplish. It advances scholarship on China. There are at least three ways in which Russian-language materials contribute to contemporary Chinese studies, and in each of these respects substantial advances were registered between 1967, when critical studies began to appear in considerable number, and 1982, when there occurred a lull in anticipation of a new and more wide-ranging round of Sino-Soviet negotiations.

First, Russian sources are valuable for their use of primary sources. Based often on a detailed reading of pertinent Chinese sources, especially the Chinese press, they serve as a useful guide for further research. In social science studies of premodern China, it has long been true that Japanese studies are indispensable because of the volume of basic information and guidance in the use of primary sources they provide. An analogous situation is developing with Russian studies of contemporary China, although the reader has to be much more wary of inferior scholarship and unsupported conclusions. Large Soviet bibliographies are worth consulting, but they are likely to omit important and recent Western and Japanese studies, just as the text of Soviet books rarely gives adequate coverage to foreign views on the topics treated.

Second, the principal contribution of Russian-language sources is their coverage of specialized topics that are overlooked or examined in less detail elsewhere. Here we have concentrated on contemporary China's social classes. On some of these, e.g., workers and officials, the Western literature is sparse. Moreover, aspects of social classes treated at length in Soviet writings are in many cases topics that have been little studied in the West. The foreign specialist who decides to do research in one of these specialized areas would be well advised to examine the existing Soviet literature.

Third, Soviet studies make a distinct contribution through their explanations of the relationships between social classes and groups in Chinese society. Guided by Marxist-Leninist traditions in scholarship and by familiarity with their own society, they look in original ways at the social structure of China. The view they offer of the dynamics of that society may often be colored by this background and the existing censorship, yet it is also informed by an appreciation for a system in many ways close to their own. Soviet sources on China not only accurately present detailed information, they manage to place it in a broad context—one that is generally believable. Nevertheless, a good deal of care must be taken in using these sources because of the distorted assumptions often carried over from the Soviet worldview, especially by the orthodox group. Specialists whom I place in the reform group also contribute in original ways to understanding the dynamics of China through their writings on traditional Chinese society and its legacy for the People's Republic.

Soviet writings on China indirectly point the way to a new field of scholarship, the comparative study of socialism. Little has been written on the similarities between the Soviet Union and China under the impact of communist leadership. The Soviets and Chinese have been denied the opportunity to write comparatively about their two countries even though within each country there appears to be a lot of curiosity about this. Because Soviet writings offer many implicit comparisons and frequently raise themes that have been studied in Soviet history, they build a foundation for studies in comparative socialism.

The sociology of contemporary China developed in the United States in the 1950s and has continued to grow. The best work has been based on émigré interviews, usually in Hong Kong, supplemented by careful examination of the Chinese media and, for a short time, in the post-Mao era, by partial field studies in communities of the PRC. Firsthand contact with life in China is now a customary feature of research. Clearly the Soviets are behind, none of their research has drawn on émigré surveys nor have they conducted field research inside China (only in 1982 were the first Soviets in fifteen years admitted to do library research).

261

Nevertheless, their rapidly expanding sociologically oriented research on China has importance for the field and deserves consideration as a contribution to scholarship.

What makes the literature treated in this book sociological? To be sure, it is not written by persons formally trained as sociologists or professionally employed in that capacity. It is not based on methods widely utilized in sociology of empirical, quantitative research, such as survey methods. Nevertheless, it addresses themes central to the field of sociology: the situation of social classes, the relations among the classes and between each class and the state, and the effects of policies aimed at transforming classes and ethnic minorities. Traditional fields of sociology are the focus of attention: social stratification, race relations, industrial relations, social psychology, the sociology of education, and others. Sources are richly detailed, drawing together statistics in Chinese newspapers and other publications. While some are narrowly focused, many writings on social classes in the PRC seek to answer general questions. There is much concern with variations over time, although in comparison to Western studies little information is given on variations among provinces and communes. For these reasons, I believe, this Soviet literature should be accepted as contributing to the sociological research on China.

The quality of this field is superior to the narrowly political literature on the PRC published in the Soviet Union and more often translated into English. Discussions of the philosophical essence of Maoism or the militarism of Beijing's policies normally cite a very limited range of sources, especially in Western languages, and do not hesitate to make strong assertions on limited factual support. They fail to consider alternative explanations. These writings are a product of the orthodox camp and share with studies from this camp cited in this book the tendency to oversimplification and dogmatism. In books published by "Nauka" for the Academy of Sciences and on specialized themes, these negative characteristics are toned down, but they are still present to a large degree. First and foremost, the difference between the orthodox and reform group is in their methods of scholarship. The standards of the reform group are superior. Reform scholars are more empirical, inductive, widely read, questioning of assumptions, and in other respects consistent with social science practitioners elsewhere. It is the reformers who in the 1970s and early 1980s built up the sociology of China inside the Soviet Union.

Even the best of these writings on social classes in China have scholarly shortcomings, the most glaring of which is their insularity. They do not engage in a genuine dialogue with non-Soviet treatments. Although in recent years specialists in China have, with the aid of improved bibliographic services from the Institute of Scientific Information in the Social Sciences, become more up-to-date in their familiarity with Western sources, there is still a time lag that is compounded by the circulation in Western academic circles of conference papers and manuscripts on the rapidly changing situation in China years before they are published. Soviets read English well and strive to know the literature in their field. Increasingly the problems they face can be attributed to restrictions on meetings with foreigners and on coverage of Western writings in published sources— both a result of the demands by party leaders for intensification of the ideological struggle. To a large extent, the choice of topics and the quest for originality are part of a self-contained field. This is an anomaly in recent international scholarship. Of course, some of the fault lies in the West—where disinterest and ignorance of Russian is the chief problem, rather than censorship and a lack of candor.

A second set of shortcomings can be attributed to gaps in scholarship. Some topics are more sensitive politically than others; for example, little is written on religion and on the benefits received by children of high officials. In other cases, such as the study of Qing society, neglect may result from the low priority in training specialists determined by centralized planners. As indicated above, the dearth of explicit comparisons is an obvious gap in scholarship. Given the fact that implicit comparisons are so central to the Soviet analysis of China, their resulting one-sidedness and unsystematic nature detract from what is achieved. In short, the unstated or implied comparisons place a greater burden on the reader and may even lead to the transmission of different messages to different audiences.

A literature written with one eye on the censors or on the leading figures in the orthodox group—especially Rakhmanin—who seek a high degree of conformity in the field, is not, in many respects, directly accessible to all readers. It helps to be aware of the overall context of Chinese studies in the Soviet Union, and of the implied comparisons with the Soviet Union. The official Soviet worldview looms not far out of sight, as does a preoccupation with developments in their own country. These circumstances account for weaknesses in the analysis of China, but they also contribute to three strengths that form the core of the Soviet contribution to the sociology of China. First, the choice of topics is based on a first-hand appreciation for what matters in a socialist society. Soviets stress problems in the development of social classes, drawing attention to many issues, as in the study of labor relations, that have been largely neglected in the West. Second, the Soviet literature advances an overview of what has happened to Chinese society. I have emphasized that this viewpoint is remarkably similar to Western criticisms of Chinese society, but it is important to add that it is difficult to find a sociological overview in the West. Specialized studies rarely point to the overall situation of one or another social class. By making social classes the focus of analysis and by keeping the overall development of China as a socialist society in mind, the Soviets have added a general dimension that is of value to the field. Third, and, I believe, most valuable in this literature is its unrealized potential as a basis for the comparative study of socialism. Western sociological writings have tried to understand China in and of itself, sometimes with reference to Chinese history but rarely with comparisons to the Soviet Union. Soviets show how similar are the questions that pertain to the two countries and, by implication, how similar are the problems created by socialist policies. Whether one accepts their direct messages or seeks indirect meaning in them, the case is clear that comparisons deserve an important place in sociological studies of China. Soviet reformers make this case and would, I am confident, realize much of the potential of this comparative field if they were permitted to. Even if they are prevented from making comparative studies the focus that they should be, Soviets guide the way for others to proceed.

Understanding Sino-Soviet Relations

For a quarter-century, informed world opinion has followed the latest developments in the Sino-Soviet split with rapt attention. Observers have reacted to each twist and turn in relations, pouncing on the latest official pronouncement, whether it contained further invectives or glimmers of hope for improved ties. Throughout this time little has been known about the mutual perceptions of the two societies on fundamental questions of domestic life.

By 1982 the Soviet literature on contemporary China had expanded to such a scale and diverged on so many points that it became possible to achieve a new understanding of Soviet perceptions. As negotiations proceeded from 1982, and the Soviet Union made the transition from the Brezhnev to the Andropov and Chernenko eras, Soviet specialists on China divided into two camps. The orthodox group has remained dominant, including all of the high-ranking officials in this field in the Central Committee of the communist party, the Ministry of Foreign Affairs, and the Academy of Sciences. Bolstered by its views of domestic conditions in China, this group was skeptical about the prospects for negotiations and hesitant to compromise. In the other camp were Soviets who had a more positive assessment of post-Mao reforms. They more enthusiastically favored negotiations and appeared to adopt a more favorable outlook on compromise.

While the Chinese were preoccupied with the pullback

of the Soviet military and its support for heavily armed allies along China's border, Soviet China specialists could not be expected to have much to say. However, if military matters were to recede, even for a time, we could expect that much would hinge on how Soviets answer questions about Chinese society, particularly what went wrong on the path to socialism? How closely have the Chinese returned to that path since Mao's death? And where is China heading as this century draws to an end? The Soviets are answering these questions. In fact, they are arriving at two conflicting sets of answers. The fate of those who are proposing the answers and of the orthodox and reform forces in general is likely to be closely intertwined with the future of Sino-Soviet relations.

Russian studies on China long appeared to be working against a reconciliation between the two communist powers. Bitter attacks on Chinese society indicated that Soviet leaders were reconciled to prolonged antagonisms. But as Chinese officials unleashed a torrent of criticism against the Gang of Four and domestic policies between the late 1950s and the late 1970s, the differences between Soviet and Chinese interpretations narrowed. Both contrast the generally positive policies of 1949-1957 with the serious errors of 1957-1976. Both criticize insufficient democracy, the muzzling of experts, and inadequate material incentives. Despite contradictory assessments of Mao and of the revolutionary movement before 1949, there has been considerable convergence in views about what went wrong in Chinese socialism. This builds a foundation for reconciliation.

In 1979-1981, as the Chinese pulled back from democratic reforms and positive appraisals of the West, the grounds for improved relations with the Soviet Union expanded. Both leaderships are concerned with preserving central control by the communist party and centralized planning. Both are concerned about a drift to the right in post-Mao China. Without detailed research on Chinese debates about Soviet society, it would be premature to conclude that the two societies are converging in their views of socialism, but the enormous gap that separated their thinking in the late years of Mao's rule has clearly been greatly narrowed.

If Soviets were to recognize that the post-Mao reforms in China are returning that country to the socialist track, it would be an important step toward reconciliation. Just reverting to the practice of calling China "socialist," as Leonid Brezhnev did at Tashkent in March 1982, was an impetus to negotiations.[36] Increasingly reformers' analyses of post-Mao reforms imply that the country is heading in the right direction; the reforms are strengthening socialism and, moreover, China had never deviated toward capitalism. Soviet reformers are making a case for reconciliation on the basis of Chinese society's return to the fold from excesses to the left. The predominant response in the Soviet Union has been more cautious. The orthodox group refuses to accept the post-Mao reforms as being, on the whole, a swing toward socialism. It insists that "Maoism without Mao" prevails and that China is drifting to the right, away from socialism.

Given the distorted interpretations of changes in China after 1976 from the Institute of the Far East and its associates, it seems unlikely that the orthodox viewpoint represents a scholarly conclusion. Rather, one must surmise that Soviet officials decided that similarities in domestic policies are insufficient grounds for reconciliation. The Chinese must first change their foreign policy in order to win Soviet approval of their domestic reforms. When in 1981-1982, the Chinese government somewhat distanced itself from the capitalist countries, this gave Soviet leaders the message they needed to speak less critically of the significance of the post-Mao reforms. Even so, the tune of the orthodox group had not changed perceptibly before a moratorium on publications about contemporary China was declared in September 1982.

Scholarship is held hostage to the fate of talks about

---

[36] *The Current Digest of the Soviet Press*, 34, no. 12 (April 21, 1982), p. 6.

reconciliation. In the 1950s "fraternal relations" meant an uncritical acceptance of Chinese policies; in the early 1960s and at times of political succession or promising negotiations "uncertain relations" meant silence over Chinese policies; and for nearly two decades "hostile relations" meant criticism of Chinese policies. "Uncertain conditions" returned in 1982, and Soviet academic specialists await word of the next position they must take. But some of them at least do so with the pride that they have not simply parroted directives from above. They have used the unusual opportunity presented by the Sino-Soviet split for specialized scholarship to advance knowledge, to help reorient the Soviet worldview and perhaps, in accord with secret hopes, to further two significant goals: the reform of Soviet society and the improvement of relations between the Soviet Union and China.

LIST OF WORKS CITED

Agrarnye otnosheniia i krest'ianskoe dvizhenie v Kitae (Moscow: Nauka, 1974).

Akatova, T. N., "K otsenke klassovoi bor'by kitaiskikh rabochikh," *Obshchestvo i gosudarstvo v Kitae* 9:3 (1978), pp. 30-37.

——,"Rol' natsional'nogo faktora v rabochem dvizhenii Kitaia 1919-1927 gg.," in *Revoliutsiia 1925-1927 gg. v Kitae* (Moscow: Nauka, 1978), pp. 122-54.

Altaiskii, M., and V. Georgiev, *Antimarksistskaia sushchnost' filosofskikh vzgliadov Mao Tszeduna* (Moscow: Mysl', 1969).

Amvrosov, A. A., *Ot klassovoi differentsiatsii k sotsial'noi odnorodnosti obshchestva* (Moscow: Mysl', 1978).

Antipovskii, A. A., N. E. Borevskaia, and N. V. Franchuk, *Politika v oblasti nauki i obrazovaniia v KNR 1949-1979 gg.* (Moscow: Nauka, 1980).

Berger, Ia. M., "Gosudarstvo i derevnia v sovremennom Kitae: tezisy," *Obshchestvo i gosudarstvo v Kitae* 7:3 (1976), pp. 474-82.

Bogoslovskii, V. A., *Tibetskii raion KNR* (Moscow: Nauka, 1978).

Borisov, O. B., "Nekotorye aspekty politiki Kitaia," *Kommunist* 1981:6, reprinted in *Opasnyi kurs* 11 (Moscow: Politizdat, 1981), pp. 7-24.

——,"Polozhenie v KNR i nekotorye zadachi sovetskogo kitaevedeniia," *Problemy Dal'nego Vostoka* 1982:2, pp. 3-14.

——, *Sovetskii Soiuz i Man'chzhurskaia revoliutsionnaia baza* (Moscow: Mysl', 1977).

——, *Vnutrenniaia i vneshniaia politika Kitaia v 70-e gody* (Moscow: Politizdat, 1982).

Borisov, O. B., and B. T. Koloskov, *Sovetsko-kitaiskie otnosheniia 1945-1970: kratkii ocherk* (Moscow: Mysl', 1972).

Bulkin, A. P., *Iadro maoistkoi "sotsiologii"* (Moscow: Nauka, 1980).

Burlatsky, Fedor, *Mao Tse-tung: An Ideological and Psychological Portrait* (Moscow: Progress Publishers, 1980).

————, "Mezhdutsarstvie, ili khronika vremen Den Siaopina," *Novyi Mir* 1982:4, pp. 205-28.

————, *The True Face of Maoism* (Moscow: Novosti, 1968).

Chertina, Z. S., *Natsional'nye otnosheniia pri sotsializme v burzhuaznoi istoriografii SShA* (Moscow: Nauka, 1982).

Clubb, O. Edmund, *China and Russia: The "Great Game"* (New York: Columbia University Press, 1971).

The Current Digest of the Soviet Press.

Davydov, A. P., "Iz istorii sovetsko-kitaiskikh profsoiuznykh sviazei i organizatsii profsoiuznogo stroitel'stva v KNR (1949-1952 gg.)," in *Rabochii klass i polozhenie v profsoiuzakh KNR* (Moscow: Institute of the International Workers' Movement, Academy of Sciences, USSR, 1978), pp. 41-62.

————, *Profsoiuzy Kitaia: istoriia i sovremennost' (1949-1980 gody)* (Moscow: Profizdat, 1981).

————, *Profsoiuzy KNR 1953-1958* (Moscow: Nauka, 1978).

Deliusin, L. P., *Agrarno-krest'ianskii vopros v politike KPK (1921-1928)* (Moscow: Nauka, 1970).

[Delyusin], *The Socio-Political Essence of Maoism* (Moscow: Novosti, 1976).

————, *Spor o sotsializme v Kitae* (Moscow: Nauka, 1980).

————, "Sud'by intelligentsii v Kitae," in *Intelligentsiia: mesto v obshchestve i politika rukovodstva KPK* (Moscow: Institute of the International Workers' Movement, Academy of Sciences, USSR, 1978), pp. 1-23.

Doolin, Dennis J., *Territorial Claims in the Sino-Soviet Conflict: Documents and Analysis* (Stanford: Hoover Institution Press, 1965).

Dvizhenie "4 maia" 1919 goda v Kitae (Moscow: Nauka, 1971).

Ellison, Herbert J., ed., *The Sino-Soviet Conflict: A Global Perspective* (Seattle: University of Washington Press, 1982).

Fedorov, I. F., and V. G. Zubakov, *Chlenstvo v KPK: kak stroilas' partiia "Idei Mao Tszeduna"* (Moscow: Politizdat, 1980).

Fomina, N. I., "Kupechestvo v sotsial'noi strukture srednevekogo Kitaia," in *Sotsial'nye organizatsii v Kitae* (Moscow: Nauka, 1981), pp. 67-99.

Ganshin, G. A., *Ocherk ekonomiki sovremennogo Kitaia* (Moscow: Mysl', 1982).

Gel'bras, V. G., *Kitai: krizis prodolzhaetsia* (Moscow: Izdatel'stvo "Mezhdunarodnye otnosheniia," 1973).

————, "O klassovo-sotsial'noi strukture naseleniia Kitaia v kanun pobedy revoliutsii," in *Kitai: obshchestvo i gosudarstvo* (Moscow: Nauka, 1973), pp. 327-45.

————, "Problemy razvitiia rabochego klassa i rabochego dvizheniia v KNR," in *Problemy i protivorechiia v razvitii rabochego klassa KNR* (Moscow: Institute of the International Workers' Movement, Academy of Sciences, USSR, 1978), pp. 65-81.

————, *Sotsial'no-politicheskaia struktura KNR 50-60-e gody* (Moscow: Nauka, 1980).

Ginsburgs, George, and Carl F. Pinkele, *The Sino-Soviet Territorial Dispute, 1949-1964* (New York: Praeger Publishers, 1978).

Gittings, John, *Survey of the Sino-Soviet Dispute: A Commentary and Extracts from the Recent Polemics, 1963-1967* (London: Oxford University Press, 1968).

Gorbachev, B. N., *Sotsial'no-politicheskaia rol' kitaiskoi armii (1958-1969)* (Moscow: Nauka, 1980).

Gorbunova, S. A., "K kharakteristike rabochego klassa Ukhania (osen' 1926-leto 1927 gg.)," *Obshchestvo i gosudarstvo v Kitae* 9:3 (1978), pp. 23-29.

Gosudarstvo i obshchestvo v Kitae (Moscow: Nauka, 1978).

Griffith, William E., *Sino-Soviet Relations, 1964-1965* (Cambridge: M.I.T. Press, 1967).

————, *The Sino-Soviet Rift* (Cambridge: M.I.T. Press, 1964).

Grigor'ev, A. M., *Revoliutsionnoe dvizhenie v Kitae 1927-1931 gg.* (Moscow: Nauka, 1980).

Gubaidulin, V. M., *Revoliutsionnaia vlast' v osvobozhdennykh raionakh Kitaia (1937-1945 gg.)* (Moscow: Nauka, 1981).

Gudoshnikov, L. M., *Politicheskii mekhanizm Kitaiskoi Narodnoi Respubliki* (Moscow: Nauka, 1974).

———, "Velikoderzhavnyi shovinizm rukovodstva KNR v voprosakh natsional'no-gosudarstvennogo stroitel'stva," *Opasnyi kurs* 5 (Moscow: Politizdat, 1974), pp. 230-44.

Hinton, Harold C., *The Sino-Soviet Confrontation: Implications for the Future* (New York: Crane, Russak & Co., 1976).

Hudson, G. F., *The Sino-Soviet Dispute* (New York: Praeger, 1961).

Ideino-politicheskaia sushchnost' Maoizma (Moscow: Nauka, 1977).

Iliushechkin, V. I., "Obshchee i osobennoe v razvitii doburzhuaznykh klassovykh obshchestv," in *Sotsial'naia i sotsial'no-ekonomicheskaia istoriia Kitaia* (Moscow: Nauka, 1979), pp. 5-24.

Issledovaniia sotsiologicheskikh problem razvivaiushchikhsia stran (Moscow, Nauka, 1978).

Istoriia Kitaia s drevneishikh vremen do nashikh dnei (Moscow: Nauka, 1974).

"Iz doklada general'nogo sekretaria TsK KPSS tovarishcha L. I. Brezhneva 'Otchet tsentral'nogo komiteta KPSS XXVI s'ezdu Kommunisticheskoi Partii Sovetskogo Soiuza i ocherednye zadachi partii v oblasti vnutrennei i vneshnei politiki,' " *Opasnyi kurs* II (Moscow: Politizdat, 1981).

Izmeneniia sotsial'noi struktury sovetskogo obshchestva: Oktabr' 1917-1920 (Moscow: Mysl', 1976).

Izraitel', V. Ia., *Problemy formatsionnogo analiza obshchestvennogo razvitiia* (Gor'kii: Volgo-Viatskoe knizhnoe izdatel'stvo, 1975).

Kapralov, P. B., *Sel'skie raiony KNR v 70e gody: tendentsii sotsial'no-ekonomicheskogo razvitiia* (Moscow: Nauka, 1981).

Kasymov, F. Kh., *Minuia kapitalizm: sovetskaia istoriografiia perekhoda narodov Srednei Azii k sotsializmu* (Moscow: Nauka, 1980).

Khanazarov, K. Kh., *Reshenie natsional'no-iazykovoi problemy v SSSR* (Moscow: Politizdat, second edition, 1982).

Kholodkovskaia, A. V., "Kampaniia 'uporiadocheniia i stroitel'stva profsoiuzov' i ee vliianie na rabochii klass (1973-1975 gg.)" in *Rabochii klass i polozhenie v profsoiuzakh KNR* (Moscow: Institute of the International Workers' Movement, Academy of Sciences, USSR, 1978), pp. 3-40.

———, *Rabochii klass Kitaia v period "uregulirovaniia" (1961-1965)* (Moscow: Nauka, 1975).

Khor'kov, V. I., *Nankinskii Gomin'dan i rabochii vopros 1927-1932* (Moscow: Nauka, 1977).

Kitai i sosedi (Moscow: Nauka, 1982).

Kitai: obshchestvo i gosudarstvo (Moscow: Nauka, 1973).

Kitai: poiski putei sotsial'nogo razvitiia (Moscow: Nauka, 1979).

Kitai: traditsii i sovremennost' (Moscow: Nauka, 1976).

Kitaiskaia Narodnaia Respublika 1973 (-1979) (Moscow: Nauka, 1975-81).

Kiuzadjan, L. S., *Ideologicheskie kampanii v KNR 1949-1966* (Moscow: Nauka, 1970).

Kiuzadjan, L. S. and T. M. Sorokina, "Vliianie traditsii na Maoizm v otsenke zarubezhnogo kitaevedeniia," in *Kitai: traditsii i sovremennost'* (Moscow: Nauka, 1976), pp. 279-319.

Klassy i klassovaia struktura v KNR (Moscow: Nauka, 1982).

Klimin, I. I., *Agrarnaia politika KPSS (1917-1937 gg.): deistvitel'nost' i burzhuaznye vymysly* (Leningrad: Leningrad University Press, 1982).

Konfutsiantsvo v Kitae: problemy, teorii i praktiki (Moscow: Nauka, 1982).

Kostiaeva, A. S., *Krest'ianskie soiuzy v Kitae* (Moscow: Nauka, 1978).

———, "Osnovnye problemy revoliutsii 1925-1927 gg. v Kitae," in *Revoliutsiia 1925-1927 v Kitae* (Moscow: Nauka, 1978), pp. 6-22.

———, "Rol' shen'shi v krest'ianskikh dvizheniiakh nakanune sin'khaiskoi revoliutsii," in *Agrarnye otnosheniia i krest'ianskoe dvizhenie v Kitae* (Moscow: Nauka, 1974), pp. 230-45.

Kozlovskii, V. E., *Dialektika perekhoda ot kapitalizma k sotsi-alizmu* (Moscow: Mysl', 1982).

Kritika teoreticheskikh osnov Maoizma (Moscow: Nauka, 1973).

Krivtsov, V. A., and V. A. Krasnova, *Li Da-chzhao: ot re-voliutsionnogo demokratizma k Marksizmu-Leninizmu* (Moscow: Nauka, 1978).

Kul'pin, E. S., *Tekhniko-ekonomicheskaia politika rukovodstva KNR i rabochii klass Kitaia* (Moscow: Nauka, 1975).

Lazarev, V. I., "Antimaoistskaia tendentsiia v Kitae," *Opasnyi kurs* 9 (Moscow: Politizdat, 1979), pp. 240-62.

———, *Klassovaia bor'ba v KNR* (Moscow: Politizdat, 1981).

———, "Kompartiia Kitaia: proshloe i nastoiashchee (k 60-letiiu KPK), *Opasnyi kurs* 11 (Moscow: Politizdat, 1981), pp. 210-31.

Lieberthal, Kenneth, *Sino-Soviet Conflict in the 1970's: Its Evolution and Implications for the Strategic Triangle* (Santa Monica, CA: Rand Corporation, 1978).

Louis, Victor, *The Coming Decline of the Chinese Empire* (New York: Times Books, 1979).

Low, Alfred D., *The Sino-Soviet Dispute: An Analysis of the Polemics* (Rutherford, N.J.: Fairleigh Dickinson University Press, 1976).

Luk'ianov, A. I., G. I. Denisov, E. L. Kuz'min, and N. N. Razumovich, *Sovetskaia konstitutsiia i mify sovetologov* (Moscow: Politizdat, 1981).

Maoism as It Really Is (Moscow, Progress Publishers, 1981).

Markova, S. D., *Maoizm i intelligentsiia* (Moscow: Nauka, 1975).

Marushkin, B. I., *Istoriia v sovremennoi ideologicheskoi bor'be (stroitel'stvo sotsializma v SSSR skvos' prizmu anti-kommunisticheskoi istoriografii SShA)* (Moscow: Mysl', 1972).

Matiaev, V. Ia., and V. P. Fetov, "Kitai: nekotorye aspekty vnutrennego razvitiia," *Problemy Dal'nego Vostoka* 42 (1982:2), pp. 38-49.

Meliksetov, A. V., "Istoricheskoe znachenie sin'khaiskoi revoliutsii v Kitae," in *Kitai v novoe i noveishee vremia* (Moscow: Nauka, 1981), pp. 95-119.

———, "K voprosu o genezise kapitalizma v Kitae," in *Go-*

sudarstvo i obshchestvo v Kitae (Moscow: Nauka, 1978), pp. 158-89.

————, "Nekotorye aspekty istoricheskoi kontseptsii Dzhona Feirbenka," *Obshchestvo i gosudarstvo v Kitae* 6:3 (1975), pp. 611-16.

————, "Nekotorye osobennosti formirovaniia rabochego klassa Kitaia k nachalu noveishego vremeni," *Obshchestvo i gosudarstvo v Kitae* 9:3 (1978), pp. 3-10.

————, *Sotsial'no-ekonomicheskaia politika Gomin'dana 1927-1949 gg.* (Moscow: Nauka, 1977).

Mikeshin, N. P., *History versus Anti-History: A Critique of the Bourgeois Falsification of the Postwar History of the CPSU* (Moscow: Progress Publishers, 1977).

Mirovitskaya, Raisa and Yuri Semyonov, *The Soviet Union and China: A Brief History of Relations* (Moscow: Novosti, 1981).

Momjan, Khachik N., *Landmarks in History: The Marxist Doctrine of Socio-Economic Formations* (Moscow: Progress Publishers, 1980).

Moskalev, A. A., *Guansi-Chzhuanskii i Ninsia-Khueiskii avtonomnye raiony KNR* (Moscow: Nauka, 1979).

————, *Politika KNR v natsional'no-iazykovom voprose* (Moscow: Nauka, 1981).

Mos'ko, G. N., *Armiia Kitaia: orudie avantiuristicheskoi politiki Maoistov* (Moscow: Voennoe izdatel'stvo Ministerstva Oborony SSSR, 1980).

Mugruzin, A. S., *Agrarnye otnosheniia v Kitae v 20-40-kh godakh XX v.* (Moscow: Nauka, 1970).

————, "K voprosu o spetsifike klassovogo sostava sel'skogo naseleniia v Kitae nakanune pobedy revoliutsii," in *Kitai: obshchestvo i gosudarstvo* (Moscow: Nauka, 1973), pp. 313-26.

Nadeev, I. N., *"Kul'turnaia revoliutsiia" i sud'ba kitaiskoi literatury* (Moscow: Nauka, 1969).

Nepomnin, O. E., *Ekonomicheskaia istoriia Kitaia 1864-1894 gg.* (Moscow: Nauka, 1974).

————, *Genezis kapitalizma v Kitae* (Moscow: Nauka, 1966).

————, "Krizis kitaiskogo obshchestva nachala XX v.: istoki

i osobennosti," in *Gosudarstvo i obshchestvo v Kitae* (Moscow: Nauka, 1978), pp. 139-57.

―――, *Sotsial'no-ekonomicheskaia istoriia Kitaia 1894-1914* (Moscow: Nauka, 1980).

The New York Times.

Nikiforov, V. N., *Vostok i vsemirnaia istoriia* (Moscow: Nauka, second edition, 1977).

Obshchestvo i gosudarstvo v Kitae (from the fourth to thirteenth "scientific conferences," 1973-1982; volumes 1-3 of each annual conference; Institute of Oriental Studies, Academy of Sciences, USSR).

Obshchestvo i gosudarstvo v Kitae (Moscow: Nauka, 1981).

Ocherki istorii Kitaia v noveishee vremia (Moscow: Izdatel'stvo vostochnoi literatury, 1959).

Opasnyi kurs 4-11 (Moscow: Politizdat, 1973-81).

Ostrovskii, A. V., "Nekotorye aspekty issledovaniia vnutrennei sotsial'noi struktury rabochego klassa KNR" in *Problemy i protivorechiia v razvitii rabochego klassa KNR* (Moscow: Institute of the International Workers' Movement, Academy of Sciences, USSR, 1978), pp. 65-81.

―――, "Problemy razvitiia rabochego klassa i programma 'chetyrekh modernizatsii,' " *Kharakter i osobennosti ekonomicheskogo i sotsial'nogo razvitiia KNR na sovremennom etape* (Moscow: tezisy dokladov nauchno-teoreticheskoi konferentsii April 24-25, 1980; Institute of the Far East, Academy of Sciences, USSR), pp. 37-40.

Ot kapitalizma k sotsializmu: osnovnye problemy istorii perekhodnogo perioda v SSSR 1917-1937 gg., vols. I and II (Moscow: Nauka, 1981).

Pavlenok, P. D., *Formirovanie i razvitie sotsial'no-klassovoi struktury sotsialisticheskogo obshchestva* (Moscow: Moscow University Press, 1978).

Perelomov, L. S., *Konfutsiantstvo i legizm v politicheskoi istorii Kitaia* (Moscow: Nauka, 1981).

Pollack, Jonathan D., *The Sino-Soviet Conflict in the 1980s: Its Dynamics and Policy Implications* (Santa Monica, CA: Rand Corporation, 1981).

Problemy i protivorechiia industrial'nogo razvitiia KNR (Moscow: Mysl', 1974).

Problemy nauchnogo kommunizma, vol. 15 (Moscow: Mysl', 1981).

Promyshlennost' KNR (Moscow: Nauka, 1979).

Rabochee dvizhenie v Kitae 1917-1949, chast' 1, ukazatel' istochnikov i literatury (Moscow: Institute for Scientific Information in the Social Sciences, Academy of Sciences, USSR, 1982).

Rabochii klass Kitaia (1949-1974) (Moscow: Nauka, 1978).

Rabochii klass v sotsial'no-politicheskoi sisteme KNR (Moscow: Nauka, 1981).

Rakhimov, T. R., "Great-Hanist Chauvinism Instead of the Leninist Teaching on the National Question," *Leninism and Modern China's Problems* (Moscow: Progress Publishers, 1972), pp. 97-115.

————, *Sud'by nekhanskikh narodov v KNR* (Moscow: Mysl', 1981).

Razvitie rabochego klassa v sotsialisticheskom obshchestve (in the series, Rabochii klass v 20 veke: istoriia i sovremennost'; Moscow: Nauka, 1982).

Real'nyi sotsializm v SSSR i ego burzhuaznye fal'sifikatory (Moscow: Mysl', 1977).

Remyga, V. N., *Sistema upravleniia promyshlennost'iu KNR (1949-1980)* (Moscow: Nauka, 1982).

Revoliutsiia 1925-1927 gg. v Kitae (Moscow: Nauka, 1978).

Rol' traditsii v istorii i kul'ture Kitaia (Moscow: Nauka, 1972).

Rumiantsev, A. M., *Istoki i evoliutsiia "idei Mao Tszeduna"* (Moscow: Nauka, 1972).

Rothenberg, Morris, *Whither China: The View from the Kremlin* (Miami: Center for Advanced International Studies, University of Miami, 1977).

Rozman, Gilbert, "Moscow's China-Watchers in the Post-Mao Era: The Response to a Changing China," *The China Quarterly*, June 1983, pp. 215-41.

————, ed., *Soviet Studies of Premodern China: Assessments of Recent Scholarship* (Ann Arbor: Michigan Publications on China, 1984).

Saltykov, G. F., *Sotsial'no-psikhologicheskie faktory v politiches-koi zhizni rabochego klassa KNR 70-kh godov* (Moscow: Nauka, 1982).

————, "Traditsiia, mekhanizm ee deistviia i nekotorye ee osobennosti v Kitae," in *Rol' traditsii v istorii i kul'ture Kitae* (Moscow: Nauka, 1970), pp. 4-23.

Sandles, Gretchen Ann, "Soviet Images of the People's Republic of China, 1949-1979" (The University of Michigan, doctoral dissertation, 1981).

Sel'skoe khoziaistvo KNR 1949-1974 (Moscow: Nauka, 1978).

Sel'skoe khoziaistvo KNR 1966-1973 (Moscow: Nauka, 1975).

Semenov, Iu., "Vnutripoliticheskie i sotsial'nye problemy Kitaia," *Opasnyi kurs* 11 (Moscow: Politizdat, 1981), pp. 288-306.

Shalin, M. A., *Antikommunizm i ideologicheskaia bor'ba na sovremennom etape* (Kazan': Kazan' University Press, 1973).

Sladkovsky, M. I., "In Opposition to Great-Han Chauvinism," *Far Eastern Affairs* 1981:4, pp. 12-29.

Smirnov, A. D., ed., *Kritika antimarksistskikh ekonomicheskikh teorii v prepodovanii politicheskoi ekonomiki* (Moscow: Vysshaia shkola, 1981).

Social Science (Moscow: Progress Publishers, 1977).

Sotsial'naia i sotsial'no-ekonomicheskaia istoriia Kitaia (Moscow: Nauka, 1979).

Sotsial'no-ekonomicheskii stroi i ekonomicheskaia politika KNR (Moscow: Nauka, 1978).

Sotsial'nye organizatsii v Kitae (Moscow: Nauka, 1981).

Sotsiologiia i problemy sotsial'nogo razvitiia (Moscow: Nauka, 1978).

Sovremennyi antikommunizm: politika, ideologiia (Moscow: Izdatel'stvo "Mezhdunarodnye otnosheniia," 1973).

Sovremennyi Kitai v zarubezhnykh issledovaniiakh (Moscow: Nauka, 1979).

Spirina, M. Iu., "Rabochii klass Kitaia v bor'be protiv gomin'danovskogo rezhima i agressii SShA (1945-1949 gg.)", *Obshchestvo i gosudarstvo v Kitae* 10:3 (1979), pp. 119-26.

Stuart, Douglas T., and William T. Tow, *China, The Soviet*

Union, and the West: Strategic and Political Dimensions in the 1980s (Boulder, CO: Westview Press, 1982).

Stuzhina, E. P., *Kitaiskii gorod XI-XIII vv.: ekonomicheskaia i sotsial'naia zhizn'* (Moscow: Nauka, 1979).

———, *Kitaiskoe remeslo v XVI-XVIII vv.* (Moscow: Nauka, 1970).

Sud'by kul'tury KNR (1949-1974) (Moscow: Nauka, 1978).

Sukharchuk, G. D., "Tsiui Tsiu-bo ob osobennostiakh razvitiia kapitalizma v Kitae," in *Gosudarstvo i obshchestvo v Kitae* (Moscow: Nauka, 1978), pp. 244-52.

Tiapkina, N. I., "O klanovoi organizatsii v kitaiskoi derevne pervoi poloviny XX v.," in *Sotsial'naia i sotsial'no-ekonomicheskaia istoriia Kitaia* (Moscow: Nauka, 1979), pp. 181-204.

———, "O traditsionnoi sotsial'noi organizatsii kitaiskoi derevni v pervoi polovine XX v.," in *Gosudarstvo i obshchestvo v Kitae* (Moscow: Nauka, 1978), pp. 207-28.

Tikhvinsky, S. L., "Bor'ba s apologetikoi velikokhan'skogo gegemonizma: vazhnaia zadacha istoricheskoi naukoi," in *Aktual'nye problemy bor'by s maoistskimi fal'sifikatsiiami v oblasti istorii* (Moscow: Institute of the Far East, 1979).

———, *Istoriia Kitaia i sovremennost'* (Moscow: Nauka, 1976).

———, *Man'chzhurskoe vladychestvo v Kitae* (Moscow: Nauka, 1966).

Tikhvinsky, S. L., and L. P. Deliusin, "Nekotorye problemy izucheniia istorii Kitaia," in *Problemy sovetskogo kitaevedeniia* (Moscow: Institute of the Far East, 1973), pp. 21-46.

Titov, A. S., *Iz istorii bor'by i raskola v rukovodstve KPK 1935-1936 gg.* (Moscow: Nauka, 1979).

Van Min (Wang Ming), *Polveka KPK i predatel'stvo Mao Tszeduna* (Moscow: Politizdat, 1975).

Vasil'ev, L. S., *Kul'ty, religii, traditsii v Kitae* (Moscow: Nauka, 1970).

———, "Traditsiia i problema sotsial'nogo progressa v istorii Kitaia," in *Rol' traditsii v istorii i kul'ture Kitae* (Moscow: Nauka, 1972), pp. 24-60.

Vladimirov, O., and V. Ryazantsev, *Mao Tse-tung: A Political Portrait* (Moscow: Progress Publishers, 1976).

———, *Stranitsy politicheskoi biografii Mao Tszeduna* (Moscow: Politizdat, 1969).

Vladimirov, P. P., *Osobyi raion Kitaia, 1942-1945* (Moscow: Novosti, 1973).

Volkova, L. A., *Izmenenie sotsial'no-ekonomicheskoi struktury kitaiskoi derevni 1949-1970 gg.* (Moscow: Nauka, 1972).

"Vtoraia Vsesoiuznaia konferentsiia kitaevedov," *Problemy Dal'nego Vostoka* (1982:2), pp. 183-89.

Whiting, Kenneth R., *Evolution of the Sino-Soviet Split: A Summary Account* (Maxwell Air Force Base, Alabama: Air University Institute for Professional Development, 1975).

Wich, Richard, *Sino-Soviet Crisis Politics: A Study of Political Change and Communication* (Cambridge: Harvard University Press, 1980).

Yegorov, K., "The Policy of Rehabilitation of Cadres and Certain Aspects of the Political Struggle in China," *Far Eastern Affairs* (1982:1), pp. 87-97.

Zagoria, Donald S., *The Sino-Soviet Conflict, 1956-1961* (Princeton: Princeton University Press, 1962).

Zak, L. M., V. S. Lel'chuk, and V. I. Pogudin, *Stroitel'stvo sotsializma v SSSR: istoriograficheskii ocherk* (Moscow: Mysl', 1971).

Zanegin, B., A. Mironov, and Ia. Mikhailov, *K sobitiiam v Kitae* (Moscow: Politizdat, 1967).

Zhukov, E. M., et al., *Teoreticheskie problemy vsemirno-istoricheskogo protsessa* (Moscow: Nauka, 1979).

Zhelokhovtsev, A. N., *Literaturnaia teoriia i politicheskaia bor'ba v KNR* (Moscow: Nauka, 1979).

———, "Rol' traditsii v formirovanii stereotipov myshleniia i povedeniia v sovremennom Kitae," in *Rol' traditsii v istorii i kul'ture Kitae* (Moscow: Nauka, 1972), pp. 349-73.

INDEX

Library of Congress Cataloging in Publication Data

Rozman, Gilbert.
  A mirror for socialism.

  Bibliography: p.
  Includes index.
  1. China—Social conditions—1949-1976. 2. China—Social con-
ditions—1976- 3. Socialism—China—History. I. Title.
HN733.5.R69 1985   305.5′0951   84-42902
ISBN 0-691-09411-X

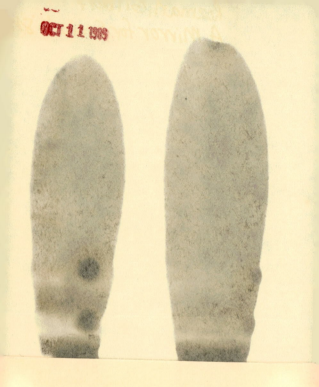